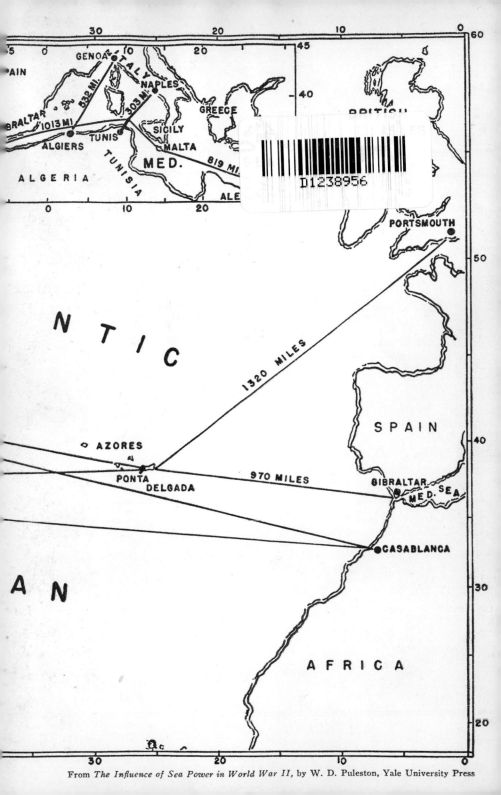

From *The Influence of Sea Power in World War II*, by W. D. Puleston, Yale University Press

The Influence of Force in Foreign Relations

CAPTAIN W. D. PULESTON

U. S. N. (RETIRED)

D. VAN NOSTRAND COMPANY, INC.

TORONTO   NEW YORK   LONDON

NEW YORK
D. Van Nostrand Company, Inc., 250 Fourth Avenue, New York 3

TORONTO
D. Van Nostrand Company (Canada), Ltd., 25 Hollinger Rd., Toronto

LONDON
Macmillan & Company, Ltd., St. Martin's Street, London, W.C. 2

PRINTED IN THE UNITED STATES OF AMERICA

Dedicated to

Fleet Admiral Ernest J. King, Commander in Chief, U.S. Fleet, and Chief of Naval Operations during most of World War II. Summoned by the President of the United States to command the Navy, which had recently suffered a series of humiliating defeats, he quickly restored its morale and led it to victory. Had his counsel been heeded in 1944 the Nation would have been spared many of its sons and the unnecessary legacy of a cold war.

Preface

This book evolved from a series of lectures delivered by the author in the spring of 1945 at the School of Advanced International Studies, Washington, D.C., since attached to Johns Hopkins University under the same title. At the conclusion of the lectures, Dr. Halford L. Hoskins, founder and Director of the School, suggested their publication and at his friendly insistence they were prepared for publication. The following decade permitted observation of the efforts of the United Nations to preserve the peace by the use of force and to compare them with classical methods employed in Europe. The lectures have been amplified and two new chapters added. The theme remains the same, the influence of force in foreign relations.

Data used were obtained from dependable and usually official reports. Source material of wars and diplomacy since 1900 has been abundant; official postwar investigations of the conduct of wars of the twentieth century have opened practically all archives. In addition, most prominent participants in these wars, civil and military, have explained their actions in autobiographies or have been aided by a friendly biographer. As well as using documentary evidence the author served with two brief interruptions from 1934 to 1945 in Washington in positions that permitted personal observation of, and occasional participation in, some of the situations described.

Besides Dr. Hoskins who inspired this book, other friends have given aid and encouragement; notably Major Andrew M. Kamarck, U.S. Army Reserve, and Lieutenant Norman S. Heaney,

U.S. Naval Reserve, who cheerfully checked facts and figures, improved diction, and made numerous valuable suggestions. Mrs. Virginia Nemeth of Washington, D.C., copied and recopied the oft rewritten manuscript. To these good friends I am indebted, but they are not responsible for facts or conclusions. The opinions expressed are my own and do not necessarily coincide with those held by the Navy Department.

W. D. P.

Lake Wales, Florida.
December, 1954.

Contents

Chapter 1

Classical Methods of Maintaining Peace

The use of force in international relations is one of the oldest devices known to statesmen. On the muzzles of his cannon, Louis XIV engraved the motto: "The Last Argument of Kings." Tiny guns like these, trundled over Europe on wooden wheels dragged by men and horses ashore and mounted on the decks of galleys and small sailing ships, established law and order throughout Europe. They made it possible for European explorers to discover and settle North and South America and to establish and protect ocean commerce. The organized force behind these muzzle-loading guns sheltered European and American civilization. Their cast-iron cannon balls, some smaller than baseballs, ordained that Europe and North and South America would be Christian, not Mohammedan. Americans should be familiar with the theories and principles of the use of force. Their independence was gained and the Federal Union preserved by war. When in 1928 Kellogg and Briand signed their hopeful pact banishing force as an instrument of policy, they were attempting to discard that instrument—force—which preserved Christianity in Europe and made the United States possible.

The literature on war is voluminous and comprehensive. Many students of history have deplored the space devoted to diplomacy and war; but the fact that the majority of historians have dwelt primarily on thrones, chancelleries, wars, forts, ships, and guns, is proof that the use of force has been the *decisive* factor in the lives of nations. In the past, no matter how high its principles, how equitable its institutions, or how delightful its customs, no nation has long retained its independence that has not been able to defend and maintain itself by force.

Today, it does not become any nation, great or small, to brand another as an 'aggressor.' Various small, 'buffer States' owe their nominal independence to the inability of powerful, aggressive states to agree upon their partition. Other small and medium-size nations were once great powers that subsequently lost their position through the folly of their rulers or the unwillingness of their citizens to defend territories acquired by more predatory ancestors. The present Great Powers of the world should be the last to criticize any nation for aggression, for their statesmen know that every Great Power—whether governed by its citizens, an absolute or limited monarch, or a totalitarian dictator—has risen on the ruins of predecessor states.

Officials responsible for foreign policies and armed forces of great nations should remember that extension of territory without careful consideration of its subsequent protection may weaken rather than strengthen a state. For example, Trajan wasted imperial resources to extend only temporarily the boundaries of Rome, which Augustus had more prudently consolidated behind its natural frontiers. And as late as 1903 Count Witte and General Kuropatkin urged Czar Nicholas to halt Russia's advance in the Far East because it was almost impossible to defend its existing frontiers. Within two years, the Russian defeats at the hands of the Japanese proved their advice had been correct.

Statesmen also should abandon their futile attempts to divide weapons into offensive and defensive types. From the time-honored bayonet to nuclear weapons, every type has been adapted to the defense and offense. Leaders responsible for the security of the State should remember that unless possessed of overwhelming strength, their armed forces must defend in one area in order to provide superior forces to take the offensive in other areas. In the present era the defense of production is essential to a vigorous prosecution of the war; and, while an active offensive is still the best form of defense, if an offensive is to be sustained it must be accompanied by an effective defense of a nation's productive capacity.

Naval officers proudly can recall that Athens, the most brilliant and democratic nation in the ancient world, built her empire and civilization upon sea power; that after the First Punic War the Romans maintained the world's most powerful navy and, while they consolidated their position in Italy with their legions, their empire was essentially a Mediterranean state dependent primarily on control of that great Middle Sea by Roman fleets. The predominant role of the Mediterranean Sea in the life of the Roman Empire is attested by the longevity of the Eastern or Greek Empire which, sustained by its sea power, outlived the Western Empire by a thousand years.

Every student of history is aware that western Europe was preserved from the Saracens at the decisive land battle of Tours in 732 A.D. Many forget that Constantinople, the eastern bastion of Christendom, resisted the advance of the Saracens until 1453. Under the protection of a professional army and navy, the trained administrators of the imperial bureaucracy preserved the Greek Church and a venerable civilization with its arts, trade, and commerce, until western Europe was able to take over its own defense and to undertake the navigation of the oceans which led to the discovery of America. In 1571, the Turkish fleet was destroyed in the decisive naval battle of Lepanto; subsequent naval campaigns restored the western and central Mediterranean to Christian Europe. Our western culture, consequently, inherited the lore of the ancient world and developed its own Christian civilization because Christian Europe was able to turn back the Saracen hordes by superior force on the land and on the sea.

Independent states are the controlling members of international society. Their governments are the agencies which direct the use of force in international affairs. In eras when states were loosely organized, they used force feebly; as states consolidated their territories and particularly as they centralized their authority, their conduct of war, that is, their use of force in international affairs, became more vigorous. In modern states, the cutting edge of the united strength of the nation is its army, navy, and air forces which are used in open war. Very often the armed forces of a hostile nation or an alliance of hostile nations are so overwhelming that their opponents yield without fighting. In this way, Austria, supported by Germany, obtained Bosnia and Herzegovina in 1908 because Russia, France, and England were unwilling to resist Austrian annexation by force. During the same period, Germany, supported by Austria, imposed an unfavorable commercial treaty on Russia.

Thus, force in international relations may either be openly applied or be simply displayed. The sword need not be drawn if rattling it in the scabbard accomplishes the nation's purpose. Force is most effectively employed when it obtains national objectives without the necessity of battles. Whether or not a powerful nation actually threatens to employ force in order to obtain concessions from a weak neighbor, the representatives of both states are acutely aware of their relative strengths, and this knowledge dominates their diplomatic negotiations. In routine diplomacy, inherent national strength that can be converted speedily into organized force is usually the unacknowledged, but decisive, factor.

Representatives of weaker states, when pressed or imposed upon by stronger ones, usually seek allies to restore the balance of power. Even first-rate nations on occasion have been obliged to join forces to oppose a more powerful, potential common enemy. One can readily gather from the history of Europe—the most Christian, civilized, and warlike of the continents—that alliances to preserve the balance of power have prevented many wars and protected the independence of numerous small nations which otherwise would have been forcibly absorbed by larger nations. To evaluate these benefits of international alliances, it must be remembered that, when groups of powers do finally resort to force, wars are longer and more bloody, and may become global. An example of this occurred in World War I. For a half century, France and England had opposed each other in all parts of the world. Twice they had been on the verge of war, but the increasing strength of Germany, leader of the Triple Alliance, which threatened both France and England, compelled them to settle their differences and to form the Anglo-French entente in 1904-05. In 1907, their increasing fear of Germany caused Russia and England, whose antagonisms also were long and deep, to compromise their differences and to form the Anglo-Russian entente which soon became merged into the Triple Entente of France, Russia, and Great Britain. As early as 1907 the European nations definitely were taking sides for the world war that began in 1914.

Becoming embroiled in war is not a novel experience for North Americans. As colonials they were involved in all major European wars of the seventeenth and eighteenth centuries. Despite Washington's warning to avoid foreign entanglements, the United States was compelled to resort to war against France, the Barbary pirates, and Great Britain during the first three decades of independence. In the twentieth century Americans have been drawn twice within a single generation into two world wars, the first originating in the Balkans, the second in Manchuria. It is unnecessary to go beyond our own history to discover the theories and principles that have governed the use of force in the past.

Between 1815 and 1914, as the United States slowly developed into a great power, she succeeded in avoiding European wars; during this same era European statesmen employing two well-proved diplomatic instruments the 'balance of power' and the 'concert of the Great Powers' prevented three major wars from becoming world wars—the Crimean, Franco-Prussian, and Russo-Japanese. Beginning in 1899 with the Hague Conference and culminating with the establishment of the United Nations in 1945, for almost half a century practically all civilized states made continuous efforts to substitute arbitration for armament and to prohibit the use of certain weapons, finally creating a super government authorized by charter to use force if necessary 'to avert or suppress' war. In this shorter period two world wars and many smaller ones have occurred. At first glance it would seem that the more nations sought to maintain peace the more often they became involved in world wars. This superficial conclusion should be rejected, but it is evident that much more than good intentions are required to preserve peace.

If we wish to understand why wars continue to recur we can not do better than to begin with the reflections of two eminent theorists on the use of force in the past who diligently studied the causes, conduct, and consequences of previous wars during the comparatively peaceful nineteenth century. One concentrated on war on land; the other, on war on the sea.

The first in point of time was a German, General Carl von Clausewitz, who fought in the Napoleonic Wars and devoted years to comparing their causes, their conduct, and their consequences with the campaigns of Gustavus Adolphus, Charles XII, and Frederick the Great. From this study came his theories on the use of force in international affairs, expressed in his book, *On War*.* The second was an American, Captain (later Rear Admiral) Alfred T. Mahan, who served in the Civil War and whose studies commencing in the 1880's culminated in his classic work, *The Influence of Sea Power on History*. The rise of the British Empire between 1650 and 1815 furnished Mahan with ample evidence supporting his thesis of sea power that dealt with the means of employing armed fleets to obtain control of the sea and, through this control, to attain domination of the land. Clausewitz used Napoleon to personify land power; Mahan used the career of Nelson, who was the embodiment of British sea power, to personify the struggle between the power which depends upon the land and that which depends upon the sea.

Both Clausewitz and Mahan sought to test their theories by the record of history, that is, by the previous experience of mankind. Clausewitz declared that the study of military history was the only substitute for actual experience in war. He considered the detailed study of individual campaigns and battles as more useful than a general and perhaps superficial knowledge of an entire war. Mahan likewise illustrated the principles of war by means of historical examples. He considered an understanding of these principles, as defined by such authorities as General Baron

* *On War*, by General Carl von Clausewitz, A. S. Barnes & Co.

Jomini (a Swiss contemporary of Clausewitz who served under Napoleon), and history both as necessary to the proper education of commissioned officers. Of the two, history, he believed, was the better teacher. It took the place of actual experience in war; it supplied practical examples (practice) with which to illuminate the principles. Mahan urged naval officers to master the principles of warfare and to 'ram them home' with historical illustrations.

Neither Clausewitz nor Mahan, however, placed much confidence in historians. Clausewitz asserted that historians rarely made truth their object. He maintained that they embellished military deeds in order to glorify their own nations or to demonstrate a relationship between actual events and their own theories. Historians, he charged, do not write history but invent it. Mahan held that historians generally had little knowledge of, and interest in, the sea; consequently, they had overlooked the profound influence of maritime strength upon great historical issues.* He also charged that naval historians had not shown the relationship existing between general history and naval history, being simply chroniclers of naval events. Mahan attempted to close this gap by emphasizing maritime influences, while showing their relationship to, and effect upon, general history. Their distrust of historians caused both Clausewitz and Mahan to draw accounts of the same campaigns from different sources in order to verify the facts as closely as possible.

The father of Captain Mahan, Professor D. H. Mahan, onetime Dean of West Point, studied the science of war in France shortly after his graduation from the Military Academy in 1824. Under the distinguished sponsorship of General Lafayette, he was enrolled at the French school of engineering and fortification founded by the great Vauban. Professor Mahan, one of the first Americans systematically to study war, became convinced that there existed both a science and an art of war, and believed that an intimate acquaintance with general literature as well as science was indispensable to the development of a thorough military

---

* At least two eminent American historians, Francis Parkman and Henry Adams, must be cleared of this charge.

leader. At the same time, he agreed with Jomini that "war, far from being an exact science, is a terrible and impassioned drama, regulated, it is true, by three or four general principles, but also dependent for its results upon a number of moral and physical complications." * His son, Captain Alfred T. Mahan, used the principles of war on land, as formulated by General Baron Jomini, in his approach to the development of naval tactics and naval science.

While the younger Mahan was somewhat influenced by his father, he rejected many of his ideas. The sharp contrast between the views of Professor Mahan and his son is shown by their opinions of the effect on France of the famous British blockade of Brest. Professor Mahan, under the influence of Vauban's ideas, praised the French forts which enabled France to "sleep on in unbroken security under the guns of her sea-bound defenses" while British blockading ships were off her harbors. His son demonstrated that the slumber of France was the sleep of death, for the nation was being slowly strangled by those British ships while its armies marched, like toy soldiers, in illusory triumphs from capital to capital in Europe.†

The different interpretations placed by the two Mahans, father and son, on the same military phenomena illustrate clearly the sharp differences of opinion which often have existed between army and navy officers on the general theory of war. Army leaders generally have subscribed to the sentiments of Napoleon that only heavy battalions and continental wars are decisive in international affairs. Naval officers, understanding the vital importance of all sea-borne trade even to continental nations, generally have believed that control of the seas is more decisive than control of the land. In this book, the relative values of sea power and land power will frequently be contrasted in order that the reader may form his own opinion on one of the most fascinating problems in universal history.

Although differing profoundly as to the value of control of the sea compared with control of the land, Clausewitz and Alfred

* *Outpost Duty*, by D. H. Mahan, Wiley and Putnam, 1841.
† *Field Fortifications*, by D. H. Mahan, Wiley and Putnam, 1836.

Mahan, both earnest students of war and both acquainted from their own experience with its practice, agreed that war was only a means to an end, that end being the achievement of national policy by force when diplomacy proves unavailing. They concluded, therefore, that statesmen ought to keep generals and admirals completely informed in peace as well as in war of the national objectives, whether political, economic, territorial, or ideological. Such knowledge would impose an obligation on generals and admirals to be ready, when statesmen might not be able to obtain national objectives by diplomacy, to secure these objectives by force, with the least possible cost, by prompt and skillful employment of armies and navies. If the leaders of the armed forces could not muster sufficient strength to support the policies of the state by force, it became their duty to advise the statesmen to moderate their ambitions.

Clausewitz divided all wars into two classes: limited; and unlimited or absolute. In the first category he placed wars with minor objectives for which a nation should not risk its total resources or independence; but an absolute or unlimited war required the full expenditure of men and money and should not be undertaken except to preserve the nation or for an objective vital to its future life. Whether limited or unlimited, operations of war would be conducted by the Chief of State in the interest of the State. A limited war might develop into an absolute war; conversely, a national objective for which an absolute war had been prepared might be achieved by a limited effort. In any case, war was not "merely a political act but also a real political instrument, a continuation of political intercourse, ..." As war is a political instrument, Clausewitz emphasized that national policy "is interwoven with the whole action of war, and must exercise a continuous influence" on its conduct as far as the strength of the armed forces will permit. But "the political objective is no despotic law-giver . . . . ; it must accommodate itself to its means and changes in these means may involve a modification of the political objective. . . ."

In preparing for an unlimited war, a nation should make every imaginable preparation in time of peace to the breaking point of a nation's resources in men and money. In commenting on President Kruger's action in commencing the Boer War, Field Marshal von der Goltz carried Clausewitz' theory a step further; he asserted that "The Statesman who, knowing his instrument [armed forces] to be ready *and seeing war inevitable* (italics supplied), hesitates to strike first is guilty of a crime against his country." * Clausewitz and Goltz in the preparation for absolute war included all cognate activities, such as economic and psychological war. If the present generation had been more familiar with Clausewitz, it would have realized as World War II progressed that there was nothing new in Hitler's concept of 'total war' except that Der Fuehrer placed the interests of the Nazi Party and his own power ahead of the permanent interest of Germany. For Hitler was the product of a revolution. Clausewitz and Goltz, on the contrary, were military officers devoted to the interests of the empire and the imperial family. To them war was a business that should be liquidated when it ceased to be profitable, with a view to being resumed under more favorable conditions; they knew that even the result of a particular war was not necessarily decisive or final. The defeated state—and every state in continental Europe has been defeated at one time or another—could anticipate the restoration of its position in a future war by more efficient preparation or by alliance with a more powerful state. The prospect of future rehabilitation inherent in a state with hereditary or long-established governments had no influence upon Nazi leaders who knew that defeat meant the destruction of the party and their own downfall.

The problems which confronted statesmen and military leaders and which were analyzed by Clausewitz and his German successors have more than historical interest. The same problems perplexed President Truman and his military and civil advisers during the Korean War. Sufficient evidence is not now available to pass judgment on the decision to limit the United Nations' effort in Korea. But it is obvious that General MacArthur could not justify his thesis that "There is no substitute for victory." War is not an end, only a means to an end. National policy has often been better

* *The Nation in Arms,* by Field Marshal von der Goltz.

served by a 'limited' than it would have been by an 'unlimited' war. Great Britain gained more by the compromise treaty of Utrecht in 1713 than if she had expended her resources further in order to dictate terms to France. Western Europe should have accepted Wilson's formula "Peace without Victory" in 1916. Bismarck did well for Prussia with a limited victory over Austria. Many statesmen have attained their political objectives without demanding 'unconditional' surrender of an enemy state. Numerous reasons can be advanced for the unconditional surrender of an army, but unconditional surrender of a state is unnecessary. When the armed forces of a state lay down their arms, that state is at the mercy of the victor; and "woe to the vanquished."

As already stated, Mahan agreed with Clausewitz that wars are only the outward and forcible manifestations of conflicting foreign policies, and they differ from periods of peace only in that nations obtain national objectives by means other than diplomacy. When first heard, this doctrine seems cold-blooded; but, if correctly understood and acted upon by sagacious statesmen, it would actually prevent many wars. It presupposes intelligent, unselfish leaders, who would not expose their nations to war until the possibilities of prolonging the peace had been thoroughly explored. It would prevent all wars occasioned by personal ambition or private pique of rulers. There would be no dynastic wars. In fact, war would then result only when national honor was involved or vital interests were threatened. As national leaders came to realize that only under extraordinary circumstances can the use of force be justified biologically, economically, politically, or morally, there would be longer periods of peace and shorter intervals of war. It might be, however, that if wars were less frequent they would be greater in intensity.

During World War I, when the Germans were accused of rabid militarism, they retorted by accusing the British nation of navalism or Mahanism. There was a certain amount of justice in the countercharge. Just as Clausewitz had shaped German military philosophy, Mahan's books and essays for almost a quarter of a century had influenced the decisions of British statesmen, admirals, and some generals. Disciples of Clausewitz demanded that Germany make "every imaginable preparation" for war. As the German fleet developed, Mahan urged his own and the British governments to augment their fleets. In 1910 he went further and suggested an increase in the British army and later even advocated compulsory military service for the United Kingdom. As Clausewitz urged unlimited violence on land, Mahan advocated the rigorous exercise of naval power at sea.

Mahan also believed that "power, force, is a faculty of national life, one of the talents committed to nations by God," and that with this power went responsibilities, among which was the "obligation to maintain right by force if need be. . . ." "Peace," Mahan thought, "is not adequate to all progress; there are resistances that can be overcome only by explosion."

In some very important respects, Mahan differed entirely from Clausewitz, and particularly from some modern disciples of Clausewitz who have distorted his doctrine. Mahan believed that "In physical coercion of material evil, the sword acts within its sphere . . . it has not power over intellect, or moral assent, nor should it dare to assume such power." Even within its own sphere, the sword, Mahan thought, should be invoked very rarely, for "war has ceased to be the natural or even normal condition of nations, and military considerations are simply accessory and subordinate to the other greater interests, economical and commercial, which they assure and so subserve."

Even before World War I there was a school of thought in Germany, claiming descent from Clausewitz, whose spokesman was General Bernhardi, that advocated war for war's sake: violence was the ultimate expression of a nation's spirit. This became the theme of many of Mussolini's bombastic speeches. Hitler carried the idea to its ultimate conclusion and would have destroyed the weak simply because they were weak and at the mercy of the "master race." Mahan, on the contrary, looked forward to a better day, and it was his "personal conviction that when moral motives come to weigh heavier with mankind than do material desires, there will be no war, and coincidentally therewith better provisions of reasonable bodily necessities to all men."

In his speculations on war, Clausewitz boldly contemplated the possibility of national defeat and possible enslavement. Nevertheless, as tutor to the Crown Prince of Prussia he urged his royal pupil to follow the example of Frederick the Great and never to despair of victory. The persistence of the influence of Clausewitz on the minds of the German people was shown by the radio broadcasts of Lieutenant General Kurt Ditmars during the last six months of World War II as the armies of Russia, Great Britain, and the United States slowly crushed the Reich. The more desperate the situation, the more frequent were the references to the conduct of Frederick the Great and the philosophy of Clausewitz. In almost the last appeal to his countrymen to continue their resistance, Ditmars reminded them that Clausewitz who had formulated the thesis of "the supremacy of policy over strategy . . . had determined the mental and spiritual character of the German officer and the General Staff over a century . . ."

It is unnecessary to remind the reader that, prior to World War II while the Clausewitz theory animated the German army, the United States, as co-author of the Kellogg-Briand Pact, had abjured the use of force as an instrument of national policy. Today the legislative and executive branches of the government have pledged the United States as a member of the United Nations to assist in preserving the peace of the world, using force if necessary. Should the most recent and most ambitious attempt at collective security fail, it will be more essential than before for American officials, if they cannot preserve the peace, to win the ensuing war. The Korean War has proved that armed force is still necessary in the conduct of international affairs, and there is a corresponding obligation upon the United States to continue to maintain its armed forces in readiness for immediate action. Potential strength is not enough in the present era of "A" and "H" bombs and supersonic planes. This country must be actually and militarily strong or it will be imposed upon, perhaps defeated, by more powerful nations. With its growth in strength will come a moral responsibility foreseen by Mahan and already acknowledged by American statesmen to help the backward and oppressed nations of the world —not in the vain hope of gaining their good will, but to avoid the vicious effect on American character of bullying small nations.

Chapter 2

Land, Sea, and Air Forces as Factors of Peace

In this book the terms 'land power,' 'sea power,' and 'air power' will be frequently used and need to be clearly defined. A nation may be considered a preponderant sea power when it exerts its strength mainly on the sea and with fleets; a preponderant land power when it exercises its strength mainly on land and with armies; and a preponderant air power when it exercises its strength mainly in the air and with aircraft. And, it is no reflection on the patriotism or ability of the citizens of small nations to state they have no chance of maintaining a preponderance on land, sea, or in the air.

The objective of land power, sea power, and air power is the same: to control land and the peoples living on the land. Land power by physically occupying the land can exercise a direct control. A sea and an air power are alike in acting not by physical occupation but by bringing pressure to bear on people.

A preponderant land power exercises its strength directly by its ground troops. Large formations of soldiers, preceded, accompanied, and assisted by aviation and fleets, invade a neighboring state, occupy strategic and commercially valuable territory, requisition all supplies, and commandeer the services of the civilian population. This control is absolute and can be continued as long as there are enough soldiers and weapons to enforce the will of the conquering land power.

A preponderant sea power, by its naval strength, protects its own coasts from overseas invasion and defends and fosters its own sea-borne trade; next, it suppresses sea-borne trade of the enemy, captures enemy merchant ships, blockades hostile ports, and confiscates goods destined to the enemy country. The pressure of sea power is more gradual than that of land power, but it can inflict deadly wounds on the economic life of an enemy nation, while protecting its own trade and enabling its industry to sustain a long war. The more dependent a country is on overseas trade, the more vulnerable it is to sea power. Countries like Great Britain and Japan which must import food, raw materials, and fuel could not exist if a hostile power should control the seas around them. Japan sought peace a month before the atomic bomb was dropped on Hiroshima, and surrendered because her sea communications were cut. But sea power can also influence continental nations, because no country can prosper without sea-borne trade. In the past, British sea power has exerted enough pressure on great continental nations, including Russia and France, so that they either changed sides or submitted.

Allied control of the sea in the last war repeatedly menaced widely separated hostile positions and forced the enemy to divert resources and 'tie troops down' in extensive entrenchments. Simultaneously, control of the sea relieved the United States of providing large numbers of soldiers to defend either coast.

Usually it has been unnecessary for a nation possessing preponderant sea power to maintain a large standing army in time of peace. After World War I began in 1914, Great Britain, under the influence of Kitchener, created a great army, which was disbanded at the Armistice; the United States did the same in World War II. It was necessary for them to mobilize and demobilize these huge armies because their allies were unable to provide large enough land armies of their own. A sea power generally is entitled to depend upon its allies to provide armies, because these are essential to their own defense and are not necessary to a nation controlling the sea and the air over the important sea lanes.

Before discussing air power further, it is important to make clear one point: nowadays, both armies and navies are three-dimensional. Victory on the ground is more easily won when air superiority over the battlefield gives the necessary observation for the ground guns and, by tactical bombing, provides a more flexible and greater range of artillery support for the infantry and tanks. But air superiority can be and has been neutralized in campaigns by superior numbers of ground troops and the character of the terrain, as in Korea. Often air superiority is rendered temporarily impotent by weather, as in the opening days of the Nazi offensive in December 1944; other arms are also affected by weather but not to the same extent. A fleet, like an army, must have both short-range artillery—guns—and long-range flying missiles—bombers and torpedo planes. But for armies and navies alike, the airplane provides just another weapon or instrument to take its place in the fighting team. When so employed, it is only a part of land or naval power just as artillery or tanks are an integral part of land power; or as the submarine, which also operates in the third dimension, is an integral part of naval power.

Naval aviation in this country, for example, has always been a part of the navy. The British Government after World War I placed the Royal Air Force in charge of the development of aviation. In 1938, they returned the Fleet Air Arm to the navy. In the meantime, their carrier planes and pilots had fallen behind their American contemporaries. On land, the practice has not been so clear-cut. But even here it has been necessary to provide a part of the air strength as a tactical air force to work closely with the ground troops. Russia, following the example of Germany in World War II, since that war has included tactical planes as a part of her army.

Air power, then, is something different from the mere use of the airplane as an integral part of the fighting team on land or water. It is the exercise of a nation's strength mainly through aviation and in the air. The basic elements of United States air power are the aviation of the U.S. Air Force, of the Army, Navy and Marine Corps, all nourished and partly sustained by the aircraft industry and civilian air transport.

To date, no great nation has depended entirely or primarily on air power to protect its territory or to advance its national interests. There are no historic instances to support or disprove claims that by air strength alone a state can become a great world power.

At present, air-borne commerce is not sufficiently important to any nation to make its loss a vital national blow. In all probability, air commerce will never become as necessary to any nation as sea-borne commerce has been to Great Britain and Japan. If great nations ever became as dependent upon supplies by air as great insular nations have been upon supplies by sea, air power would be more nearly comparable with sea power, for a nation possessing superior combat aviation could probably destroy or interrupt the air commerce of an adversary. But a nation whose geographical position, genius for commerce, and aptitude for aviation would lead it to create a great commercial air fleet, probably would have the ability and foresight to create a combat air fleet to defend its air-borne trade.

The most important aspect of air power is its ability to strike directly from the skies at the inhabitants and economy of a nation. Whereas formerly sea power could strike only at water-borne commerce and the coastal fringes of an enemy's economy, today, like air power, its carrier planes can strike directly at the population and industry within ranges of carrier planes. Air power can strike at the entire economy in depth, within range of its planes taking off air fields nearest the enemy. This is the modern equivalent of an army's encircling a besieged city and possessing artillery adequate in range to destroy any part of the city.

Ardent exponents of air power would rely on this ability of an air force as the main means to win wars. During World War II, Marshal of the Royal Air Force, Sir Arthur Harris, recommended a complete reversal of "the old principle that wars are to be won by seeking out and overcoming the enemy's armed forces . . ." * He proposed that, when the British Government had obtained "4,000 heavy bombers," they "ignore alike the German Army and Navy, except insofar as it was necessary to defend England,

* *Bomber Command*, by Sir Arthur Harris, Collins, London, pp. 278-279.

and secure our (English) bases and sea communications while striking continuously at the enemy's industrial potential."

In World War II, every effort made by any belligerent power to win the war or even major campaigns by air attacks alone failed; on the other hand, superior aviation integrated with land and sea forces was the decisive factor in many battles and campaigns. Nazi air attacks could not prevent evacuation of the British Expeditionary Force and, operating independently, overcome the United Kingdom in 1940. Similar failures of first the British and then the British-American air attacks on the Reich in 1942 and 1943 completely discredited the Harris theory of winning a war by air attacks alone. The invention of atomic and hydrogen bombs temporarily revived this fallacy, for at first only very long-range bombers could deliver nuclear weapons, whose radius and powers of destruction were so great that even bombs dropped from rapidly flying planes could land near enough to a target to have devastating effects. Air enthusiasts exhumed the Harris theory. But in a short time, ships' batteries, shore artillery, then field artillery and carrier planes were adapted to deliver atomic bombs and shells. Long-range heavy bombers now offer just one of many means of delivering devastating attacks using nuclear weapons; as the pioneer and principal deliverer they may be the most available at the present time, but their monopoly no longer exists.

Gunpowder was first used in cannon. The French were the first to build clumsy but effective muskets that would fire smaller projectiles; and the infantry regained its former status relative to artillery. Modern industry and science will doubtless provide additional means of delivering nuclear bombs and it will become more a question of delivery than construction of nuclear or even more deadly weapons. One fact can be accepted: virile nations may be defeated and destroyed, but they will not be terrified into abandoning powerful weapons. History is positive on that point. Hydrogen bombs can inflict no greater horrors than did the Vikings with their battle-axes, or the Saracen pirates in the Mediterranean, or the Hungarian bowmen on their ponies; nuclear weapons only devastate faster, not more completely. Europeans fought back, and finally emerged from the Dark Ages. As late as

1913 we were told that war had become so horrible it could never happen again. Wars have been more frequent since that date than in the nineteenth century.

Air power alone proved equally indecisive in the Korean War. However, air power is still too young for the experience of World War II to be taken as conclusive. Also, air power was handicapped by political decisions of the United Nations in the Korean War. The present and future potentialities of air power need, therefore, further analysis. Comparison of air power with land and sea power will help in estimating its strength and weakness.

The elements of land power include huge continental areas sufficiently large to be almost self-sustaining in raw materials; a population patriotic, virile, hard working, and with enough of the martial spirit to make good soldiers; an industry sufficiently developed and technically advanced to produce modern weapons. Without these elements, no nation can become a great land power. Even though great land powers depend primarily on their field armies, they also need naval and air units as adjuncts to their armies to assist in the defense of their sea and air frontiers.

A nation aspiring to sea power must have, first, the capacity to produce goods or commodities for export; and, second, the shipping facilities necessary to carry these goods abroad and to return with raw materials. This implies an extensive merchant marine, which in time of war provides transports, tankers, and supply ships which support the combat navy. But during war the merchant ships also require naval escort, so they are in that respect a liability. Formerly colonies were considered necessary to a sea power, serving as overseas bases and sources of raw material. Colonies also require protection from the home country. Access on equal terms to foreign markets can be as profitable economically as possession of colonies. For example, Argentina has been until recently as valuable a customer of the United Kingdom as if she were a member of the British Empire. Way stations or naval bases are requisite to a naval power, even at the price of expensive naval facilities, fortifications, garrisons, and the continuous hostility of neighboring states. A sea power should not have more of these overseas bases than are needed; they are expensive and their garrisons absorb thousands of soldiers. In time, improved machinery and atomic power will enable fleets to remain almost indefinitely at sea. Even in World War II, United States men-of-war regularly fueled underway; huge floating dry docks, and repair ships following close behind the combat task forces, transformed any open roadstead into a temporary advance base.

The elements of air strength require more discussion. Land and sea weapons developed slowly, and land and sea power evolved gradually as nations were integrated into empires or great states. Compared with other weapons, airplanes have improved with extraordinary rapidity. The development of aviation has been so rapid and so forced by two world wars that we cannot evaluate it as accurately as other land and sea weapons which evolved more slowly. It is clear, however, that only a powerful nation with a scientific, industrious, martial population can supply the crews and planes necessary to create a preponderant air force. Bases are even more important for air power than they are for sea power because of the enormous fuel consumption of airplanes and the greater vulnerability of their mechanism. The attrition that an air force suffers from simply operating under combat conditions is quite often comparable to the losses from actual combat with enemy.

Not since the fall of the Roman Empire has one nation possessed both preponderant land and sea power. In subsequent wars, the great powers have exercised force in international relations either by preponderant land power or preponderant sea power. In wars of alliances, in the beginning one group has usually possessed superior armies; the other, superior fleets; and the first phase of the war is frequently a struggle between superior land power and superior sea power.

Land power may be more essential to one nation; sea power, to another. Germany, France, and Russia have always needed more powerful armies than navies. France was defeated by Germany in 1871 and in 1940, although her navy was much superior. Russia was defeated by Germany in 1915-16, although her allies possessed complete control of the sea; and in 1939 Poland was crushed although her allies dominated the oceans. Nor could the greater sea power of Great Britain prevent the German invasion of Russia in 1941, although it did mitigate its effects and stiffen the resistance of the Soviet armies. Nor could superior armies and air forces defend the United Kingdom if the British navy lost control of the sea and its imports were suppressed. It is not sufficient to contrast the abstract value of sea with land power, but it is essential to ascertain the actual value of each attribute to a particular nation.

For our purpose it is desirable to contrast the value of sea power and land power; however, obviously all great nations do not have the choice of becoming a great sea power or a great land power. Russia, today, the greatest land power on earth, could only by the utmost exertion become a great sea power because her sea fronts are too widely separated. If Russia attempted to maintain a preponderant navy, she would need at least four fleets—one for the Baltic Sea, one for the Black Sea and Mediterranean, one for the Persian Gulf, and one for the Far East. If these fleets were ever threatened by an enemy from the eastern Atlantic, the Mediterranean, or the western Pacific, it would be almost impossible for them to concentrate; their physical separation means that, to be effective on the offensive, each of four Russian fleets would have to equal the strength of a probable enemy. As if to compensate for this handicap on the sea, the solid continental mass of the Soviet Republics, now that they have developed a modern industry of their own, makes them almost immune to blockade, and therefore practically independent of threats of sea power. For a sea power to attempt to blockade Russia would suggest a whale trying to strangle an elephant.

The United Kingdom cannot become a great land power. During the One Hundred Years War with France, England strove to be a continental power and failed; not until the middle of the seventeenth century did she turn her whole energies toward the seas. More recently, Japan made a disastrous mistake in attempting to become a great land and sea power.

It is easy to understand how invading armies can take complete possession of a conquered nation, levy contributions, conscript labor, and compel the disarmed inhabitants to submit to their conquerors. It is most difficult to realize the slow, irresistible, boa constrictor effect of control of the sea upon even a continental nation like France or Germany with numerous land neighbors. One of the most dramatic contests between land and sea power ended with the overthrow of France under its great warrior and statesman, Napoleon, whose genius delayed for over a decade, but could not avert, the defeat of his empire. Many factors contributed to the downfall of the First French Empire, the foremost being the complete cessation of French ocean trade which deranged the entire economy. This condition compelled Napoleon to resort to the Continental System, in a desperate effort to embargo British trade with continental Europe, and thus to compel the British Government to see peace.

The Continental System practically prohibited British trade with the continent, but the British diverted their merchant ships and goods to the Western Hemisphere and smuggled their own and transhipped neutral goods into Napoleon's allied and satellite states: the Emperor himself connived at the importation of overcoats and boots for the army. In the last phase of that great contest the Royal navy limited its blockade to France proper. Its more important task was to escort its own and friendly neutral ships to other European ports. British sea-borne trade was temporarily reduced, and in 1809-11 there was an economic depression, but new sources of trade produced a gradual revival.

The Continental System interrupted a flourishing Anglo-Russian trade in ship timber, hemp, and other commodities. This interruption caused more hardships in Russia than England. The Czar informed Napoleon he would denounce the system, although he knew such action invited war with France. In an attempt to enforce compliance, Napoleon invaded Russia. The subsequent retreat from Moscow and the ensuing revolt of Europe against France brought the downfall of the French Empire. If Napoleon had won the battle of Waterloo, he would have only postponed defeat; already he had exhausted the manhood of France and antagonized all Europe in his vain attempts to force Great Britain to cease the capture of ships and cargoes and to raise the blockade which was strangling France.

There is a close parallel between the careers of Napoleon and Hitler. Both were products of a revolution, both were parvenus in power. Both overran western Europe and negotiated nonaggression pacts with Russia. Neither could invade the British islands, suppress British trade, or compel the British Government to make peace. Both were denied access to world markets and correspondingly were more dependent upon the raw materials of Europe, especially of Russia. Both exacted the heaviest tribute from conquered states, quartered soldiers in allied and hostile cities; both for a short time were able to make force or a show of force support the expenditures of war. As they expended their resources, they gradually lost strength and were compelled to demand increasing supplies from adjacent states, including terrified and obsequious neutrals.

In 1812 Napoleon, and in 1941 Hitler, invaded Russia. Other factors influenced their decisions. But British sea power was the compelling cause in both cases; sea power gave the British Isles comparative immunity from the threats of Hitler, as well as from those of Napoleon; sea power compelled them both to resort to a war of endurance, during which they became increasingly dependent upon the benevolent neutrality and economic assistance of Russia. The genius and tact of Napoleon enabled him to continue the struggle until the Czar denounced the Continental System. The impatient Hitler confronting an England he could not conquer, distrusting Stalin who was increasing the Red armies, and confident that his land and air forces could win the decision, invaded Russia in 1941. The Reich soon became enmeshed in the same fatal sequence of events which, after a longer struggle, had caused the downfall of France under Napoleon. It is improbable that a western European coalition can defeat either Great Britain or Russia, for Britain restores its strength continuously, even in war, by its sea communications, and Russia from its enormous territory and population. Moreover, in the effort to defeat one, the chances are that the other will be drawn into the war, and no nation or coalition of nations in Europe can simultaneously defeat the sea power of Great Britain and the land power of Russia.

Control of the land by armies is absolute. Invading troops take possession of flourishing cities and seize the products of enemy factories, mines, and fields. Control of the sea is less complete than control of the land. Its object is to protect friendly ships and capture or destroy hostile ships. The extent of the oceans prevents remote areas from being continuously patrolled, and navies have never been able to control directly any portion of the seas except that under the guns of their widely deployed ships. With the use of carrier planes, the size of the area that can be controlled at any one time by naval fleets has greatly multiplied. However, it is still only a small fraction of the water's surface. Generally the superior fleet can control the traveled sea routes, the main crossroads of the oceans, and the great sea terminals, but only after it has defeated or forced the enemy fleet to retire to its own harbors.

After defeating or blockading the enemy fleet, no navy has ever been able to suppress enemy trade entirely. At the height of British sea power in the Napoleonic Wars after the Battle of Trafalgar, it was always feasible for some French convoys to evade the British blockade. At the height of American sea power in World War II when we dominated the seas around Japan, some Japanese ships were still able to get through to China, Manchuria, and Korea. Nor has any navy ever protected its own merchant marine completely. It was always possible for a few French privateers or small squadrons to escape the British blockade and capture British merchant men. Losses suffered by the British Merchant Marine during the Napoleonic Wars were continuous and severe. During twenty-one years of war with France, the British lost annually an average of nearly five hundred merchant ships. In addition, during the three years that the United States was in the war, 1812-15, their ships took about 1,600 British merchant men. During the years 1812-15, inclusive, Great Britain probably lost about 1,030 ships per year, an average of approximately 2.8 ships per day. During World War II, Nazi submarines were able to operate and inflict losses to the end of the war. In 1942, the submarines sank allied ships faster than we were able to build them.

Although not as continuous or as certain as control of the land, control of the sea effectually suppresses the overseas commerce of an enemy. And no European nation to date, not even a continental nation like France or Germany has been able to sustain a long war when deprived of its overseas trade. In 1917, the Kaiser resorted to unrestricted submarine warfare in a desperate effort to avoid the effects of Great Britain's control of the Atlantic Ocean and the Mediterranean Sea. This action brought the United States into the war with disastrous results to Germany.

Control of the sea will not immediately force an enemy to sue for peace. If a nation or group of nations controlling the seas can simultaneously invade the enemy country, the decision will be gained earlier. Control of the sea contrasted with control of the land is transitory and incomplete; it is slower in its results, but history proves that its influence has been quite as decisive.

Control of the air is even less continuous and complete than control of the sea. Airplanes cannot remain aloft as long as surface ships can remain at sea. Control of the air must be in depth (or altitude) as well as in the horizontal plane: this multiplies the difficulties of control rather than merely adds to them. Airplanes are more subject to weather.

The great weakness of ships is their dependence upon bases where they can refuel, refit, and repair. Without such bases, a magnificent fleet, when it expends its fuel, would be no more use than a collection of painted ships on a painted ocean. So, next to ships, the most important element in sea power is the possession of adequate bases. Airplanes are even more dependent on bases than ships are. In the near future some combat ships will be propelled by atomic power that will render them less dependent on overseas bases. On account of the size and weight of a shield that will protect personnel from atomic rays, it will be very difficult to drive piloted planes with nuclear power.

As in the case of sea power, with the possession of favorably situated bases and sufficient superiority in airplanes, an air power can maintain control over small areas of land and water. But, as mentioned, their control is even less continuous and effective than that of sea power. The most spectacular triumph of air power alone in World War II was the air-borne invasion of Crete, a clear-cut victory of airships over surface ships. It is fair to add that this air invasion was only across a sixty-five mile stretch of sea, that the surface ships had little supporting aviation; and to observe that the German air losses were heavy, and that the Luftwaffe did not undertake to follow this success with the capture of Cyprus, only 350 miles distant. During most of World War II, the Axis controlled the air between Tunisia and Sicily. Yet time and again Allies were able to reinforce Malta by sea, and the Axis never succeeded in taking the island. During the Korean War we had practically unchallenged control of the air over the entire Korean peninsula, yet the Chinese Reds were able to continue to supply and to maintain an effective army at the front. Continuous control of the air has not yet been obtained over territory of a resolute enemy, with efficient fighting planes and well sited and defended air fields.

From the evacuation of Dunkirk through May 1941, the German Luftwaffe was at liberty to concentrate its full force on the United Kingdom. During that time, London was bombed unmercifully. For fifty-seven successive nights that city was the target of the Luftwaffe. No city in the United Kingdom was safe. Destruction of Coventry added a new word to the English language, 'coventried.' The only restriction on the use of German aviation was the latent threat from Russia which compelled the German High Command to retain a considerable portion of their air force on the eastern frontier and limited the losses they could accept in the effort to subdue the United Kingdom. Except for this armed truce on Germany's eastern frontier, Air Marshal Goering could and did employ the full might of his very efficient air forces.

In spite of all their planes and the numerous well-equipped air fields in France and the Low Countries which formed a vast crescent around the south and east coast of England, German aviation could not compel the British people to sue for peace. Many factors contributed to the failure of the Luftwaffe; the magnificent behavior of the Royal Air Force and the robust determination of the British people were not the least, but the decisive factor was the ability of the British navy and merchant marine to maintain the overseas communications of the British Isles. In spite of the destruction of port facilities, of the railway system ashore and repeated disruption of the coastwise shipping, the British navy and merchant marine supplied the United Kingdom during this terrible ordeal. In the longest and fairest trial between superior air forces combined with inferior surface ships, and inferior air ships combined with superior surface ships to control the water approaches to a powerful nation, the surface ships won. The air battles for Britain proved that control of the air through aviation alone is not sufficient to crush a determined insular nation which can maintain its overseas communications.

If the Germans had gained control of the waters around the British Isles for six to twelve weeks, the British Government would have been compelled to yield in spite of the courage and determination of the British citizens.

Then in 1943 and 1944 the Allies won preponderance in the air and had the opportunity to try to subdue Germany by air power alone. This experience will be more fully discussed in Chapter 5; here it is sufficient to say that this attempt of air power alone to win the war was also a failure. It did put pressure on Germany and force her to use hundreds of thousands of laborers, many of them prisoners of war, to repair bomb damage and to produce antiaircraft weapons; and it tied up tens of thousands of soldiers in manning the defensive weapons. On the other hand, to mount the Allied effort likewise absorbed the labor of hundreds of thousands of men and diverted aircraft and men from aiding directly the armed forces on land and on sea. Whether on balance the Allies invested more of their men, material, and effort in these attacks than the Germans did in repelling them and effecting repairs is difficult to say. No one has yet made a factual comparison of the relative expenditures in men and money.

The first target of land, sea, or air forces should be the opposing armed forces. The absence of Lee's cavalry, which was off raiding the northern countryside, cost him dear at the battle of Gettysburg. Chiang Kai-shek's armies concentrated on defending cities in the Chinese civil war while the out-numbered Reds refused to be bound to cities and picked off Chiang's armies one by one. In all of the French naval wars, their navy never accepted, or at least never consistently acted upon, this fundamental principle, although on several occasions the French navy had been numerically superior to the British navy. In 1778-79, the French fleet had temporary command of the English Channel. It did not seek to destroy or blockade the British fleet. A few troops were landed on the southwest shores of England and subsequently re-embarked and returned to France. Very soon the British shipyards had refitted and the Admiralty commissioned enough ships to make their fleet superior.

The French Mediterranean fleet nearly always has substituted territorial objectives, such as the capture of the island of Minorca or the invasion of Egypt, for the real objective which was the British Mediterranean fleet. A French Admiral, de Castex, after World War I, realized this fact and said that Mahan's greatest contribution to naval warfare was his demonstration of the principle, forgotten by the French, that the enemy fleet was the primary objective of a superior navy.

In the early part of World War II, the Japanese fleet made the traditional mistake of the French fleet despite the fact that the Japanese officers were well acquainted with the teachings of Mahan. Instead of using their utmost endeavors to destroy the American navy in the Pacific, they joined with their army to seize vast tracts of territory extending from Burma and French Indo-China to the Solomons which, unless they could defeat our fleet, they could hold only temporarily. Meanwhile, Admiral King was reinforcing Admiral Nimitz. On June 4, 1942, at the Battle of Midway, the American navy gained control of the entire eastern Pacific by its defeat of the Japanese fleet. From that moment, all of the Japanese insular possessions were in pawn to the American fleet, which was continuously increasing in strength. Thus Japan's violation of a fundamental principle opened the way for the American advance in 1943 and 1944.

The defeat of the enemy fleet is the first step in a naval war. After the fleet is defeated or driven into port, the enemy country can be blockaded and the enemy merchant marine destroyed. The destruction of the merchant marine and the suppression of the sea-borne commerce of an insular empire, such as Japan, will compel its surrender without landing a soldier ashore.

The destruction of the enemy merchant marine, which is the second object of naval war, can never be thoroughly done until his combat fleet has been destroyed. There had been numerous officers, particularly in the American navy in its early days, who advocated that privateering and attacks on enemy sea-borne commerce be substituted for a battle with the enemy fleet. Privateering was not an effective means of attacking enemy commerce and did not justify the men and ships it absorbed even during the Revolution, when our navy was so small that it could not hope to battle with the British fleet on the oceans.

In the 1914-18 war, the reaction of Germany to the British blockade was to begin ruthless submarine war. On account of the novelty of the weapon, the absorption of British men and resources in Kitchener's armies, and the lack of vigorous defensive measures, this campaign almost succeeded. It might have been successful except for intervention by the United States. The submarine threat to the Japanese Empire and the British Isles will always be formidable, and each navy will be compelled to set apart a large part of its forces, particularly aviation, to combat this menace. Even so, submarine war against merchant shipping cannot take the place of the complete destruction of the enemy navy and the entire suppression of his sea-going commerce. In our war with Japan, American submarines were the first arm of the fleet to take the offensive. No branch of our navy did more toward defeating Japan than our submarines. In the first three years of the war, almost half of the tonnage Japan possessed in January 1942 was sunk. This destruction of Japanese merchant ships, while our surface fleet was defeating the Japanese surface fleet, undoubtedly shortened the second phase of the war in which our navy and land forces occupied bases near enough to Japan to blockade effectively that insular empire. This major success should not be allowed to conceal the fact that the navy should have done better with its submarines.

Not until June 1943, when Admiral Nimitz discontinued the

use of the exploders provided by the Bureau of Ordnance, could a submarine commander depend upon his torpedoes to explode after hitting or running just under the keel of an enemy ship. With incredible obstinacy the Bureau of Ordnance did little to improve the torpedoes after these defects had been reported. Finally, machinists' and gunners' mates at Pearl Harbor made necessary modifications.

In addition, the depth mechanism in torpedoes launched by planes and submarines proved unreliable, causing many torpedoes to pass harmlessly under enemy ships. Considerable responsibility for these defects in torpedoes must be shared by former commanders-in-chief of the fleet, who never insisted upon testing these weapons under conditions that would exist in war. In striking contrast, Japanese fleet and squadron commanders fired torpedoes with exploders in the war heads from destroyers, submarines, and aircraft to ascertain the ruggedness of material. They found from actual experience that it was necessary for a plane to descend to very low altitudes to launch a torpedo successfully. Our officers waited until war began to discover the limitations of their weapons.

We can take pride in the skill and daring of our submarine commanders and the assistance they rendered Admirals Spruance and Halsey in the two fleet engagements that destroyed the bulk and dispersed the remnants of the combined fleet. They provided both Admirals with early and generally reliable information, and then sank two enemy flagships. We should still regret that much more was not done, by diverting more submarines from their attacks on enemy merchantmen to act as scouts and attack enemy combat ships. The serious losses our submarines inflicted on the enemy's commerce and the resulting continuous reduction of the mobility of the Japanese fleet and the slowdown of the Japanese industry naturally made Admirals Nimitz and Lockwood reluctant to divert sufficient submarines to work with the 3rd and 5th Fleets.

Had sufficient submarines been available to Spruance in May and June 1944, he would have been spared the disappointment of letting the Japanese fleet escape a major air attack for fear of an attack on his amphibious forces; and in October Halsey and Kinkaid would have been provided with more accurate and continuous information of Kurita's movements. Undoubtedly, submarine commanders were reluctant to halt their sinkings of merchant men which acts were dealing a vital blow at the enemy, but their attitude can no more be condoned than that of the air commanders who labored under the delusion that planes alone could win a war.

The effect of control of the sea on continental powers like Germany and France differs from that on the British and Japanese islands. By virtue of their land neighbors, continental nations can obtain supplies by land; and in the naval wars of the seventeenth and eighteenth centuries, it became a regular practice to land goods in neutral ports and transship them by land to the blockaded nation. This subterfuge deranged the usual trade routes and added greatly to the cost of the goods, but it did tend to nullify the effects of the blockade. The doctrine of continuous voyage was the natural legal remedy for this evasion of international law. Under this doctrine, which all Americans should cherish for it shortened the Civil War and did much to preserve the Union in 1861-65, the guilt or innocence of the cargo, and possibly the ship, is fixed by the *eventual destination* of the goods. If goods were eventually destined for the enemy, they could be seized at any place on the open seas. During the Civil War, blockade runners, mainly British, consigned goods to Bermuda and the Bahama Islands which were actually destined for the South Atlantic States. The American Government revived this doctrine in order effectively to blockade the Southern States. Great Britain had employed this same doctrine in her wars against France, Holland, and Spain; she could not question its validity. Under it, the American navy seized British ships in the Atlantic or Gulf of Mexico if their cargoes were plainly intended to serve the Confederacy.

Another device of traders to avoid the rigors of sea power was to shift merchant ships of a belligerent to a neutral flag—an obvious fraud intended to infringe on the rights of a belligerent. Such vessels were seized and sent in for adjudication. The ingenious neutrals (or "thieving traders," according to Admiral Nelson) arranged another artifice. In 1856, after the Crimean War, Great Britain and France having been allies, the British Government yielded to the request of France and agreed to a new doctrine that a neutral flag covers enemy's goods, except contraband of war. This was the so-called "Free Ship, Free Goods" doctrine, earlier advocated by the Netherlanders. This would permit belligerent nations with an inferior navy to evade the effect of blockade and nullify the value of a superior fleet and control of the sea. Fortunately, the United States did not sign this treaty. If it had done so, it would have been compelled to disavow its action, or the United States navy would have been unable to blockade the Southern States during the Civil War.

In the exercise of air power, the same rule holds true; the main target is the air forces of the enemy. The successful examples of the use of air power so far (Crete, Pantelleria) are those in which this mission was accomplished. The unsuccessful examples, the German air offensive against the United Kingdom in 1940 and the Allied air offensive against Germany in 1943, were those in which this objective could not be attained. It might be commented that Goering in 1940 at least tried. There was a tendency among the Allied airmen, as shown in the above-cited quotation from Harris, even to deny the necessity of attacking enemy aircraft. As a result, the German jet planes in the last months of the war almost succeeded in securing control of the air. If Hitler had devoted the effort and resources that were put into the V-1 and V-2 into jet fighters, he might have succeeded.

As shown above, sea power by nature is less complete, less absolute, than is land power. It is accordingly more tolerable for other nations to bear. In the seventeenth century, Bacon's statement that sea power "was an abridgment of the sovereignty of all nations" was true. Nevertheless, the whole world acquiesced in British sea power between 1815 and 1914. During this time, the British Empire was enlarged by the simple process of landing a few soldiers or marines on any piece of territory she desired outside of continental Europe or the Western Hemisphere. Because of the isolated position of most of these acquisitions and the moderation with which Great Britain exercised this enormous power, no European nation or alliance was sufficiently injured to challenge her preponderant sea power by force.

Great Britain did not hesitate to employ sea power against Russia, her traditional rival, when it seemed necessary. During several Anglo-Russian crises, the Admiralty dispatched superior naval forces to shadow all Russian naval forces that might threaten British ships or trade.

At the Hague Conference of 1899, Captain "Jackie" Fisher, British naval representative, flatly refused to consider a proposal to suspend all military or naval movements while a controversy was submitted to international arbitration. His reason was simple; the British navy was always on a war footing, and he did not propose to give a possible rival three to six months' notice to recruit sailors and put ships into commission. The British attitude was supported by the German delegation for a similar reason. The German army could always be mobilized faster and strike sooner and harder than either the French or Russian. The General Staff in Berlin did not propose to sacrifice this advantage while an International Court deliberated on the merits of an international dispute. A few years later when Germany challenged British naval supremacy with its building program, Fisher proposed to King Edward that the British "Copenhagen" the German fleet, that is, destroy it by a surprise attack in harbor as the British did to the Danish fleet a century before, or surprise the fleet while at sea and take it into custody. Edward VII recoiled at the idea, and Fisher claimed he was speaking in a jocular manner. But with Fisher's knowledge of the growing strength of the German navy and the determination of the German army to strike first on land, in all probability his proposal was seriously made.

The British Government adopted a balance of power policy which included supporting Turkey to prevent Russia from reaching the Mediterranean. But unless her dominant position on the seas was threatened, she exercised her enormous sea power with great restraint; and during a century when all other first class powers were creating tariff barriers she adhered to a policy of free trade. This moderation was not entirely altruistic. With the start the United Kingdom had gained in modern industry, her great merchant marine and the possession of steaming coal near tidewater, British industry could meet all foreign competitors. Furthermore, the leaders of Great Britain realized that if she was too drastic in exercising her belligerent rights on the sea, she might inspire a European coalition which could in time out-build her navy, threaten her foreign trade and her very existence.

Under the present conditions, it is doubtful if any nation could maintain a navy sufficiently strong to exercise the almost universal control of the sea that was exercised by Great Britain between 1815 and 1900. If the United States attempted to create and maintain over a long period a naval force powerful enough to control the eastern Atlantic, the Pacific, the Mediterranean Sea and the Indian Ocean, it would probably ultimately cause such hostility among the European and Asian countries that they would gradually create a coalition against the United States.

Although no nation since Rome has possessed preponderant land power and sea power, these national attributes are not in themselves mutually exclusive. The possession of ample land power of itself certainly does not prejudice the chances of a nation aspiring to sea power or air power, or both. Currently, the conditions essential for naval strength likewise favor the creation of air strength. The United States land, sea, and air forces, therefore, should not be considered competitive but cooperative and complementary, for each is only a means to the same end; at their utmost, they exist only to protect and advance the interests of the American people. By supreme exertions the United States could simultaneously create the greatest army, navy, and air force in the world. But the possession of more armed forces than are necessary is a national extravagance which directly reduces the standard of living. It is unlikely, moreover, that these preponderant forces would add to our national security. Possession of preponderant land, sea, and air forces by the United States would almost certainly excite apprehension abroad; and this apprehension might create a hostile world coalition which in time could create larger navies, armies, and air forces. The United States should, therefore, carefully consider what branch or branches it should emphasize with reference, first, to protection of its own territories and essential interests and, second, to the sensitivity of other powers.

The American High Command bears the responsibility for determining the relative proportions of the land, sea, and air forces. Its members have a free choice. In the global wars ending in 1918 and 1945, United States armed forces held their own with their enemies and contributed as much as their allies. American designers and industry provided weapons equal in quality and in greater quantity; in the improvement of old and production of new munitions, Americans with aid from their British allies excelled; their factories already famous for mass production revealed equal facility in retooling to provide in astronomical quantities new and modified weapons and munitions, designed by research departments to meet the needs of the armed forces at sea, in the field, and in the air. The United States need not fear destruction from a "secret weapon" if it utilizes the inventive talents of its citizens, the research in pure science of its universities, and the application of scientific developments by its industrialists. If the Joint Chiefs of Staff agree on the proper balance of land, sea, and air forces, and Congress provides funds, the nation can furnish the personnel and material to meet any emergency and to meet its manifold international commitments in the foreseeable future.

The younger generation can face the future confidently. They will meet recurring emergencies; some eras will be more dangerous than others; but their ancestors faced equally perilous situations: their forefathers transformed the weapons of their ground troops from smooth bore to rifled cannon, from muzzle-loading muskets to rifles and machine guns, and shifted from ox-drawn to motorized transport: their sea forces progressed from sail to steam, from wood to steel, and integrated submarines, torpedo boats, and planes, hailed as destroyers of the navy, into its fleets; the Wright brothers invented the airplane, and when Americans turned their minds to it they created an air force equal, if not superior, to any other. Unless future generations lose their inherited enterprise, ingenuity, and intrepidity, Americans can lead in any or all branches of conventional or, when it comes, push-button warfare. They can base their future on strength, not weakness, provided their statesmen, generals, and admirals cooperate in peace and are prepared for war.

Chapter 3

Maintaining Peace; a Joint Responsibility of Civil and Military Leadership

Three major wars occurred in the first half of the twentieth century, the Russo-Japanese, World War I, and World War II, all intimately related. The defeat of Russia by Japan in 1905 upset the balance of power in Europe and increased the international tensions that caused World War I. The consequences of World War I, the disappointment of two victor nations, Japan and Italy, with their share of the spoils, and the resentment of defeated Germany led first to war breaking out in Manchuria in 1931, spreading to Ethiopia in 1935, to central and southern China in 1937, to Europe and the British Empire in 1939, and engulfing the United States, part of the Western Hemisphere, and most of the rest of the world, in 1941. These wars are sufficiently separated to afford a reasonable perspective, so that they offer an abundance of material to illustrate the joint responsibilities of statesmen, generals, and admirals.

These wars are worthy of study for they wrought kaleidescopic changes among the Great Powers. France was invaded and partly occupied in World War I; it was crushed and fully occupied in World War II but was restored by its allies, after each war, to its former boundaries. In 1905, Russia, under Czar Nicholas II, was defeated by Japan and in 1914-17 by Germany, and subsequently transformed by a proletarian revolution into a Soviet Republic. In alliance with Nazi Germany it began World War II in 1939 only to be attacked by Hitler in 1941; it was saved by the stubborn courage of its people, the desperate resolution of its leaders, and large Anglo-American aid. Great Britain exhausted her resources maintaining the world's greatest navy, an army of four million men, and an infant air force in World War I. Before completely recuperating she was plunged into a second global conflict and survived only by expending the remainder of her wealth and parting with much of the Empire. The United States, after successfully avoiding European entanglement for a century, entered World War I as an associate power, that is, a limited partner only. She became a charter member of the United Nations in the second conflict and, before its close, pledged herself to fight any aggressor nation, any time, anywhere. She promptly became involved in a "cold" war with a former ally, and in a limited, bloody war in Korea.

Events during the three major wars of the twentieth century, reinforced by occasional references to other wars, will be used to illustrate the relations of statesmen, generals, admirals, and air marshals. In time of peace, statesmen formulate their foreign policies which are usually in accord with the desires of their citizens or subjects; if not, propaganda is employed to gain public support. The military leaders simultaneously should strive to prepare the armed forces to meet any opposition that these policies may excite; if unable to make reasonably adequate preparation, the military leaders should advise the statesmen either to increase the forces or modify the policy. In time of war, the statesmen should still prescribe the political objectives, but should leave the military measures to attain the objective to the generals, admirals, and air marshals. As the war progresses, it may be necessary to abandon or modify the objective; if the enemy wins the military decision, it will be imperative for the statesmen to intervene to save what they can. It is nearly always possible for an astute statesman to avoid some of the consequences of defeat. By clever diplomacy, Talleyrand preserved the ancient frontiers of France after Napoleon's downfall in 1815.

The classical definition of national policy is still applicable, but the former division between tactics and strategy can no longer be applied to battles which range from the Mariannas to Borneo or from Normandy to Egypt. Only a panoramic view of the campaigns of World War II will bring them into a correct focus. The only term sufficiently comprehensive to describe them is triphibious operations. For our purpose, tactics may be defined as the use of weapons to win battles; strategy, the use of success in battle to win the war; foreign policy, the use of victory over the enemy to attain the national objective and secure the peace. These definitions delineate the responsibilities of the soldier, the sailor, the aviator, and the statesman in their joint efforts to protect the continental United States, its citizens and its possessions overseas, and to contribute its share to world security.

It is primarily to attain political objectives that a nation goes to war. Military campaigns naturally should be planned to attain those objectives. It is sometimes said that political considerations tend to interfere with military operations. This statement can be true only if the statesmen or military chiefs have failed to understand the reciprocal effects of diplomacy and war upon each other. Political considerations, properly conceived, should dominate military moves. However, there is always an obligation on the part of the statesman not to involve his country in hostilities without making sure that the army, navy, and air leaders are prepared to meet the enemy with at least an even chance of victory. Moreover, after war begins, statesmen should refrain from suggesting campaigns for other political objectives unless the armed forces available are prepared to undertake them with a reasonable prospect of success.

In modern cabinet governments, three ministers of state have been primarily concerned with problems of war: the Foreign Minister, the War Minister, and the Navy Minister.* In an autocratic government, no consideration need be given to the legislature, but

* Since World War II a few countries including the United States have combined land, sea, and air forces in a single department under a Minister of Defense.

even an absolute ruler must consider the temper of his people: public opinion must always be taken into consideration. Napoleon at the height of his power never failed to keep informed of the feeling of Parisians toward himself and his foreign policies. Even an autocrat must divide the labor of maintaining peace or waging war among several ministerial chiefs. If they disagree as to the conduct of war, it is necessary for the chief of state, or government, whether Kaiser, President, Prime Minister, Generalissimo, or Fuehrer, to choose among them.

In parliamentary England, the first Pitt demonstrated that in war a cabinet responsible to a parliament could be made to function as efficiently as an autocratic government. Pitt left domestic affairs and the management of Parliament to the Prime Minister, the Duke of Newcastle. Taking into his own hands the direction of three ministries—the Foreign Office, the Ministry of War, and the Admiralty—Pitt displayed rare ability in choosing able generals and admirals, in supplying them with the necessary ships and troops, and in defining for them the political objectives of the British Government. Nor did he hesitate to dismiss an incompetent leader. The resulting victories made it easy to obtain parliamentary appropriations. Under Pitt, Great Britain waged the Seven Years' War which, even after a poor start, became the most successful in her history. Although his successors relinquished Havana and Manila, Pitt added large parts of India, Canada, Florida, and numerous islands to the British Empire.

It should be pointed out that Pitt did not tell his generals and admirals how, when, or where to fight. He did little more than supply them with troops and ships, keep them informed of the government's policies, and protect them from unjust criticism at home. The occasion which brought him nearest to interfering in operations occurred after an initial repulse in an attack on Belle Isle. Pitt needed that island to exchange for Minorca taken by the French; to recapture Minorca would have been more difficult than the conquest of Belle Isle. With the peace conference in mind, Pitt immediately forwarded reinforcements from England and directed that the attack be renewed. It was. Belle Isle was taken and later exchanged for Minorca. Like all war leaders,

Pitt undoubtedly made mistakes, but he never interfered with the tactical decisions of a general or an admiral.

When William Pitt, the younger, became Prime Minister, he was more interested in domestic and financial reform than in foreign affairs. He did not expect the probable conflict with France so clearly discerned by Edmund Burke. Pitt neglected the army and navy but considerably strengthened the fiscal position of the United Kingdom. He made every effort to avoid war with France; and, by maintaining comparative prosperity, he prevented the revolutionary feeling prevalent in Western Europe from spreading to England. Even though he lacked his father's wisdom in supporting the national policy with adequate arms and military leadership, he realized that the strength of Great Britain lay in control of the sea, and understood that only the Royal navy could cope with the armies of Napoleon. Pitt's courage and indomitable spirit were imparted to his colleagues in the Cabinet. They were more efficient administrators than he and carried the Napoleonic Wars to a successful conclusion after his death.

Both Pitts came to power toward the end of a century of war in which Great Britain gradually established itself as the dominant sea power. These two British ministers, father and son, without being acquainted with the theories of either Clausewitz or Mahan, clearly understood with Bacon that an insular "nation which controls the sea can take as much or as little of the war as it chooses," and they based their whole foreign policy on retaining control of the sea.

Even in Imperial Germany, where the doctrine was formulated that war is a continuation of policy by force, there often has arisen the sharpest difference of opinion between statesmen and the military. This is not surprising: it is always easier to accept a principle than to agree upon its application in a critical situation. The conduct of war is never easy, and as the crisis of a conflict approaches it becomes increasingly difficult to reach sound decisions. This is illustrated by the various expedients adopted by the German High Command after Admiral Scheer convinced Quartermaster General Ludendorff in 1916 that there was no method of bringing the war to a satisfactory end without resorting to unrestricted U-boat warfare. The opposition of Chancellor Bethmann-Hollweg, who feared American intervention, delayed the submarine war until January 9, 1917, when the Kaiser summoned the German High Command to Pless to discuss the situation.

The Chancellor then reported that the Allies had rejected the German peace offer, that President Wilson's offer of mediation probably would fail, that there was no prospect of obtaining a separate peace with any of the enemy states, and no evidence that any of them would yield.* The army leaders already had reported that there was no way of gaining an immediate decision on land and that if the war were prolonged, the Allied control of the sea would prove ruinous to Germany. Admiral Holtzendorff, Chief of the Naval Staff, then stated his belief that unrestricted submarine war would have decisive results within five months. Field Marshal von Hindenburg believed that the submarines would require twelve months, but thought the German army could resist for a year, provided that the submarines substantially reduced the flow of munitions from the United States to France. The rapidly increasing supply of munitions from the United States, mainly artillery, enable Anglo-French forces to inflict unbearable losses on the Germans in trench warfare. That is to say, American industry plus Anglo-French sea power, in Hindenburg's opinion, was winning the war. All members of the conference were agreed that the United States would declare war if unrestricted U-boat warfare was resumed and that unless Germany won within the next year American intervention would be likely to give the Allies victory. Having considered all factors, Hindenburg recommended and the Kaiser decreed unrestricted submarine war.

It should be noted that the Kaiser had rejected all previous recommendations for unrestricted submarine war by his naval and military chieftains; only when his civil advisor, the Chancellor,

---

* In his memoirs, Admiral Tirpitz asserts that if the German High Command had known that Russia was on the verge of collapse, unrestricted U-boat warfare would not have been ordered. When the decision was made there was ample evidence in Petrograd of the impending collapse. German intelligence, very efficient in the beginning of the war, apparently did not ascertain the desperate situation existing in Russia.

admitted that German diplomacy could not find a way to evade defeat did he unloose the U-boats. In spite of the determined efforts of the Germans, their submarines were defeated by January 1918.

In the meanwhile, the Russian army had collapsed; and, before accepting defeat, the German High Command decided to make one more maximum effort to win the war on land. They reinforced their armies in France by several army corps taken from the eastern front and, in March 1918, launched the spring offensive against the Anglo-French armies. By July this effort also had failed, and Allied Generalissimo Foch had taken the offensive. On August 8, 1918, Hindenburg told the Kaiser that his diplomats would have to obtain *the best terms possible,* because the military were unable to gain the decision.

In August 1918, the question was not that of negotiating a satisfactory peace with the Western Powers. Germany requested terms and accepted the best ones she could get. The defeat of Germany in 1918 does not invalidate the doctrine of Clausewitz, which emphasized the uncertainties of war and envisaged defeat as well as victory. The only question was: Had the best possible use been made of the military resources to secure the victory? The German High Command contended that their army and navy had been overcome by sheer weight of numbers and they used this valid argument, together with the unwarranted assertion that the home front had collapsed before their armies had been defeated, to re-establish their prestige after the war.

Difficulties between civil and military have occurred in nations other than Germany. During the Casablanca Crisis in 1908, Georges Clemenceau, then President of the Council of France, boldly confronted Germany, but not until he had been assured by the War Minister General Picquart that the army was ready for war (which it was not) and had received assurances from the British Government that if Germany were the aggressor public opinion in the United Kingdom would demand intervention on the side of France. Although an anti-clerical free-thinker, he also appointed General Ferdinand Foch, a devout Catholic whose brother was a Jesuit priest, to head the École de Guerre.

The paths of Foch and Clemenceau separated shortly afterward. In May 1917, during some of the darkest days of the war for France, Foch was made Chief of the General Staff. Six months later President Poincaré called upon Clemenceau to become President of the Council. Foch and Clemenceau were chosen for the same reason: their courage and known determination to fight to the bitter end and their conviction that victory was still attainable. The final German offensive in April 1918 found this indomitable pair at Doullens with other Allied leaders. Clemenceau, well aware of the gravity of the situation but full of courage, was enchanted when Foch declared he would fight the Germans, "in front of Amiens, in Amiens, and behind Amiens." Later in the Chamber of Deputies he defended Foch when the German armies broke through the French front and again reached the Marne. His loyal support saved Foch from removal by the Chamber and may have saved France from defeat.

But the bond between these great sons of France, so strong in adversity, could not stand success. In September 1918, Foch informed Clemenceau that victory was in sight and asked what the peace terms would be so that necessary military measures could be taken to secure them. Clemenceau tartly replied that he, the Civil Head of the government, would manage the peace terms and denied his military conferee any knowledge of the Cabinet's intentions. Again, in October, Foch asked specifically to be informed of the government's intentions concerning the Rhineland, and whether France would persevere in an attempt to create a neutral, independent buffer state between herself and Germany. These were proper questions for the Generalissimo to ask, and Foch was entitled to answers. He also requested that the foreign office send a representative to his headquarters to keep him informed on "all necessary points. For the armistice, from political and diplomatic aspects as well as from the military point of view, bears in it the seeds of the ensuing peace." Throughout his career as a deputy and an editor, Clemenceau had been on guard lest a popular French general overthrow the Republic. He assumed that Foch was trying to dictate to the government when he (Foch) was striving solely to garner the fruits of victory for France.

Clemenceau probably desired as much as Foch to extend and strengthen French frontiers, but he knew that both President Wilson and Prime Minister Lloyd George would oppose this aggrandizement of France. Had Clemenceau consulted fully and freely with Foch, together they could have done more for their country.

The relations of Lloyd George with his military confreres was in striking contrast to those of Clemenceau with Foch. The British Prime Minister had little confidence in either General Haig, Commander-in-Chief of the British Army in France, or General Robertson, Chief of the Imperial General Staff. His refusal to reinforce Haig in January and February of 1918 was primarily responsible for the German break through the British army in March and April. But as the prospect of peace appeared, he supported heartily the recommendations of the First Sea Lord, Admiral Roslyn Wemyss. The last minute cooperation of Lloyd George with his naval colleague enabled Great Britain promptly to attain all her objectives, namely, the surrender of all U-boats, of the High Sea Fleet and of a large proportion of the German merchant fleet. Similar cooperation between Clemenceau and Foch probably would not have obtained all of Foch's desires for a stronger frontier. If these two patriotic Frenchmen had begun in September 1918 to work together for France, they could have put considerable pressure on Lloyd George to support their demands. Once Germany had been deprived of any means of threatening Britain on the sea, Clemenceau could not persuade Lloyd George to help France protect herself from Germany on the land: the British Prime Minister and his Cabinet had no intention of making France preponderant in Europe.

The makers of the American Constitution created in the presidency a strong executive office in which the powers of commander-in-chief of the army and navy and the control of American foreign policy were consolidated. As long as an American president is supported by Congress and public opinion, he has all the powers necessary for concentrating the energies of the United States in the vigorous prosecution of a war and for maintaining the necessary coordination between diplomacy and military operations, that is, between national policy and strategy. Autocratic governments are usually better adapted to waging war than oligarchies or democracies, but thanks to the 'founding fathers,' the United States can enjoy the advantages of a democracy in peace and a centralized government in war. Lincoln, Wilson, and Franklin D. Roosevelt made full use of Presidential powers at critical periods in American history.

In the words of Secretary of State John Foster Dulles, "Our Army, Navy and Air Force necessarily constitute our ultimate reliance." The armed forces of the United States are a means to an end: a means by which the United States Government seeks to protect the continental United States, to further American interests abroad, and to make its contribution to world peace. It necessarily follows that the size, composition, strength, and disposition of the armed forces in peace or in war and the determination of the relative strength of the army, air force, and navy is even more a political than a military problem.

This fact does not in the slightest degree lessen the dignity and the high responsibility of army, navy and air officials. Least of all does the recognition of the navy's mission detract from the wonderful naval traditions that have inspired succeeding naval generations. Founders of the American navy recognized their mission, and one of the most renowned, Stephen Decatur, expressed the idea in his toast: "My country . . . may she ever be right, but right or wrong, my country!" Decatur meant that the navy existed solely for the benefit of the country and that, regardless of the cause of war, the navy must bear its part in the defense of the United States.

At the same time, it is a narrow interpretation of duty, for the Chiefs of Staff to abstain from stating their views on foreign policies to the President, the Secretaries of State, Defense, Army, Navy or Air. Under the United States Constitution, the President is charged with the conduct of foreign affairs while he is also Commander-in-Chief of the Army and Navy. It is his constitutional responsibility to recommend to Congress in time of peace such appropriations as will insure that the military establishment is sufficient to support the national policy. To assist him in coordinating policy and force, he has in his cabinet the Secretaries of State and Defense. To coordinate the plans of the army, navy, and air force, he has the Secretary of Defense, the Joint Chiefs of Staff, and his own personal Chief of Staff. Although the President is assisted by these high-ranking officials, who jointly can be termed the American High Command, the final responsibility for determining foreign policy and conducting war is not joint but individual: it is the personal responsibility of the President of the United States. In a world war, American policy and strategy must be fitted into the over-all plans of any allies, and again it is the President who represents the United States in the final decisions in these matters. If he uses his Cabinet Ministers and the Joint Chiefs of Staff, he will be well equipped to meet his responsibilities.

The President and the Secretaries of State and Defense will determine the policies and provide the necessary force and the Joint Chiefs of Staff, under their Chairman, will direct the armed forces necessary to support or carry out these policies. The President thus has a civil and a military component to assist him as Commander-in-Chief of United States Armed Forces.

Only Congress can appropriate the necessary funds, and the President must secure the support of Congress to any policy involving expenditures of the nation's money. When the President and the Congress cooperate, it is comparatively easy for the President to secure proper coordination of the civil and military components of his High Command, who are his appointees. It is essential that corresponding coordination be established in each echelon from the highest to the lowest level in the departments at Washington; then the President's policies and the action taken to support them will be developed in an orderly, continuous manner.

The State Department, under the President, has the basic responsibility for originating, developing, and carrying out policies until it becomes necessary to summon the armed forces. With its ambassadors, ministers, and consuls, its staff in Washington to evaluate their reports, it is well prepared to advise the President and other departments. Thus as the policy-forming department it has the continuing responsibility of weighing the possible and probable consequences, from day to day, as courses of action previously initiated unfold. Such is the authority and the unending responsibility of all foreign offices.

This process is identical in peace or war. The difference is only in the preponderant consideration given to military factors in diplomatic crises and during war. The whole rhythm and continuity of government is dependent upon an easy passage from peace to war or war to peace. This is shown by a statement of Secretary Stettinius to the Foreign Affairs Committee on December 12, 1944, that included in the department's policies the following: "The fullest possible support in the conduct of our foreign relations for our armed forces, so that the war may be won at the earliest possible moment." Unfortunately, in time of peace when the Secretary of State should be just as careful to insure that the armed forces are ready to support his foreign policies, he is often absorbed in less important matters. In their vanity several of our Secretaries of State have assured Americans that their skillful diplomacy was all the nation needed to maintain peace. This is the unforgivable sin in a statesman, because the failure to appreciate the role of force in foreign relations may lead the nation into a disastrous defeat and threaten its existence.

Secretary Kellogg took the leading part in persuading the public that he and Briand could banish war from the world. World War II was required to convince Americans, their Congress, and two administrations that diplomatic fiats cannot change human nature. Since that experience, at Dumbarton Oaks, at Cairo, at Teheran, at San Francisco, in the Capitol, and in the White House, it has been affirmed that it may be necessary to maintain peace by force and that the United States is ready to preserve the peace by force. When Stettinius announced the intention of the State Department to give fullest possible support to win the war, he added another departmental objective: "Establishment at the earliest possible moment of a United Nations Organization capable of building and maintaining the peace, by force if necessary, for generations to come . . ." And, under the guidance of Stettinius, at Dumbarton Oaks, provision was made and authority given to the Security Council of the United Nations to use force to avert or suppress war.

Practically every international problem that arises in peace or war involves political, military, and economic consequences. For example, with few exceptions all naval operations to suppress enemy and protect our own sea-borne trade involve the rights of neutrals. These questions cannot be separated into components involving only military, only economic, or only political factors, each in its own compartment. However, during World War II, the Joint Chiefs of Staff refused to consider the consequences of State Department policy toward neutral states on the ground that only economic and political factors were involved. They persisted in this untenable attitude, although one of the principal purposes of controlling the sea is to put economic pressure on enemy states. During World War II our Joint Chiefs of Staff were so occupied directing triphibious campaigns and so accustomed to saying "Aye, aye, Sir!" to the State Department that they failed to give enough attention to the navy's responsibility to suppress enemy trade.

Before and after the United States entered World War II, Chiefs of Naval Operations disavowed interest in political decisions on the assumption that these were the sole prerogative of the State Department. This narrow concept of their sphere of responsibility is not in accord with the principle, long accepted by civilized states, that war is the means of obtaining national objectives by force when peaceful methods fail. This voluntary isolation of the Joint Chiefs of Staff from consideration of the effect of political decisions in causing war or on its conduct, also is directly contrary to the advice given to President Theodore Roosevelt by Mahan. He urged the President to appoint as head of the army and navy only officers who understood foreign policy and were competent to advise the President of the reciprocal effects of American national policies and the strength of the armed forces on each other.

It is necessary for the Joint Chiefs of Staff to take cognizance of the political consequences of their recommendations to the President; it is equally incumbent on the Secretary of State to take cognizance of the military consequences of his recommendations to the President. Political and military consequences cannot be separated in their joint effort to achieve victory in war and then maintain peace. During hostilities the Chiefs of Staff should make their military decisions while keeping the military factors solely in mind, because in war military factors are decisive in most instances. If the State Department advises the President against their plans for political reasons, the Chiefs of Staff should consider carefully whether the military advantages outweigh the political disadvantages. If not, they should change their plans; if so, they should adhere to their decisions and take the problem to the President for final judgment.

If the Joint Chiefs of Staff act otherwise, they abdicate in favor of some amateur strategist in the Cabinet, who may overrule carefully conceived military plans. This is not an imaginary danger: Lloyd George and Winston Churchill overruled Field Marshal Robertson and Admiral Fisher, and Briand overruled Joffre in World War I. The political consequences of a victory at the Dardanelles would have been very great, but sufficient forces could not be provided without endangering the western front. The inevitable defeat was a great political advantage for Germany. This experience did not prevent Lloyd George and Briand from diverting troops from the western front to win a useless victory in Palestine. The contempt of British and French civil authorities for military advice resulted in enormous, unnecessary waste of life and money in four minor theaters during World War I, the Dardanelles, Mesopotamia, Palestine, and Salonika.

In World War II, Churchill never ceased suggesting diversionary attacks even when the Combined Chiefs of Staff opposed his ideas. After General Eisenhower had landed in Normandy, Churchill continued to urge the diversion of Army Corps earmarked for landing in southern France for a campaign to take Vienna. He pictured "a bloody prospect for the forces attacking from the south (of France)," but said nothing about the heavier losses that crossing the Alps would have caused. The General felt that the Prime Minister was really concerned with postwar political consequences. His reply to Churchill should be remembered by officers who may find themselves in a similar situation.

He told Churchill that "strategy can be affected by political considerations, and if the President and he (Churchill) should decide that it was worth while to prolong the war, thereby increasing its cost in men and money, in order to secure the political objectives they deemed necessary, then he would instantly and loyally adjust his plans." *

Some commentators on the war have supported Churchill's views because of the subsequent occupation of the Balkans by Red forces. Stalin could have been denied the Balkans more safely by simply reducing or stopping the flow of supplies to him in the late autumn of 1943 when his armies had driven the Germans almost out of Russia. The unfounded fear that he would make a separate peace with Hitler prevented Anglo-American action which would have been justified by the needs of American forces fighting Japan in the Pacific.

If Churchill's plan to wage a campaign for the Balkans in 1944 had been accepted, it might easily have had disastrous consequences to his own country. The V-bombs, Hitler's last secret weapon, were not under control until after Holland had been recovered late in 1944. They were falling on London until Eisenhower's army had overrun their sites in France. Had this advance been delayed, the effect on the expeditionary force certainly would have been serious, and might have been fatal. In his book, *The Crusade in Europe,* Eisenhower records that the depressing effect of the bombs was not confined to the civilian population. Soldiers at the front began to worry about friends and loved ones at home; he then conjectured that if the Germans had begun using V-bombs six months earlier, the invasion of Normandy "might have been written off." Yet from the very beginning of the plan for invading France, Churchill had done his utmost to postpone it by dilating upon its dangers and suggesting alternative methods of winning the war.

The Constitution of the United States provides a ready means of giving proper weight to political and military factors in determining national strategy. An interdepartmental committee with

* *Crusade in Europe,* by Dwight D. Eisenhower, Doubleday, p. 284.

representatives of the State, Defense, Army, Navy, and Air Departments with representatives at each lower echelon from the Secretaries down, vested with authority to express the views of their Secretaries in the continuous exchange of information and discussion of plans, could either reach agreements, or fix precisely the areas of disagreement, that could be passed to higher authority for action in case of agreement, and for a decision in case of disagreement. The path of authority and responsibility in the Executive Branch is plainly marked: it can function efficiently if properly officered. Similar complex problems involving widely different factors are daily solved in American corporations; they need not baffle the civil and military components of the United States High Command. Interdepartmental committees were found necessary and organized during World War II. The top and second echelon staffs of such a structure already exist in the National Security Council and its staff. There is still need for subordinate staffs in the lower echelons. Space for the Secretaries of Defense and State and the Chairman of the Joint Chiefs of Staff could be provided in the former State, War and Navy Building adjacent to the White House where the highest echelon of the United States High Command would be readily available and would have easy access to the Commander-in-Chief of the Armed Forces in peace and in war.

The American Constitution centers the diplomacy and conduct of war in the Presidency. No better system can be devised; but it makes exceedingly great demands upon the man in the White House, particularly in the critical period preceding hostilities and toward the end of the war when the terms of peace should be determined and means provided to enforce them. When hostilities are fully joined, the President's primary purpose should be to maintain the morale of the people, provide the means for victory, support competent leaders against unjust criticism, and replace the incompetent.

The United States was involved in World War I, World War II, and the present cold war, primarily by the failure of civil officials, particularly Presidents and Secretaries of State, to consider the military factors that enter into every problem of foreign relations. Failure of the civilian officials to give proper consideration to the military factors that enter into these problems stems from the undue subordination of the military to the civil officials in the government of the United States. This undue subordination is caused by our ancient fear that American liberties would be subverted by huge standing armies. To avoid a remote danger, Americans have incurred an ever-present peril of becoming involved in unnecessary wars or being plunged unprepared into unavoidable wars with foreign nations.

Liberties of some nations have been crushed by standing armies; other nations have been destroyed by failing to prepare their armed forces in time of peace. The framers of the Constitution provided against both dangers. To guard against a domestic despot, the Constitution provided that only Congress can declare war; only Congress can provide and maintain a navy; only Congress can raise and support armies, and then only for a period of two years. This time limitation was not placed on the navy, for it was manifestly more difficult for sailors embarked on ships to overthrow the government than for troops in barracks ashore.

The framers of the Constitution were familiar with war; most of them had witnessed two global wars, the Seven Years' War and our Revolutionary War. They knew from their own experience that a Congress, composed of many members, could not conduct our foreign relations in peace or direct military operations in war. So, having given Congress the authority to declare war and to provide for the armed forces, they made the President Commander-in-Chief of the Army and Navy. To further safeguard their liberties, they divided between the President and the Senate the power to negotiate treaties, which outline our foreign policies and become the supreme law of the land.

The framework of our government is the best ever devised to protect citizens from potential domestic despots and foreign aggressors, provided that there exists a correct and sympathetic understanding between American civil and military officials. But if either branch ignores or dominates the other, our institutions will be threatened from without or within.

Our nation is over 175 years old. Only once in that time did the specter of a military dictator appear. President Lincoln dissipated this phantom in one biting sentence by reminding the ambitious Commander, General Hooker, that only successful generals became dictators. In other nations, military dictators have been triumphant. It is necessary for us to be on guard, particularly if we are to maintain huge regular armies indefinitely. But we should not involve the nation in the peril that will inevitably follow if the conduct of diplomacy and war is left entirely to civilian officials who ignore their legally constituted military advisers.

As previously stated, this lack of understanding between military and civil officials exists in many other countries. It invariably results in the undue subordination of either the civil or military branch. In Germany and Japan, the civil authorities have been controlled by the military; in England, France, and the United States, the military have been dominated and usually ignored by the civil branch. Unfortunate and sometimes disastrous consequences have resulted when either branch is dominant.

The present undue subordination of American military officers is not due to the American Constitution. The action of the framers of the Constitution in making the President Commander-in-Chief of the Army and Navy and responsible for the day-to-day conduct of foreign relations was sound. They knew that General George Washington would be the first President if the Union was established. The organization is just as efficient today provided a President, who enters the White House with no military experience, is guided by the Chiefs of the Armed Forces that he selects and appoints in accordance with laws passed by Congress, and thus gives proper consideration to the military factors that enter into every problem of foreign relations.

Our first President was not only the best American general of his generation; he was one of the few great generals who understood the value of sea power. His experience in the Revolution convinced him that all governments in time of peace should prepare for war. John Adams, our second President, had no military experience. He set the precedent of leaving military matters to military officers. He recalled General Washington from retirement to be Commander-in-Chief of the Army, and Commodore

Truxton to be Commander of the Caribbean Squadron, in our quasi-war with France in 1798.

Thomas Jefferson reversed this precedent. Disdaining naval advice, he constructed a navy of gunboats, then discovered he had to build forts to protect them from larger enemy ships. President Madison, a disciple of Jefferson, learned by sad experience during the War of 1812, and he recommended construction of ships of the line. From Madison to Woodrow Wilson our Presidents, notably Lincoln and McKinley, were usually guided in military problems by their military advisers.

As a war President, Wilson's conduct was uneven to the point of caprice. In the autumn of 1914 when the people and Congress both wished to strengthen the army and navy, he opposed their efforts with the following sophism, "Europe prepared for war. Europe is at war. The United States did not prepare for war. The United States is at peace," leaving his listeners to infer that "Preparation for war leads to war." He ended by defying Congress to "turn America into an armed camp." Wilson was one of our most intellectual Presidents; he simply had not bothered to study war.

By the summer of 1916, he had learned that European nations would not heed his well-reasoned notes and he began to prepare the armed forces. His delay led the German General Staff to risk war with the United States in the belief that Germany could defeat Great Britain and France before the United States would be ready to fight.* After entering the war, Wilson urged the use of force without stint. He appointed the Honorable Newton D. Baker, who quickly became a very efficient Secretary of War. Wilson gave Baker and the Chief of Staff, General P. G. March, his full support. At the same time he retained, as Secretary of the Navy, the Honorable Josephus Daniels, who regarded the navy as a floating university for American sailors and who concentrated his mind on demobilization before the navy was fully manned. At the peace conference, Wilson took General T. S. Bliss as one of his advisers. When it was suggested that he add Admiral

* See pp. 42-43.

Benson, Chief of Naval Operations, he replied that he took Bliss as a personal friend, not as a representative of the army.

Wilson forged the first link in a fatal chain of events that involved Americans in World War I; a similar chain to be described in the next chapter involved them in World War II. It is summarized at this point so that American readers can conveniently compare the events that led them into two World Wars, and learn from their own history that it is extremely dangerous to unduly subordinate the military to the civil or the civil to the military in the Executive Department of their government.

Between the two World Wars American military officials were more and more ignored. In 1921-22, Secretary of State Hughes ostentatiously refused to consult the Navy General Board or Chief of Naval Operations. On his personal responsibility he scrapped American ships nearing completion while permitting England to tear up blueprints. Without consulting military advisers, he agreed to Japan's suggestion that America not modernize her fortifications and naval facilities in the Far East while agreeing that Balfour could continue construction of the British base at Singapore.

In 1930, Secretary Stimson, over the objections of naval officers, increased the Japanese quota of submarines. (During World War II Japanese submarines sank two of our largest carriers.) A year after facilitating an increase of the Japanese Navy, Stimson was surprised when the Japanese Government ignored his protests about their invasion of Manchuria. Yet he and Hughes had directly contributed to the strength of Japan and to the obsolescence of American ships and their bases in the Far East. In 1933, Franklin Roosevelt approved all naval limitations and sought to increase them; he continued his efforts to reduce the navy until 1936.

Meanwhile Japan was increasing her army and navy; in 1937 she deliberately bombed the *USS Panay* in broad open daylight. The President and Secretary Hull accepted her thinly disguised excuses. As late as 1940 after Congress had appropriated for a two-ocean navy, Roosevelt would not support Admiral Stark's request for additional men to man the new ships. These actions of Republican and Democratic administrations encouraged the

Japanese military to attempt to take advantage of our unpreparedness. They seized and attempted to hold territory in the western Pacific in the belief that Americans would not make the necessary sacrifice of life to recover them.

The domination by the German and Japanese military proved more disastrous to their nation than the domination by American civil officials to the United States. But is it necessary for our country to be dragged into unwanted war? Why should not the government find a proper balance between the civil and military components of the High Command?

It is the duty of all officers, particularly high-ranking officers, to keep themselves informed at all times of the trend of international events and especially to observe foreign interests that conflict with the interests of the United States in such a way as to furnish the earliest indications of an approaching war. It is also within the province of the military component of the High Command to indicate possible enemies and to estimate the strength and disposition of the forces necessary to combat these potential enemies and to protect American interests at home and abroad whenever diplomatic means have failed.

Mahan's last admonition to his brother officers at the Naval War College was ". . . to master, and keep track of, the great current events of history contemporary with yourself. Appreciate their meaning. Your own profession, on its military side, calls, of course, for your first and closest attention; but you all will have time enough to read military history, appreciating its teachings, and you can also keep abreast of international relations, to such an extent that when you reach positions of prime responsibility, your glance—your *coup d'oeil,* to repeat the French idiom—will quickly take in the whole picture of your country's interests in any emergency, whether they be pressing or remote . . . That you may more effectually concentrate upon this necessary knowledge, avoid dissipating your energies upon questions interior to the country . . . The sphere of the Navy is international solely. It is this which allies it so closely to that of the statesman. Aim to be yourselves statesmen as well as seamen . . ." *

* *Naval Strategy,* by Captain A. T. Mahan, Little, Brown & Co., 1889.

The essence of Mahan's advice to high-ranking naval officers was: "Aim to be yourselves, statesmen, as well as seamen." Amplifying this thought, it can be said that the crowning glory of Nelson, Sampson and Dewey was their appreciation of the political effects of naval campaigns. In his long service in the Mediterranean, Nelson never contented himself with simply thwarting the moves of the opposing admiral. He constantly considered the effect of the movements of his fleet on the plans of Napoleon. At Santiago, Sampson justified the risks of close blockade by his knowledge of the political consequences in Europe if Admiral Cervera were allowed to escape and return either to Puerto Rico or to the Canaries. After his victory at Manila Bay, Dewey showed a complete understanding of its political consequences in his solutions of the vexatious questions raised by the German Admiral von Diedrich.

A great American general, Stonewall Jackson, demonstrated by example that generals also should keep the political consequences of campaigns and battles continually in mind. During the Civil War, he observed closely the words and deeds of President Lincoln and not only directed operations against the northern armies, but also constantly played upon the apprehensions of the President for the safety of the city of Washington. Many reasons have been given for the disagreements that arose between Lincoln and General McClellan, but Stonewall Jackson's threats to attack Washington were their basic cause. It may be added that during World War II, General Eisenhower showed the same acute understanding of the intimate connection between military operations and international politics. High-ranking naval and military officers thus cannot content themselves with knowing only the technical part of their professions.

At every international conference between 1921 and 1937 where American defenses were further reduced, the political representatives of the United States Government were accompanied by naval officers, many of whom were not sufficiently informed on world conditions to indicate to their civil colleagues to what extent the limitation of armaments weakened the influence of the United States in international affairs. If the senior officers of the American navy had followed the advice of Mahan to the extent of appreciating the meaning of current events, they would not have spent their time haggling over the size and number of a few British and American cruisers. They would have appreciated the fact that Japan was the future enemy and Great Britain a potential ally. They would have informed the Department of State in forthright language that, if the island bases in the Far East were not fortified, the power of Japan to enforce its will on China would be increased, and consequently the open door in China, the avowed aim of American foreign policy in this part of the world, would be supported only by scraps of paper.

It is certainly possible, and even probable, that the Department of State would not have accepted the advice of the Navy Department on Far Eastern matters even if such advice had been tendered, but the fact that naval officers did not first keep in touch with the trend of events and then report their bearing on American foreign policy places on them a substantial share of responsibility for the character of the subsequent war with Japan. The failure of the Navy High Command obviously does not excuse the officers of the Department of State, who should never have committed the United States to any course of action unless they were certain that the American naval strength could sustain such a program if challenged.

If Mahan had addressed officers of the U.S. Foreign Service, he probably would have advised them to give their first and closest attention to their own profession, but to keep informed of current military and naval developments, and to understand the function of force in international relations. Career men in our State Department should be particularly alert in time of peace when their day-to-day recommendations to their Secretary influence decisions that combine to form the pattern of the nation's foreign policy. By maintaining cordial relations with their corresponding echelon in the Department of Defense they will avoid the danger of exposing the country to war which its armed forces are unprepared to wage. Instead, by making sure that the armed forces are ready and their overseas bases protected, they can time their diplomatic moves to obtain national objectives without drawing the sword or, by a firm note, deter an ambitious nation from assailing our most distant frontier.

Triphibious operation of United States land, sea, and air forces brought victory in the Pacific and Atlantic in World War II. Americans today need for their future protection a similar integration under the President of the Departments of State and Defense. Then, under the direction of the Commander-in-Chief of United States Armed Forces, when our Statesmen can no longer protect Americans at home and abroad by peaceful means, the armed forces can intervene successfully with the least expenditure of lives and treasure.

Chapter 4

Diplomatic Rivalry in the Pacific; Japan vs. The United States, 1893-1941

Chapter 1 discussed former methods of preserving peace. Chapter 2 compared methods of utilizing superior land, sea, or air forces as the primary means of providing national security. Chapter 3 outlined the several and joint responsibilities of statesmen, generals, air marshals, and admirals in maintaining or preserving peace. Chapter 4 will contrast the methods employed by Japan and the United States between 1893-1941 in their vain endeavor to settle an almost continuous conflict of national policies by peaceful means. Incidental reference to the effect of policies of other nations will be necessary.

When Mutsuhito became Emperor in 1867, the modernization of Japan began. He started a series of reforms that, before his death in 1912, transformed his hermit nation with feudal institutions into an empire recognized as one of the world's great powers. He was determined that his country should participate in world affairs and should not be divided into spheres of influence by European powers.

In 1872 he decreed compulsory service for the armed forces; he patterned the army, first, after the French model; later, after the German model; and his navy, after the British. He secured the assistance of British officers for his navy and German officers for his army. They organized the Navy and War Departments, the fleet and the field army. Major Meckel, a brilliant disciple of Clausewitz, headed the German mission. Simultaneously, the Emperor ordered his envoys in Europe to begin negotiations to abrogate extraterritorial rights previously granted foreigners. In 1876, he compelled Korea to open its ports to Japanese ships and merchants and China to acknowledge Japan's title to the Luchu Islands.

While he ruled by Imperial Edicts with improvised bureaus to enforce his decrees, he dispatched a group of young Japanese to study European forms of government. In 1889 he voluntarily bestowed upon his subjects a Constitution, very similar to that of the German Empire. The Emperor reserved for himself the power to direct foreign relations, to declare war, to make an armistice, and to negotiate a peace. He retained command of the army and navy but, to insure professional competence in the armed forces, provided in the Constitution that ministers of the army and navy must be chosen from generals or admirals on the active list. The Constitution also provided that a Minister of Finance who failed to provide funds for the armed forces would be impeached.

The Constitution gave the nation an Imperial Diet of two houses, one of hereditary Peers and one of Representatives elected by qualified voters. The Diet met annually but could sit for only three months; when it was not in session, the Emperor could issue edicts that had the force of law; he also retained the right to summon or adjourn the Diet, or to dissolve the House of Representatives. Mutsuhito's government was an improvement over the shogunate's feudal system; considered solely as an instrument to protect the nation from foreign aggression it was well designed, but the Constitution he granted his subjects differed entirely from that of the United States.

Few American diplomats realized that the Emperor's fundamental purpose was to create a government that could protect Japan from foreign aggression, and to that end civil officials in Japan had been deliberately subordinated to the military. The radical difference between the constitutions of Japan and the United States added to the difficulty of finding a peaceful solution to conflicting interests of Japan and the United States.

Japanese and American rivalry began for the hegemony of the Hawaiian Islands. By 1890 Japanese formed one fourth of the population of those islands, and a naval squadron regularly cruised in Hawaiian waters to protect their nationals. President Harrison had accepted the Hawaiian Islands for the United States, but President Cleveland disavowed the act. Japan, even when preparing for war with China, did not hesitate to challenge the American position in Honolulu.

With his modernized army and navy, Mutsuhito in 1894 quickly defeated China, only to be deprived of the fruits of victory by a coalition of France, Russia, and Germany. Shortly after, China leased Port Arthur to Russia and the Russo-Japanese struggle for Korea began. While preparing for war with Russia, Japan lodged a formal protest against American annexation of the Hawaiian Islands in 1898, but supported Hay's Open Door Policy in China. Then, her growing need of economic and diplomatic aid in her struggle with Russia temporarily silenced her criticism of the United States. In 1902, by an alliance with Great Britain, she halted the Russian penetration of Korea. When it was resumed, Tokyo decided war with Russia was inevitable.

The High Command knew they would never have a better opportunity to defeat Russia, for the Czar could double his Far East Fleet and reinforce the army in Manchuria, which would make the task of defeating Russia in the future practically impossible. Even then they could not assure the Emperor of victory. Mutsuhito approved their plans for war at that time. Few American observers noted that the Emperor and his advisers were willing to risk defeat in an uncertain major war, rather than to abandon their national objectives.

The Japanese war plan included a surprise attack on the Russian fleet based on Port Arthur. If they had presented a formal ultimatum, Admiral Alexieff, Russian Commander-in-Chief, could have parried the blow. If they had attacked without warning, they would offend the neutral opinion, particularly American, that they had been cultivating briefly. To solve this dilemma the Japanese Foreign Office directed the Ambassador at St. Petersburg to present two notes simultaneously to the Russian Foreign Minister on January 13, 1904. The first, to propitiate neutral opinion, stated that the Japanese had no alternative "than to terminate the present negotiation" and "reserved the right to take such action as they deemed best." The second, designed to lull the suspicions of the Russians, read: ". . . having exhausted every means of conciliation . . . they had resolved to sever diplomatic relations with Russia," adding that "it was the intention of the Ambassador and Staff to leave on February 10." Many Russian officials thought that Japan would not dare to risk war. The second note convinced most others that Japan would only sever diplomatic relations. Admiral Alexieff was not alarmed. Diplomatic duplicity enabled Togo to launch a successful night attack with his destroyers.

In Tokyo, cooperation between army, navy and the Foreign Affairs departments continued throughout the war. Under the prudent but resolute Togo, a comparatively small insular navy defeated in succession two hostile fleets, each approximating its own tonnage. Field Marshals Nogi and Oyama, after forcing Port Arthur to surrender, advanced as far as Mukden. Japanese diplomats, by moderating somewhat their demands, obtained from the Russian colossus by force what they had been unable to obtain by negotiations. As a result of the war, Japan occupied Korea and Port Arthur, and firmly established herself in the mainland of Asia.

Although Japan had enjoyed the sympathy of the United States during hostilities and President Theodore Roosevelt had acted as mediator during the Peace Conference, as soon as peace was concluded with Russia, Japan renewed her protest against exclusion of her citizens from the United States. The President's patient explanation of the economic and racial reasons for exclusion did not reduce the tension.

Annexation of the Hawaiian Islands had advanced the United States one third of the way across the Pacific; purchase of the Philippines in 1899 carried the flag to the western Pacific. The bulk of our naval strength was concentrated in the Atlantic; the Panama Canal was not finished; our ships burned coal and there was little steaming coal on the West Coast. Following the system of the British in controlling the Mediterranean, the United States established naval bases in Hawaii, Guam, and Luzon; those at Honolulu, Pearl Harbor, and Manila Bay were heavily fortified so that they would require a large expeditionary force and a siege to capture. The Army-Navy Joint Board, well aware of Japanese resentment, also realized that the small army garrison in Luzon could not resist indefinitely the much larger Japanese army if the Japanese navy could control the western Pacific. When the fortifications of Manila Bay were designed, they could resist any frontal attack that naval guns of that time could deliver. The Asiatic Fleet was provided with submarines, destroyers, and a few cruisers to help the army delay the Japanese advance, while the North Atlantic Fleet was prepared to escort reinforcements either through the Magellan Straits or the Mediterranean Sea.

In 1908, President Theodore Roosevelt sent the Atlantic Fleet to the California coast. The passage of the fleet through Magellan Straits and its subsequent world cruise confirmed American naval opinion that when the Panama Canal was opened the fleet could reinforce Corregidor before it could be taken by the Japanese. Apparently the Japanese reached the same conclusion, their threats ceased, and the Root-Takahira Agreement, pledging each government to respect the other's possessions in the western Pacific, was signed. But two years later, when President Taft authorized Secretary of State P. C. Knox to sponsor the purchase of the Chinese Eastern Railway by an international group of bankers, Russia and Japan quickly reached a secret agreement on joint action to protect their interests in Manchuria. The readiness of former enemies to unite to protect their interests did not cause the American Secretary of State or his successors to be more wary in their dealings with either nation.

The siege of Port Arthur demonstrated that naval guns dismounted and properly emplaced ashore could sink a fleet or force it to sea; the garrison of Luzon was increased; and in 1917, General J. F. Morrison, one of the Army's best tacticians, after combined maneuvers in Luzon, was convinced that, with 6,000 regular infantrymen and Filipino scouts, he could hold Bataan Ridge as long as the stores and ammunition in Corregidor held out. Holding Bataan would prevent the Japanese from lobbing shells into Corregidor, where there was ample space for six months' stores and munitions for the Corregidor garrison and the infantrymen on Bataan. It was believed that in six months the navy could relieve the siege or at least replenish the stores.

In 1912 Emperor Mutsuhito died, leaving Japan a powerful insular empire, with a patriotic, industrious people, an efficient army and navy capable of protecting the nation from European aggression, and a Constitution peculiarly designed to further Imperial interests.

The Japanese victory over Russia diminished the prestige of Europeans in the Far East and increased the national spirit of China. Sun Yat-sen, "the George Washington of China," organized a party to overthrow the Chinese Imperial Government and to establish a Republic of China. In 1912 a railroad from Tientsin to Nanking, financed by a foreign loan, was built, operated, and controlled by Chinese engineers and labor. This achievement encouraged the revolutionists who carried through a successful revolution. Sun Yat-sen was elected President, but soon resigned in favor of Yuan Shih-kai, who ruled autocratically but efficiently, and opposed Japanese demands until his death in 1916.

The impact of other nations, particularly Great Britain, on Japanese-American relations became more pronounced during World War I. In 1916 President Wilson requested and Congress appropriated for an "incomparable Navy." After we entered the war, the President, at the request of the British Government, suspended work on all other types to speed the construction of destroyers. He explicitly stated that construction of capital ships would be resumed when the U-boat menace was overcome. Colonel E. M. House, who represented the President during discussions with British officials at the Versailles Peace Conference, reported that the question of the relative size of the British and

American navies was one of the "most serious and delicate of the entire peace conference." *

After the armistice, Wilson sponsored a navy primarily to compel Lloyd George to accept the "principle of the freedom of the seas." If that so-called principle had been accepted, the value of a preponderant navy to any nation would have greatly diminished. Lloyd George, realizing this, never consented but intimated to Wilson that when a League of Nations was formed, the problem of freedom of the seas would automatically disappear. And when Lloyd George abandoned his opposition to the League, Wilson lost interest in a navy.

During the Versailles Conference, Admiral Sir Roslyn Wemyss, First Sea Lord, brusquely demanded of Admiral W. S. Benson, Chief of Naval Operations, the reasons for increasing the United States navy. American naval officers were suspicious of the Anglo-Japanese alliance that many British officers considered necessary to protect their interests in the Far East. Late in 1920, American fleet construction reached a stage where Parliament would be compelled to increase its naval appropriations largely or to see its navy surpassed. Anglo-American naval rivalry exceeded that between either country and the Japanese. But neither Parliament nor Congress was willing to provide funds for a naval race.

President Harding was elected on a platform advocating economy and opposing entry into the League of Nations. Republican leaders, including the new Secretary of State, the Honorable Charles Evans Hughes, soon ascertained that only drastic reduction of the naval program could effect substantial economies. Also many influential Republicans, including ex-President Taft, favored participation in the League.

The prospect of simultaneously pleasing the great majority of Americans by reducing expenditures and conciliating pro-League Republicans inspired the Administration to invite Great Britain, France, Japan, and Italy to participate in a conference to discuss the "limitation of arms" and "to reach a common understanding" concerning Far Eastern policies. Lloyd George accepted, and ap-

* *Intimate Papers of Colonel E. M. House*, edited by C. S. Seymour, 4 Vols., Houghton Mifflin Co.

pointed the Right Honorable Arthur J. Balfour, who had negotiated the Japanese alliance of 1902 while in the Foreign Office,
and as Prime Minister renewed it in 1905, as Chief of the British
Delegation.*

The Japanese Delegation was headed by Admiral Baron Kato,
Chief of Staff for Admiral Togo at the battle of the Sea of Japan.
During World War I he had been Commander-in-Chief of the
Combined Fleet and Minister of Marine with personal access to
the Emperor. As sagacious as Balfour or Hughes, Kato was better prepared by technical knowledge to guard the interests of his
nation.

Secretary Hughes, well equipped by native ability and experience in law and government to protect his country's interest, handicapped himself during the negotiations by his determination
that the Conference over which he presided should limit naval
armaments. He insured subsequent senatorial ratification by se-
lecting Senator Henry Cabot Lodge, Chairman of the Foreign
Affairs Committee, and Oscar Underwood, Democratic leader in
the Senate, as delegates. He also included the Honorable Elihu
Root, former Secretary of State, co-author of the Root-Takahira
Agreement, who believed that both Japan and United States had
rights and interests in China, but that Japan's interests were
greater and, therefore, she had more reason for their exercise.
Root had justified Japan's 21 Demands on China in 1916 (which,
had they not been resisted by the United States, would have made
China a Japanese satellite), asserting that western powers, including the United States, had been unfair to Japan and should abandon their sentimental attitude of defending China. Root's
convictions made him Tokyo's advocate, and as an Elder Statesman of the Republican Party, he exercised much influence on the
delegation, particularly on Hughes.*

Hughes painstakingly prepared for the Conference. Ambassadors kept him informed of reactions of foreign governments as
the discussions continued. In particular, the Honorable C. B.
Warren in Tokyo carefully noted Japanese opinion; on November

* For details, see *Life of Balfour*, by Blanche Dugdale.
** For Root's views, see *Elihu Root*, by Philip C. Jessup, G. P. Putnam's Sons.

19, and again on November 23, 1921, he reported to Hughes that the Japanese Cabinet was satisfied with Hughes' proposals and stated specifically that he could "see no reasons for making concessions to Kato as here (in Japan) the strongest desire is for an agreement. If Kato takes an extreme position, I do not believe he will be supported." Sentiment in Great Britain and the United States also favored naval limitations. France and Italy had been compelled to reduce their navies to support their armies; but their delegations had a very large influence on the pact, on account of their naval rivalry in the Mediterranean and French insistence on retaining submarines.

Hughes played his hand boldly. Ignoring naval colleagues, he fixed naval ratios according to the tonnage of ships built, being built, or planned by the five nations; the excess would be scrapped. He limited tonnage of aircraft carriers and prescribed a ten-year naval holiday during which no ship over 10,000 tons carrying a gun larger than 8″ could be built. Balfour immediately accepted "in spirit and principle"; Kato, more prudent, accepted only "in principle." The British delegates proposed to abolish submarines; although American naval officers were opposed, Hughes obligingly agreed. France then insisted she must have 90,000 tons of submarines and 300,000 tons of other than capital ships.

From that moment the Anglo-French dispute threatened to wreck the Conference. Japan supported the French contention that the submarine was the most effective ship for a weaker navy. To save the limitation already accepted on capital ships, Hughes abandoned all effort to limit construction of other types. Probably he hoped eventually to prevail on other nations to extend the limitations to smaller ships. But he had no other American ships to scuttle. Foreign nations immediately lost interest in scrapping and diverted the funds saved on capital ships to construction of smaller ships.

Improvement in battleships since the erection of the fortifications for Manila Bay had made it necessary to modernize the fortifications, to strengthen those of Guam, and to increase naval facilities at both places. The War Department was aware of this necessity and the Navy Department was actually mounting 7″

guns on Guam when Secretary Hughes, to please Admiral Kato, froze fortifications and naval facilities in United States possessions in the Far East. Balfour certainly, and Root probably, endorsed Kato's request. Balfour reserved for his country the right to build and fortify a first-class naval base at Singapore. Hughes in 1922 continued to follow Root's policy of concessions to Japan.

China, eventually the victim of this Conference, was a temporary beneficiary. Great Britain announced its intention to return its base at Wei Hai Wei; Russia relinquished concessions in Tientsin and Hankow, canceled the remainder of the Boxer indemnity, placed the Chinese Eastern Railway under Russo-Chinese management, and lent President Sun Yat-sen economic advisers and military instructors. Japan, by postponing the trade conference until 1930, retained her tariff differentials in China. But for a time Chinese officials, aided by contributions from wealthy Chinese merchants living abroad, built railways in Manchuria with Chinese money and labor.

Japanese intrigues and internal strife following the death of Sun Yat-sen prevented his party, the Kuomintang, from organizing and consolidating an orderly government. Chiang Kai-shek, the military commander of the Kuomintang's army, in alliance with Communists, defeated some war lords and was joined by others who also were determined to resist Japan. Again China seemed on the verge of a stable Union. But with the breaking of the alliance between the Kuomintang and the Communists in 1927, Mao Tse-tung organized a Communist army that maintained a guerrilla war against Chiang. American diplomats in Washington and the Far East did all they could to support China, but disorders incident to civil war gave Japan and Russia excuses to intervene. The Chinese boycott of British goods alienated London's sympathies and increasing disorders compelled the United States to despatch troops to Shanghai. In 1931 the Japanese invaded Manchuria. China's deep-seated internal troubles and the determination of some European countries and Japan to take advantage of them proved too much for Chiang and the Kuomintang.

Next to the Chinese, Americans suffered most from the Limitation Armament Conference of 1922. They were told by Hughes that equal naval sacrifices had been made by all nations. Accepting this statement, the American press, except for the Hearst papers, and the public generally extolled Hughes. Naval officers who realized that the United States had scrapped 28 capital ships of roundly 780,000 tons; Great Britain 17 of 528,000 tons, only two of which were modern and these had not progressed beyond the blueprint stage; Japan only 415,000 tons and had received a bonus of frozen American fortifications and naval facilities in the Far East, were convinced that Hughes had purchased his temporary triumph by sacrificing potential control of the sea and leaving China at the mercy of Japan and Russia.

President Coolidge repeatedly offered to extend the limitations on capital ships to other types. In 1927, replying to the President's invitation to a Conference at Geneva, Foreign Minister Briand, the French apostle of peace, praised the generous idealism of the President but explained that France, as a member of the League, could not discuss land, sea, and air disarmament with the United States without jeopardizing the success of the League's Disarmament Program. Mussolini, more frank, said there would be no reduction in Italy's armaments until her relations with France improved. Neither France nor Italy accepted the President's invitation.

A meeting at Geneva of Great Britain, Japan, and the United States resulted in Anglo-American recriminations with both groups appealing to the Japanese delegates who enjoyed being arbiter. The British delegation charged Americans with attempting to prevent them from building necessary cruisers because Congress was unwilling to spend money on the navy. This charge was correct. Americans replied with equal truth that London was trying to limit the size of future American battleships so that they would be inferior to *H.M.S. Nelson* and *Rodney* then under construction. The Japanese won an increase in their allowance of submarines from 60 to 70 per cent. This absurd result was a natural consequence of Anglo-American rivalry.

For four years Coolidge had watched Great Britain, France, Italy, and Japan increase their cruisers, destroyers, and submarines. Americans gradually learned of the unequal sacrifices made by Hughes, and the subsequent increase in naval expenditures by other nations; none of whom would pay their debts in full to the United States. At the conclusion of the Geneva Conference, the President ordered the Secretary of State to make a "clear, strong statement of the American position." Kellogg included in it the following: "Pursuant to the Washington Treaty, the United States made drastic cuts in its capital ship navy program and scrapped the largest capital ship navy in the world. It made greater sacrifices than any other country." Within six years of a formal statement by Hughes, one Secretary of State, that equal sacrifices had been made at the Washington Conference, candor compelled another, Kellogg, to deny its veracity.

Shortly after his refusal to accept Coolidge's invitation to the Conference Briand proposed, informally, using the press as a medium of communication, that France and the United States renounce "a recourse to arms as an instrument of policy." The subsequent extension of this proposal into the Kellogg-Briand Pact outlawing war will be discussed in Chapter 7. Its main effect on Japanese-American relations was to make it more difficult for the United States navy to obtain naval appropriations. But Coolidge's ire was finally aroused. He informed Congress of the insincerity of other signatories, requested and quickly obtained appropriations for ten 8" gun, 10,000-ton cruisers. But his term was almost over, and his successor, the Honorable Herbert Hoover, promptly accepted an invitation of Prime Minister Ramsey MacDonald to reduce naval forces still further. During Hoover's administration not a single additional ship was authorized for the navy.

The Honorable Henry L. Stimson, the new Secretary of State, led the American Delegation to London in 1930; following the example of Hughes, he ignored or dominated his naval colleagues. The Japanese again gained concessions, and scarcely had Stimson reached home when they marched into Manchuria. Stimson persuaded Washington correspondents to deal gently with the Japanese invasion assuring them he could prevail upon moderate statesmen in Tokyo to restrain the army. Stimson was quickly hoist by his own petard. Japanese diplomats made excuses for generals that Stimson was forced to accept, but their troops were not halted. The British Foreign Minister, Sir John Simon, advised Stimson to reconcile himself to the action because he knew that British opinion would not support intervention and he did not believe American opinion would.

Simon evaluated sentiments of Americans more accurately than Stimson. After World War I Americans had been rapidly disillusioned by the dissensions between Allied leaders at the Versailles Peace Conference. They learned that their comrades-in-arms had been fighting primarily for national objectives—not for Wilson's 14 points. They were called Shylocks by people they had fought to help. Journalists in the United States retorted with a plausible but unwarranted assertion that the United States had been dragged into the war by Anglo-French propaganda, and the influence of American munition makers on President Wilson. Hughes, Kellogg, and Stimson in turn had increased the confusion among Americans by accepting the fetishism prevailing in the State Department, that foreign statesmen could be persuaded to abandon national objectives by eloquent appeals to their better natures.

In spite of the obvious failure of the Harding-Hoover policy of naval disarmament and the evident determination of Japan to expand in China, between his election and inauguration President-Elect Franklin D. Roosevelt wrote President Hoover that "as to disarmament, your policy . . . (is) satisfactory . . . time is required to bring it to fruition." Later after consulting Stimson, Roosevelt announced that he would make no radical change in our Far East policy. In February 1933, Ambassador Hugh Gibson, at Geneva, indicated the faith of Hoover and Roosevelt in the Kellogg-Briand Pact, when he announced: "We believe this conference should and can successfully devote itself to the abolition" of offensive weapons. Mr. Gibson's eloquence proving futile, President Roosevelt himself appealed on May 16, 1933, to the heads of foreign governments for peace by disarmament in order to end economic chaos. He proposed the elimination of all offensive weapons and that all nations "enter into a solemn and definite pact of nonaggression."

The Kellogg-Briand Pact was only five years old when Roosevelt reported to Congress, "The way to disarmament is to disarm . . . I have asked for an immediate agreement among nations on four practical and simultaneous steps. First, . . . weapons of offensive war be eliminated. Second, that this first definite step be taken now. Third, while these steps are being taken no nation increase existing armaments . . . over treaty limitations. Fourth, . . . no nation during this period shall send any armed force of whatever nature across its border." Hoover and Stimson had been trying since 1931 to get Japan to respect China's borders, so had the League of Nations, but Roosevelt was as positive as Kellogg had been that powerful, unsatisfied nations could be persuaded to disarm and to abandon efforts to expand.

Roosevelt held these views as late as December 1935, perhaps later, for in his instructions to the Honorable Norman Davis, Chairman of the U.S. Delegation to the London Conference, he included the following: "The Washington Naval Conference of 1922 . . . brought to the world . . . the first . . . agreement for . . . reduction of armament . . . The London Treaty of 1930 carried on the good work." Roosevelt recommended a further naval reduction of 20, 15, 10 or at least 5 per cent. He ended by saying he would not submit to the Senate any new treaty calling for larger navies.*

While Roosevelt was accepting Hoover's plan of further disarmament, Winston Churchill urged a bold approach to a reasonable solution of European questions before Germany rearmed, and while the World War I Allies had forces sufficient to compel a decision by force. In November 1932 he advocated that, before there was any further disarmament, Germany's grievances (some of them well-founded) be removed because "It would be far safer to reopen questions like those of the Danzig Corridor while victorious nations still have ample superiority (of armament) than to wait—until once again vast combinations equally matched confront each other face-to-face."

English and American public opinions by this time were for

* For F. D. Roosevelt's determination to limit armaments, see *The Papers and Public Addresses of F. D. Roosevelt*, by S. I. Rosenman, Random House.

peace at almost any price. Soon after Roosevelt's first inauguration, students at Oxford made a formal pledge "not to fight for King or country." Conservative and labor leaders alike neglected the armed forces. Between 1923 and 1937, Stanley Baldwin, a successful businessman and patriotic politician, alternated with Ramsey MacDonald, laborite, as Prime Minister. Both opposed any increase of armaments—Baldwin, in hope of reducing expenditures and in fear of losing an election; MacDonald, because he wished to divert funds from national defense to social security. A year after Roosevelt instructed Davis to obtain additional naval reductions, Churchill finally taunted Baldwin into admitting to the House of Commons that he had not advocated rearming for fear of losing the previous election.

Churchill's attack on Baldwin for failing to strengthen the armed forces was justified by the Prime Minister's acts. His arguments carried less weight with members of Parliament because, as Chancellor of the Exchequer under Baldwin from 1924 to 1929, Churchill had permitted subordinates in the Treasury to starve all three Services. Next to Baldwin, Churchill was the most influential member of the Cabinet during that time and, therefore, largely responsible for this action and the failure to complete the fortifications and facilities at Singapore. Only after he had been dropped from the Cabinet did he attack Baldwin and urge strengthening the Empire's defenses.†

Roosevelt's order to Ambassador Davis to obtain further naval reductions, impracticable under any circumstances, became impossible, for Adolf Hitler was chosen Chancellor of the Reich almost as Roosevelt entered the White House. A formidable nation, defeated and disgruntled Germany, joined two dissatisfied victors, Japan and Italy. The support Roosevelt first gave to disarmament and the confidence with which he assured Congress that he could personally persuade other heads of governments to disarm, subsequently hampered his first, feeble efforts to strengthen the army and navy.

Anglo-American concessions in 1930 did not reconcile Japan to

† *Main Fleet to Singapore,* by Captain Russell Grenfell, RN, Faber and Faber, London, pp. 68-69.

a 3 to 5 naval ratio with Great Britain and the United States. In 1934, her government renounced all limitations on her navy; a year later, incensed by a very mild rebuke from the Lytton Commission of the League of Nations for invading Manchuria, she announced her intention to withdraw from the League. The death of Hindenburg strengthened Hitler's hold on the German Government and the Reich followed Japan out of the League in 1935. The failure of the United States, Great Britain, or the League to do more than formally protest the invasion of Manchuria, convinced Japanese army officers that British and American people were for peace at any price.

In 1936, Japan formally asserted its determination "to secure the position of the Empire on the East Asia Continent by diplomatic policy and national defense," and to "develop the Empire in the South Seas." In July 1937, its government began by invading Central China; so in the first year of his second term, Roosevelt was compelled to pay more attention to foreign affairs. In May, Neville Chamberlain, Chancellor of the Exchequer, succeeded Baldwin as Prime Minister and began to rehabilitate the British armed forces. Simultaneously he sought a formula that would satisfy Germany and Italy. Hitler was steadily increasing the Reichswehr.

The British vainly looked to the United States for leadership in the Far East. The State Department contented itself with begging nations with interests in the western Pacific to observe certain principles. Chamberlain privately commented, "It is always best and safest to count on nothing from the Americans but words." * Hoover or Stimson truthfully could have said the same about the English people and government. The Japanese, well aware of sentiment prevailing in both countries, turned a machine gun on the British Ambassador in China traveling with his entourage with the Union Jack flying; later army bombing planes sank the *USS Panay* in broad daylight. Roosevelt and Hull, after accepting obviously false excuses on Christmas Day, congratulated the American people on their forbearance. The American press that

* *Life of Neville Chamberlain,* by Keith Feiling, London.

pilloried Chamberlain for appeasing Hitler said little when Roosevelt set the example by appeasing Japan; and in 1938 the House of Representatives, influenced by public opinion, narrowly rejected a resolution proposing a constitutional amendment that would have restricted the power of Congress itself to declare war until such action had been approved by a national plebiscite.

The President's only reaction to the Panay incident was to direct the Chief of Naval Operations, Admiral W. D. Leahy, to send Captain R. E. Ingersoll to London to consult the Admiralty on joint action to resist the Japanese advance in the Far East. In January 1938, Anglo-American Naval Officers recommended that a British fleet be stationed at Singapore and an American fleet at Honolulu to cooperate in the western Pacific. Both navies had been neglected for several years. The British navy had maintained a larger construction program but had been deprived of control of its Fleet Air Arm; and, although having authority to create a first-class base at Singapore, the British Government had neglected both its naval facilities and fortifications. Finally, at the last moment defense was entrusted to an Air Force Commander, with a meager force of bombers.

The Anglo-American combined plan suggested two cripples leaning on one another. It was aptly named Rainbow One, because it was based in large part on hope. Hope of joint action itself was abandoned in May 1939 when London informed Washington that responsibilities in the Mediterranean would prevent the concentration of a fleet in Singapore and Washington accepted the obligation of defending the western Pacific alone.

Some economic pressure against Japan was applied. In June 1939, the State Department secured the cooperation of American airplane manufacturers to place a "moral" embargo on planes and spare parts to Japan on account of the indiscriminate bombing of undefended Chinese cities. In July 1939, it cleared the way for more economic pressure by notifying the Japanese Foreign Office of its intention to abrogate the Commercial Treaty of 1911. In February 1940 the treaty was neither renewed nor replaced. The State Department was then legally prepared to apply economic sanctions, but hesitated to do so lest it precipitate war for which we were far from ready.

Early in 1938, the President had apologetically recommended to Congress an extra 39 million dollars for defense because other nations were increasing their armaments at "an unprecedented and alarming" rate; he was careful to explain that only a small part of these funds would be expended on battleships and cruisers up to July 1940. Despite the weakness of the armed forces he wrote two expostulatory notes to Hitler during the Czech crisis. Two days after dispatching the last one he learned that Great Britain, France, and Italy had agreed that the Sudetenland should be returned to Germany. At the same time, Roosevelt's ardent admirers insisted that these two notes entitled him to some of the praise lavished on Neville Chamberlain for preserving the peace. After the invasion of Poland no one volunteered to share Chamberlain's responsibility for appeasing Hitler. Chamberlain, as Chancellor of the Exchequer under Baldwin, must share some of the blame for Britain's unpreparedness, but the major share goes to Baldwin and MacDonald. A succession of French premiers including Briand, Blum, and Daladier were equally responsible for the unpreparedness of France. To Neville Chamberlain must go the credit for making the first determined effort to increase the efficiency of British armed forces between two world wars. And, by appeasing Hitler temporarily while vigorous efforts were made to improve radar stations, fighting squadrons, and the navy's air arm, he provided barely enough to enable Churchill to win the battle of Britain.*

In the United States, Hughes, Kellogg, Hoover, and Stimson must share the blame with Roosevelt for American unpreparedness in 1941; but in a much smaller degree, for he entered the White House almost nine years before Pearl Harbor. During his first four years he did his utmost to make further reductions in the Japanese, the British, and the American navies. As the Japanese would have only reduced 3 tons to 5 tons for the other two,

* The claim has been made (*To the Bitter End*, by H. B. Gisevius, Houghton Mifflin Co.) that if Chamberlain had not appeased Hitler the German army would have revolted. This assertion is, to say the least, doubtful.

the reduction meant that Anglo-American fleets would be reduced 10 tons to 3 for the future foe. Not until the eve of his third term did he commence to prepare the armed forces for war.

The conclusion of a nonaggression pact by Hitler and Stalin in August 1939 followed by the invasion of Poland in September surprised Tokyo as well as London, Paris, and Washington. Hitler's action diverted the attention of Roosevelt and Hull to Europe. Japan controlled Manchukuo, North China, and the major cities, ports, and railways in Central and South China. Chiang Kai-shek had retreated into the interior transporting a few factories ahead and scorching the earth behind him. His resistance absorbed enough Japanese resources to prevent their taking prompt advantage of the European war; their officials paused to appraise the situation.

On September 3, the President announced American neutrality; shortly after he proclaimed a limited national emergency and made a small increase in the armed forces. He promised the nation he would keep ships and citizens out of dangerous areas. Congress and the public were unwilling to trust the question of peace or war to the President. And for some reason he did not explain to the public the reasons for his foreign policies as he did so effectively for his domestic programs.

While Hitler's armored and motorized forces, with Stuka bombers overhead, slashed through Poland, Anglo-French forces after a feeble effort to advance on the western front, sheltered themselves comfortably in trenches "de luxe." At sea, the Anglo-French navies had no difficulty in establishing an efficient convoy system and maintaining control of the sea. U-boat sinkings were small. In Washington the War Department, still under the spell of the French army of 1918, reported to the President that the Nazis could not break the Maginot Line. The navy was equally confident that Anglo-French fleets could control the sea and suppress the U-boats. Admiral Leahy had advised the President that the navy was ready for war. When Ambassador Grew in Washington on leave advised the President that if Japan was denied oil from the United States or other commercial sources, she would probably take it by force from the Dutch East Indies,

Roosevelt replied: "Then we could easily intercept her fleet." *

The menace of Europe caused the American Republics to rally around the United States; Sumner Welles, Under-Secretary of State, assured them that the Western Hemisphere could defend itself from all aggression by relying upon "freedom, democracy and Christian faith." All was tranquil along the Potomac.

Germany and Japan were discussing terms of an Anti-Comintern Pact to include Italy when, without informing Tokyo, Hitler announced the Red-Nazi Pact in August. The Japanese Cabinet resigned, stating that "Japan must form new policies." A compromise followed; General Abe became Prime Minister, and clung to the objective of establishing "a new order" in the Far East; Admiral Nomura, friendly to England and America, became Foreign Minister. In January 1940 a new Cabinet with Admiral Yonai as Prime Minister took office. Under Abe and Yonai, the army continued its advance in China. In February, Japan increased her demands on the Netherlands East Indies.

The German successes in western Europe in the spring of 1940 confirmed the confidence of the Japanese army in the Wehrmacht, but in Washington they caused a complete reversal of army and navy opinion. On June 26, the Joint Planning Committee and the Joint Board doubted if the British Empire would survive the winter of 1940-41. The General Staff reported to the President that the Nazis could invade England, take Gibraltar, cross the Straits into Africa, seize Dakar, cross the South Atlantic into Brazil, then occupy Venezuela, threaten the Canal Zone, Mexico, and the great cities of the middle west. On their weird hypothesis, General Marshall subsequently gave priority to airplanes and bases in the Caribbean and South America over Pearl Harbor or Manila.

Admiral Stark too succumbed to Marshall's defeatist philosophy. Apparently they convinced the President, who later suggested to Churchill that in case the United Kingdom surrendered, the Royal Navy be dispatched to bases in the Commonwealth. Some American officials feared to send surplus stocks of World

* From Grew's unpublished diary. Quoted from *The Road to Pearl Harbor*, by Herbert Feis, Princeton University Press, p. 41.

War I rifles and 3″ field pieces to England lest they fall into German hands. After Churchill pledged his Cabinet to fight to the end, Roosevelt promptly sent all surplus field guns, rifles, and munitions to England. A large majority of Congress approved the action and authorized the President to embody the National Guard and Reserves in the regular army and appropriated generously for the armed forces. But fears that the President, eager to aid Great Britain, might deprive the armed forces of essential equipment, caused Congress to require that the head of a Service certify that transfer of equipment would not jeopardize national security.

Imminence of two political conventions added to domestic confusion; Roosevelt, before he had revealed his intention to run for a third term, appointed former Secretary of State Henry L. Stimson and the Honorable Frank Knox, influential members of the opposition party, to his Cabinet. Personal rivalries in the Democratic Party, Roosevelt's pledges to union labor before and after his nomination, and partisan strife during the Presidential campaign, hampered efforts to change industry from producing consumer goods to munitions.

In September 1940, Churchill renewed his request for 50 overage destroyers. The Republican candidate for the Presidency, The Honorable Wendell Willkie, agreed to refrain from criticizing the action, enabling Roosevelt to comply with Churchill's request without political risk. In October, however, Democratic bosses in some big cities insisted that Roosevelt give one more assurance to mothers and fathers that "Your boys are not going to be sent into any foreign wars," or lose the election. This pledge was made to a Boston audience in October 1940 and subsequently handicapped the Commander-in-Chief of the Army and Navy. Roosevelt had some reason for accepting the advice of city bosses. Public opinion was against our entry into the war. Both political parties asserted in their platforms their intentions to keep out of war. Willkie did not suggest in any of his speeches that the United States enter the conflict.

Economic factors were having a cumulative effect on Japanese-American relations. Shortage of strategic materials appeared and in July 1940 were placed under government control. Secretary of the Treasury, The Honorable Henry Morgenthau, was openly seeking means of aiding Great Britain. He and Lord Lothian, the British Ambassador, immediately appreciated that together Great Britain, the United States, and the Netherlands could halt the flow of oil to Japan. Morgenthau recommended this action to the President, and was supported by Secretaries Knox and Stimson. Under-Secretary Welles, General Marshall, and Admiral Stark opposed; they feared that if deprived of oil by such an embargo, Japan forcibly would seize it in the Netherlands East Indies and probably precipitate hostilities. The President decided against the action.

When exports of scrap iron and oil were prohibited except to Great Britain and the Western Hemisphere, aviation gasoline and its ingredients were not included.* Prohibiting the export of scrap iron alone was a blow to Japan's munition industry and Ambassador Horinouchi protested to Hull that it was an unfriendly act.

While Americans were engrossed in the national election, Japan's ambitions were increasing. Instructions to her representative at the meeting drawing up the Tri-Partite Anti-Comintern Pact included the following: "The sphere to be envisaged in the course of negotiations with Germany and Italy as Japan's Sphere of Living for the construction of a Greater East Asia New Order will comprise: the former German Islands under mandate, French Indo-China and Pacific Islands, Thailand, British Malaya, British Borneo, Dutch East Indies, Burma, Australia, New Zealand, India, etc., with Japan, Manchuria and China as the backbone."

On September 27, 1940, the Anti-Comintern Pact was signed by Germany, Italy, and Japan. It included a proviso that if one of the powers was attacked by a power, not then in the European war or in the Chinese-Japanese conflict, the three countries would help each other with military means. This was so plainly aimed at the United States that Secretary Hull simply announced that its consummation was the culmination of developments that had been known for several years. A few days later, Hull informed

* *Road to Pearl Harbor* by Herbert Feis, Princeton University Press, Chapter XII.

the British Ambassador that the United States wished to see Great Britain succeed in the war and that American acts and utterances involving the Pacific would be influenced by this desire.

When Ambassador Horinouchi left for Tokyo in October 1940, he told Hull that never had Japanese-American relations been so critical; he refused to return to Washington and other diplomats declined the appointment. Thereupon some senior admirals persuaded Admiral Nomura, a former Foreign Minister, to take the post with its heavy responsibility for they were not then ready to accept the inevitability of an American war. These Flag Officers knew that their navy could easily gain temporary control of the western Pacific and enable their army to occupy the Philippines, Malaysia, and much of the Bismarck Archipelago. They also knew it would be difficult, if not impossible, to retain control of the western Pacific; furthermore, if a superior American fleet regained control of the seas in that area, these temporary conquests would be lost and the Japanese Islands blockaded. Responding to the requests of brother officers, Nomura patriotically undertook his task.

Before Nomura left Japan, Admiral I. Yamamoto, Commander-in-Chief of the Combined Fleet, with the approval of Admiral O. Nagano, Chief of the Navy General Staff, ordered Rear Admiral Onishi, Chief of Staff of the 11th Air Fleet, to prepare a plan of campaign so that the Combined Fleet could act promptly and effectively if negotiations failed and war with United States ensued. Simultaneously, officers of the British Royal Navy at Stark's invitation joined American officers in Washington to prepare Rainbow Five that became the Anglo-American plan for World War II.

Soon after the beginning of Roosevelt's third term, in response to requests from Churchill, he obtained the passage by Congress of the Lend-Lease Bill with an initial appropriation of 7 billion dollars. Churchill, momentarily satisfied, endorsed the President's campaign pledge made in Boston asserting that Great Britain would finish the war alone and did not wish the aid of American troops then in training camps. This pretense was soon abandoned in London and Washington. Admiral Stark, asserting that it would be folly to appropriate funds for lend-lease goods and then allow them to be sunk, contended that the Lend-Lease Legislation was a mandate from Congress to deliver these goods to the United Kingdom. Therefore, he urged the President to provide United States naval escort for them. Stark desired to get the United States into the war for he feared that the Nazis would compel the British Government to surrender before the American armed forces were prepared. Then he was convinced Germany and Japan would join to attack the United States, who would be left to fight alone.

As Roosevelt and Harry Hopkins inaugurated lend-lease, Hitler and Stalin were watching each other warily. Stalin, having defeated Finland, was remodelling his army to remedy the defects that war had revealed. He gave his generals a freer hand, with orders to improve the army. As the British resistance to Germany increased he raised Russia's claims in the Balkans. Hitler was further embarrassed by Mussolini's invasion of Greece and the visit of Yosuke Matsuoka to Moscow on his way to and from Berlin. Von Ribbentrop carefully explained to the Japanese envoy on his arrival that the Nazis had wanted to complete their alliance with Japan in 1939. As that proved impossible, Hitler was obliged to conclude an agreement with Russia, but that alliance was not important, and while the relations between Moscow and Berlin were *correct* they were not *friendly*.

Matsuoka explained with equal casuistry that he had only visited with Stalin and Molotov on their invitation. During their conversations he had emphasized that the Anglo-Saxons were the greatest hindrance to the establishment of a New Order in the Far East, that with the downfall of the British Empire difficulties between Russia and Japan would disappear. Stalin had replied that Soviet Russia had never gotten along with Great Britain and never could. Matsuoka sought to convince Stalin that the Anglo-Saxons were the common enemy of Russia, Germany, and Japan; Stalin genially agreed. In Berlin, Matsuoka listened carefully to Hitler's arguments, that ran substantially as follows: The Nazis were already victorious in Europe; Britain's only hope was aid from Russia or the United States; both Britain and the United States were striving to get Russia on the side of the British; he corroborated Ribbentrop's statement that Nazi-Communist relations were correct but not friendly; in Finland and the Balkans the Reds had demonstrated their unfriendliness; he knew Sir Stafford Cripps was trying to arrange an understanding between London and Moscow. Hitler said he placed no dependence on his agreements with Moscow, only in the strength of the Wehrmacht and he could quickly crush the Red army and the Soviet state.

Hitler again thanked Matsuoka for the 'spiritual' aid Japan had given the Reich by causing the United States to hesitate to enter the war officially. Then he employed his most effective arguments. Now was the time for Japan to realize her aims in the Far East. England was tied down in Europe. Russia could not intervene since 150 Nazi divisions stood on her western frontier. The United States had three choices: she could arm herself; she could assist England; or she could wage war on another front. If she helped England she could not arm herself; if she abandoned England the latter would be destroyed and the United States would face the Axis powers alone. If, however, Japan did not improve this opportunity and the European conflict ended in a compromise, England and France in a few years would recover; they would be joined by America and Japan would face them alone.

Frankly admitting that there was always some risk in war, Hitler climaxed his argument by reminding Matsuoka that Japan was the strongest power in the Far East; that she would never have a better chance to attain her objectives. After the Axis victory Germany would satisfy her colonial ambitions in Africa and give Japan a free hand in Asia and the South Seas.

Matsuoka was impressed with Hitler's presentation; he was already convinced that Japan, on account of her industrious and increasing population, her commercial enterprise and the strength of her armed forces, was entitled to more territory and access to sources of raw materials. But Hitler failed to convince Matsuoka that the time to strike had arrived, so he told Der Fuehrer that he knew Japan could not solve the South Sea problem until she had taken Singapore. In time it would be attacked. He requested his conversation be considered confidential, for many of his colleagues did not agree with him, and would turn him out of office if they learned his views; finally, he cautioned Hitler not to be alarmed if he pretended to be friendly with Anglo-Saxons.

From Berlin, Matsuoka left for Moscow where he and Stalin had a final meeting where a 'reinsurance' pact was made between the Reds and the Japs. No difficulty was encountered, because Stalin wanted to avoid a war with Japan and Japan wanted to avoid war with Russia. Shortly after Matsuoka returned to Tokyo, Hitler invaded Russia. Two days later, with Secretary Knox's approval, Stark advised the President "to announce and start escorting (convoys to England) immediately . . . that such a declaration, followed by immediate action . . . would almost certainly involve us in the war." Stark emphasized much more delay might be fatal to Britain's survival. Stark reminded the President that he had been "asking this [getting in the war] for months in the State Department and elsewhere," because he was convinced that only a war "psychology . . . would speed up" American preparations for war sufficiently.

While Stark was giving this advice to the President, Secretary Stimson reported his own and General Marshall's views. They were convinced that Germany would only require from one to three months to beat Russia; during this time, the President "should push with vigor . . . movements in the Atlantic," particularly the occupation of Iceland and equipping bases in Brazil. Not a word about the Pacific. Roosevelt's own estimate of the situation on July 1, was "the Japs are having a real . . . fight among themselves . . . to decide whether to attack Russia, . . . South Seas . . . or sit on the fence and be more friendly with us. . . . He considered it essential to keep peace in the Pacific in order to control the Atlantic for he did not have enough Navy to go round . . ." Like Stimson, Roosevelt was hoist by his own petard. He was primarily responsible for not having enough navy to go around.

The President's statement indicates that he fully accepted the views of Stark and Marshall that our first task was to save Great Britain. In Tokyo, Prince Konoye was recalled as Premier and, after consulting chiefs of the army and navy, recommended, and the Emperor approved, the following program: To accelerate the advance into French Indo-China and to use force if French officials did not yield; to delay any attack on Russia; to prepare necessary forces to attain their objective. The Foreign Office explained to the Kremlin that their obligations to Germany did not require any change in their relations with Russia; Stalin was quite content with this *modus vivendi;* Hitler fighting Great Britain and Russia had no way of compelling his nominal ally, Japan, to participate.

The arguments given by Hitler to Yosukea Matsuoka eventually determined Tokyo's decision, and they afford an interesting contrast between the reactions of Washington and Tokyo to the invasion of Russia. After the war, Churchill admitted that from the beginning he had worked to get the United States into the war on the side of England and to keep Japan out if he could. But, if necesary, he would gladly accept the entry of Japan as an enemy if at the same time he could be sure of getting the United States as an ally. As far as Great Britain's interests were concerned, it is easy to understand Churchill's policy.

The President at the Argentia Conference in August 1941 accepted the suggestions of Churchill, who was striving to involve the United States in the war. Hitler offered Matsuoka various concessions, but Japan avoided war with Russia and, temporarily, with the United States or Great Britain, until Japanese forces were ready to strike.

Churchill had nothing to offer to the United States materially; and he loftily ignored strategical suggestions from American officers that Roosevelt had sent to London. Churchill obtained the entry of the United States on his own terms because Roosevelt, Hull, Stimson, Knox, Marshall, and Stark (in short, the U.S. High Command), after the collapse of western Europe, convinced themselves that to save the nation they must first save the United Kingdom. It did not take the British Foreign Office or the adroit Prime Minister long to discover this attitude; the rest was easy.

Admiral Stark went further than the rest. He attributed to American psychology the lag in military production that was really due to the recent Presidential campaign and Roosevelt's attitude toward labor. When Hitler steadily refrained from declaring war in spite of United States provocation, Stark urged the President to openly increase our aid to England in order to provoke hostilities, so that Americans would expedite the production of munitions.

Stark reversed General Washington's advice: "In time of peace prepare for war." Stark recommended that Roosevelt plunge the nation into war unprepared so that Americans would hasten their armament program. And the Chief of War Plans, Admiral R. K. Turner, was ready with a plan to provoke war with Germany in case we got into war with Japan first, and Hitler still remained neutral. But Hitler was only waiting until he could be sure of Japan's entry; he declared war soon after the attack on Pearl Harbor. Thus the United States was spared the effort of provoking a war with Germany, in order to save Great Britain, so as finally to produce sufficient weapons to protect the United States. Our devotion to our future ally, Great Britain, was only matched by the distrust among the Tripartite Nations.

Hitler's invasion of Russia relieved Japan of any menace from the north; concentrating her efforts in the south, she quickly occupied French Indo-China, whence she threatened the Philippines, Malaya, and the Dutch East Indies. At the Argentia Conference in August 1941, the President joined Churchill in a message to Stalin promising "to help your country . . . against the Nazi attack," and agreed with Churchill's suggestion to send a joint ultimatum to Japan, if she continued her advance in Siam. Shortly before, the United States, Great Britain, and the Netherlands had blocked Japanese funds in their countries; this action restricted oil supplies to Japan. Even as tempered by the State Department, Roosevelt's ultimatum which he personally read to Ambassador Nomura on this occasion convinced Nomura that further Japanese expansion southward would cause the United States to declare war on Japan, and he so advised his government. In September, negotiations were temporarily suspended. The Japanese southward advance continued, but when negotiations were resumed they pivoted around the Imperial Navy's reserve of oil.

For months three groups in Japan had been arguing about their foreign policy. The army wanted to enter the war as an ally of Germany; the navy, including Admirals Nagano and Yamamoto, hesitated; they were confident that their navy could gain and maintain control of the western Pacific for about two years. Thereafter, they could not depend upon retaining control. The Emperor and Imperial Household sought a compromise solution. The restriction on the flow of oil to Japan confronted the Japanese navy with a crisis; its oil reserves would last only two years. If negotiations were prolonged, the reserve would be depleted correspondingly. Its only hope of resisting Anglo-American navies was to gain an initial advantage by some form of surprise, to seize oil wells in the East Indies, and with their fleet tankers, to replenish their reserves. Accordingly, Admiral Nagano advised the Emperor to put a definite time limit on the discussions in Washington.

In September, Japan formulated her minimum demands; the United States refused to accept. On November 5, Japan made a final offer; that too was rejected. On November 11 the nation was informed of the critical situation by Secretary Knox and Under-Secretary Welles in public addresses. On November 20, Ambassador Nomura suggested a temporary agreement to preserve the peace while a permanent solution was sought.

Meanwhile, General Marshall and Admiral Stark asked the President and Secretary Hull to prolong the negotiations, because they needed several weeks to increase their defenses of the Philippines. At first Hull agreed, but when Chiang objected and was supported by Churchill, Hull recommended and the President ordered the negotiations ended. Oddly enough, about this same time, the Japanese navy needed a few days to perfect its preparations; its Foreign Office complied with a navy request to prolong the discussions in Washington. Again the absolute contrast between Japanese and American diplomats in responsiveness to requests from the armed services was revealed.

Hull's refusal meant that the long Japanese-American conflict of interest would be settled by force. Like their diplomacy the approach of the two nations to the crisis was diametrically different. The Japanese had decided where and how to strike, and had trained each task force for its specific part; they only needed to decide upon the time to attack. They simply followed the precepts learned from European instructors of the army and navy and with their own native industry and patience improved on their instructors. They were apt students of European methods.

The U.S. High Command, having decided to make its initial effort against Germany even if Japan attacked first, allotted insufficient forces to the Pacific; Churchill expended forces in the Mediterranean he had promised to the Far East; most important, Roosevelt had decided to wait an overt attack. But neither international law nor custom requires such action. Over half of the wars of the past two centuries began without or before a declaration of war. Before our war with Spain, President McKinley concentrated the Asiatic Fleet in Hong Kong and gave orders to Dewey to be ready to destroy the Spanish Fleet at Manila. Sampson at Key West and Schley at Hampton Roads were ready on telegraphic signal to strike Cervera's Fleet if it approached the Atlantic or Caribbean coasts. It was the fatal election pledge made in Boston at the insistence of Democratic city bosses that gave the initiative to the enemy.* Many of the President's warmest friends regretted that speech. Among them was Secretary Stimson, a patriotic but often misguided statesman devoted to the President, who lamented his lack of courage to lay the whole question before the American public.

As early as September 1941, the Japanese combined fleet had completed preparations for its wide-flung attacks and the various task forces were trained for their specific duties. About November 5, when the final decision on war or peace was made by the Cabinet, the operation orders were issued to senior Commanders and they proceeded with their forces to their various stations. The forces were ready and could be launched on short notice.

An attack force commanded by Admiral Nagumo, formed

* For details, see *Roosevelt and Hopkins,* by R. E. Sherwood, p. 191.

around six aircraft carriers, had been practiced in launching torpedo and bombing planes especially to disable the fleet in Pearl Harbor. Assuming that this attack would succeed, a South Seas Attack Force under Admiral Kondo was ready to, and did, clear the way for, and protect, landing forces in the Philippines and Malaya. A Northern Defense Force interposed between Vladivostok and northern Japan. Admiral Yamamoto retained under his own command in the Inland Sea the main body of the Combined Fleet. He gave to the South Seas Attack Force two battleships, two aircraft carriers, two heavy cruisers, and a squadron of destroyers to observe and to attack if necessary the *Prince of Wales* and *Repulse,* British capital ships known to be at Singapore. He added to Kondo's Force the 11th Air Fleet of three flotillas, two in Formosa and one in Saigon.

Yamamoto's plan, executed on December 8, Tokyo time, was completely successful with losses much less than estimated. There was about a week's delay in capturing Wake; a four months' campaign was successfully completed within ten days' of schedule.

Only a few more details of this disgrace of United States armed forces need to be recalled. First the operation was planned and controlled by Admiral Yamamoto from his flagship in the Inland Sea where he was in easy communication with the Foreign Office and the Chief of the Naval General Staff. Not until November 26, after receiving Hull's last note, did the Foreign Office despair of reaching an understanding. Then fleet movements began. Envoys in Washington prolonged the negotiations to give the fleets time to get into position.

Even then the Foreign Office through the Navy Department had complete control of the situation. D-Day was set for December 8, Tokyo time; "H" hour was dawn at Honolulu, December 7, Honolulu time; and 1:00 P.M. December 7, Washington time. Not until December 4 would the task forces reach assigned stations. Surprise was considered essential to success; therefore, if Admiral Nagumo encountered any American ships before December 6 (D-2), he was ordered to return; if he encountered any after December 7 (D-1), he was authorized to decide whether to return or to proceed to attack. This was the only initiative allowed to the Commander of the striking force.

The utmost care was taken to insure success. It was possible that the United States ships would be protected by steel nets that would intercept torpedoes; therefore, bombing planes were also provided; aerial torpedoes were provided with stabilizers; and veteran air pilots were especially trained to launch torpedoes in shallow water.

If the Japanese plan had been carried out precisely at 1:00 P.M., December 7, Washington time, Ambassadors Nomura and Kurusu would have presented Secretary of State Hull with formal notice that negotiations were ended and that Japan was free to take measures she considered necessary. Tokyo planned to declare war minutes afterward, and had the Embassy in Washington been as efficient as the fleet, the Japanese Government could have claimed that the attack followed the declaration of war. Decoding the long message compelled the ambassadors to request a delay in the meeting with Secretary Hull. They arrived about an hour after Pearl Harbor was attacked, for the Imperial Japanese Navy carried out its program on schedule. The Pearl Harbor attack had thus been planned almost exactly like the attack on the Russian fleet in the Russo-Japanese war. The weapons were somewhat different, but the theory and policy of the application of force remained the same.

The Roberts Board, which investigated the Pearl Harbor attack, was limited by the President to investigating actions of army and navy officers. On ex parte testimony, some of it unsworn, it promptly exonerated all members of the High Command in Washington from the President down from any blame for the disaster at Pearl Harbor. Subsequently, employing the time-tested legal procedures common in all military services and basing their conclusions on sworn testimony of responsible officials, the Army Pearl Harbor Board held that the Chief of Staff, General G. C. Marshall, had "failed to keep General Short fully informed as to the international situation" and that he "was personally concerned . . . with the delay in getting to General Short the important information reaching Washington" on December 6. A Naval Court of Inquiry, also using Service legal procedure, held that Admiral Harold R. Stark, Chief of Naval Operations ". . . did not transmit to Admiral Kimmel, Commander in Chief Pacific Fleet, during the very critical period November 26 to December 7, important information. . . ." Evidence given under oath before a Joint Congressional Committee in 1945-46 reveals beyond any reasonable doubt sufficient errors of omission and commission by the civil and military components of the U.S. High Command in Washington and the Pacific to justify the un-favorable conclusions of all three Boards.

In his recent book *The Big Secret of Pearl Harbor*, Rear-Ad-miral R. A. Theobald makes an excellent summary of the facts of the debacle. It is impossible to agree with his conjecture that "President Roosevelt encouraged and expected" the Japanese at-tack on the fleet. Vice-Admiral F. E. Beatty, Aide to Secretary Knox during the autumn of 1941, in a letter to the *U.S. News and World Report*, which published Theobald's book, agrees with the facts but challenges many of Theobald's conjectures. Al-though clearing Roosevelt of the more serious charge, Beatty confirms other evidence that Roosevelt did desire to get the coun-try into war with Japan because "our efforts to cause the Germans to declare war on us had failed." Therefore, the President ap-proved Secretary Hull's note handed to Ambassador Nomura on November 26 containing the demand that Japan evacuate China and other terms "so severe we (the Administration) knew that nation could not accept." In Beatty's judgment, "We did not want her to accept them." Admiral Turner confirms and ampli-fies Admiral Beatty's statement; he testified that if after Japan declared war Hitler still hesitated to do so, he had a plan that would provoke German entry.

Defenders of Roosevelt's policies and the consequent conduct of the U.S. High Command have excused their actions by assert-ing that these devious methods were necessary to wake Americans to their dangerous situation. These highly placed officials should not be allowed to use the public as a whipping boy to escape censure for failing to measure up to their responsibilities; to do so would lower the standard Americans are entitled to demand of those who aspire to the honorable but exacting posts in the High Command. Americans for their own future safety should pay more heed to foreign affairs. They should remember that, while at present they are satisfied with their possessions, all other nations are not equally content. In the nineteenth century their forebears threatened Spain to get Florida and Great Britain to obtain Oregon territory; and fought Mexico to secure Texas, New Mexico, and California. At all periods of history some powerful states have been dissatisfied with their position and ready to go to war to improve it. Because they are satisfied today they should not make the dangerous assumption that all other nations desire peace. It only takes one strong, dissatisfied state to start a war; the American public should bear this fact in mind and be more willing to accept the burden of preparing for war in time of peace; if they do, the High Command in the future will have no excuse for resorting to various devices such as giving the enemy the first blow to ensure public support for an unavoidable conflict.

The surprise attack on Pearl Harbor has entirely overshadowed the debacle in the Philippines whose officials knew several hours before the enemy struck that war had begun. Under the over-all plan of making the major effort in the Atlantic, the chance of the small land, sea, and air contingents of the American forces holding Manila Bay and enough surrounding country to furnish a naval and air base was poor indeed. This chance vanished when General MacArthur, with characteristic optimism, persuaded the War Department to increase his responsibilities. Late in November his mission was enlarged to include: support for the navy in raiding Japanese sea communications and destroying Axis forces; air raids against Japanese forces and installations within tactical operating radius of available bases; and cooperation with Associate Powers in the defense of territories in accordance with approved policies and agreements.

In fairness to the War Department, it should be emphasized that MacArthur's responsibilities were enlarged at his own request. But his difficulties were increased by the expressed desire of the Administration "that Japan commit the first overt act." This led him to forbid air reconnaissance over Formosa before hostilities. MacArthur's overconfidence in his Filipino troops, added to the overconfidence of the Chiefs of Staff in the ability of thirty-five to fifty long-range bombers to repulse any expeditionary force, were the fundamental reasons for the speedy annihilation of the air force, the subsequent destruction of the navy yard, and the resultant uselessness of Manila Bay as a naval or air base. From 1939 to 1941, innumerable air fights had shown that unescorted bombers could not operate if opposed by fighters and flak. In addition, it was shown that, for sustained operations, bombers needed well-equipped bases, with dispersal fields and ample spare parts; and these bases (and bombers when grounded) needed to be protected from enemy air attacks. Nevertheless, Marshall and Stark accepted Arnold's and MacArthur's estimate that these B-17's hastily flown to the Philippines, where only a few partially equipped and poorly protected air fields existed, could deter or repulse the Japanese expeditionary forces escorted by carriers and supported by their planes and by fleets of land based Naval aircraft that covered the advance of the surface ships. And they so reported to the President.*

During the Japanese attacks in the Philippines, records were destroyed and subsequent oral accounts of senior officers are conflicting; the following statements are taken from the official history of the fall of the Philippines authorized by the War Department.

About 5:00 A.M., December 8 (Manila time) Brereton proposed to MacArthur to attack the Japanese Air Base in Formosa; this attack was deferred until a photo reconnaissance of the target could be made; about 11:00 A.M., an attack was authorized; meanwhile the bombers had taken to the air to avoid being bombed on the ground, the bombers were back on Clark Field shortly after 11:30 A.M.; MacArthur then planned to have the bombers attack Formosa at daylight on the 9th, but later gave Brereton permission to attack in the afternoon of the 8th. The bombers were being refueled and their crews having midday meals when, about 12:15 P.M., 108 bombers escorted by 84 fighters of the Japanese 11th

* Congressional Investigation, Pearl Harbor Attack, Vol. 2, p. 649.

Air Fleet, based on Formosa, struck. Despite warnings from observers in North Luzon that large formations were flying toward Clark Field and Manila, the first flight of bombers was unmolested by fighters or flak; 15 minutes later a second flight of bombers repeated the attack; all bombers remained at altitudes beyond the range of antiaircraft batteries. After the second attack a squadron of fighters came in flying low, machine-gunning and bombing. Only three American fighters managed to take the air.

Thus, on the first day of the war, ten hours after the attack on Pearl Harbor had been reported, the Far East Air Force was reduced by half; installations on the only air field in Luzon that could service bombers had been destroyed; the communication system necessary to operate the force as a fighting unit had been disrupted. Still hopeful, MacArthur reported to Washington that he was planning a massive attack on Formosa on the 9th.

Fortunes of war favored the Japanese: fog shrouded their base in Formosa at daylight on the 8th. But had Brereton been allowed to attack when he first requested to do so, if he could have found the airfields in the mists, he might have struck a serious blow on the enemy's highly efficient 11th Air Fleet, which later spearheaded the land and sea forces that overran the Philippines. Instead, this Japanese air force with one blow on December 8 gained control of the air over Luzon, two days later it destroyed Cavite Navy Yard, drove our submarines out of Manila Bay, and directly contributed to the surrender of Corregidor and the Bataan March. The air debacle in Luzon on the first day of the war is more humiliating to America's Armed Forces and the High Command in Washington than the surprise attack on Pearl Harbor.

Various reasons for the collapse of American Forces in the Far East and their temporary neutralization in the Hawaiian Islands have been given. The one to be remembered is the insistence of President Roosevelt that the enemy be allowed to "strike the first overt blow." The assumption on which this decision was made was that the American people would not unite behind the President until they were attacked. There is no doubt that Americans prefer peace to war; that they are satisfied with their present possessions and do not want to commence a war of conquest. Secretary Stimson has told how the War Cabinet had sought a way "to maneuver the Japanese" into an attack that would do little damage, but would unite the people.

This theory still exists. The former Chairman of the Joint Chiefs, General Omar Bradley, and his successor, the present incumbent Admiral A. W. Radford, have announced that the United States will concede the first blow in the next war to the enemy and depend upon our power to make instantaneous, deadly, and sustained retaliation. Apparently Roosevelt's new theory that a democracy must await attack has been accepted. Such an attitude invites Russia to follow the Japanese methods and deliver a surprise attack on United States defense installations, on its concentrated and vulnerable industry, and on its populous cities. The blow might not be fatal but it would certainly raise havoc; and with a little luck it might so disarrange our defenses that the Red air force could follow up these attacks and gain such a decided advantage that at best, we would have to fight a long war of attrition; at worst, we would be left at Moscow's mercy. An alternative to this suicidal program is outlined in Chapter 5.

Chapter 5

The Impact of New and Improved
Weapons on International
Relations

In previous chapters the inability of civilized states to preserve
the peace until the end of World War II have been discussed. In
this chapter, the effect of new and improved weapons resulting
from developments in electronics, air power, and atomic weapons
on efforts to avert a future war will be considered. Since World
War II, strictly speaking, no new weapons have been invented,
but all have been improved. As nuclear weapons are by far the
most devastating and since, at present, only Russia and the United
States have a stockpile of them, this discussion takes as a concrete
example a conflict of Russo-American interests or ideologies culminating in war. There have been sufficient clashes of policy between these two powerful states since 1945 to give awesome
realism to a prevision of such a titanic struggle. A Russo-American war would be proof of the inability of the United Nations to
avert or suppress war among major powers, so the American High
Command would have only a single objective: to win the war at
the least cost. Both countries would have allies, but the burden
of the war would fall on the United States and Russia since they
are best able to sustain it.

With our experience in World Wars I and II freshly in mind,

we know this grim struggle could not develop into a war to end all wars, or to establish another super State. It would be, from first to last, an unlimited war for survival between the monolithic communistic, land Empire occupying the heartland of Eurasia and its unhappy satellites, and a continental American Republic with only air and sea frontiers, and its uneasy allies. It could determine a long-disputed question: whether control of the great Eurasian land mass was more effective in modern war than control of the oceans, that is, apply another test to the conflicting theories of Mahan, the prophet of sea power, and Mackinder, the theorist of geopolitics.

In an international sense, it would be a war between two powerful alliances whose states are members of the United Nations; fundamentally caused by an irrepressible conflict between people believing in democratic self-government and people subjected to totalitarian government. Since the end of World War II this conflict has defied diplomatic settlement. It would resemble in some aspects our Civil War with the great difference that the loser might not be readmitted to the Union on equal terms by the victor. If it were not for their satellite states and allies, in the beginning a Russo-American war would be restricted to an air-sea contest. As some of our allies are exposed to greatly superior numbers of Red troops, it is necessary to go to their aid not only as a matter of honor but of interest, and the fundamental tactical question will be what aid can we give them without unduly jeopardizing ourselves. The United Kingdom confronted a similar problem when France began to falter in June 1940.

The Secretary of State, the Honorable J. F. Dulles, on January 12, 1954, in a public address announced that our reaction to any local aggressions by Russia or her satellites would no longer be defensive action at the place attacked but instant retaliation "at places and with means of our own choosing." This was an extension of protection of our own country by retaliatory atomic attacks to defending the entire free world from Red aggression. Obviously, this is a huge commitment. Previously we had trusted that our power of retaliation would deter Russia from attacking the United States. The defense of Washington was our presumed ability to destroy Moscow.

The limited application of the retaliatory defense had many disadvantages. Its extension has multiplied them. For defense by massive retaliation depends for its success on new weapons not yet tested in actual war; and unpleasantly suggests Air Marshal Harris' proposal to win World War II by bombing Germany's industrial areas, which failed. The difficulty of providing a defense against airplanes prior to World War II led Great Britain and some European states to neglect their fighting planes and air defenses and to depend too much upon retaliation by their own bombers. One of the most impressive lessons of World War II is that fighter planes, antiaircraft guns, and radar communications inflicted unbearable losses on first the German and then Anglo-American bombing planes.

Many military officers have contributed to the neglect of American defenses by repeating a maxim that "The best defense is offense." This is true but, like all maxims, needs amplification. Before an effective offense can be launched, the home country that supplies the armed forces must be defended from a counterattack. Clausewitz long ago pointed out that defense was the stronger form of war on land, provided the general could create a situation that compelled the enemy to make an attack from an unfavorable position. His great pupil, von Moltke the First, proved the soundness of this doctrine at Sedan. Mahan, who again and again insisted that navies are most effective on the offensive against enemy combat ships, urged the construction of coast defenses for our most important harbors and cities before constructing the combat fleet; for otherwise he was convinced that public opinion would insist that our fleet be dispersed to protect them and not allowed to take the offensive. In the Spanish War, in response to public demand, the Flying Squadron was organized and stationed in Hampton Roads, while monitors were sent to various northeastern cities. To use a gridiron analogy, an effective line is as essential to victory as a good back-field for, unless the line holds, the backs will be smothered before they get underway with the ball, or a passer will be tackled before he can locate a receiver.

The concept of relying on retaliatory attacks, without first providing an effective defense, carried to its logical conclusion would result in destroying enemy industry but, simultaneously, giving hostile planes practically a free hand to destroy our more efficient but more concentrated and, therefore, more vulnerable industrial plants. One must repeat: such an exchange would be a very poor trade for the United States, and the surest way to lose the war.

The Joint Chiefs of Staff, according to their Chairman, Admiral A. W. Radford, are with their Canadian colleagues constructing a modern defense system, including a warning system, a communications network that will coordinate fighter-intercepters and anti-aircraft weapons. This is the improved version of the British system that won the air battle over Britain in 1940 and the similar German system that inflicted unbearable losses on the British night bombers in 1941-42, and the Anglo-American night and day bombers in 1943.

Defense will not stop all attacks but can stop enough to permit civilian producers to continue at their tasks, provided the civil defense system is effective and the government does not surrender. When Poland and western Europe were smitten with bombs and attacked by the Nazi motorized forces, panic-stricken civilians crowded the highways and interfered with the defense. The French Cabinet, rather than expose Paris to air attacks, declared it an open city and soon after surrendered one and one-half million young French soldiers to spare Paris and the nation further bombing. To gain a brief respite, the French Government of that day led its citizens into slavery and degradation. As devastating as "A" and "H" bombs may be, their consequences are not to be compared with the wretchedness of an enemy occupation that inevitably follows when a nation lays down its arms and surrenders to an enemy.

After the novelty of air attacks wore off, bombing of Chinese, English, German, and Russian cities increased rather than diminished the morale of civilians and their willingness to continue the war. An unexpected tactical result of indiscriminate bombing of cities like London was the creation of great areas of rubble that acted as fire screens and prevented the spread of fires from incendiary bombs. Meanwhile, the Royal Navy and Air Force prevented an invasion of England. The rubble of Stalingrad was quickly turned into a series of tactical strongholds that enabled defenders to resist Nazi ground troops who attempted to follow up the air bombardment while the construction of bridges, submerged a few feet under the Don, permitted a continuous flow of food, munitions, and troops into the city during darkness. In more than one battle in Europe the preliminary air bombardment hindered the subsequent advance of tanks, mechanized regiments, and foot soldiers.

The exaggerated emphasis on retaliatory attacks as a means of defense has led to an astonishing neglect of the most elementary defensive measures. Until very recently, little if any effort was made to interfere with foreign espionage or sabotage. Even though the public and the government are now much more alert to the danger than ever before, there is a reluctance to undertake the necessary quietly effective police measures. Meanwhile, smaller "A" bombs have been produced. Consequently, it is probably easier for enemy agents to plant a small "H" or "A" bomb in an industrial or communication center than for an enemy bomber to deliver it. There is a simple and easy way to locate suspicious strangers; it has been employed for years in many European countries that require every person to carry an identification card with a portrait and fingerprints. Thousands of Americans are required to have identification cards for drivers' licenses, to enter certain establishments, and to prove their memberships in certain clubs or societies. The practice could be extended, and citizens could be required to inform their local police when they leave their home town and show their identification cards to keepers of hotels, motels, boarding houses, even flop houses. This system would make it much easier to locate evil-disposed foreigners who could start a disastrous series of explosions. The recent attack by Puerto Rican revolutionaries on members of Congress in their own chamber shows how easy it is for actual subversives and saboteurs to operate in the United States.

The necessary elements of an extremely effective civil defense system already exist in the United States. The problem is only to fit these parts together. In every state, county, city, and town there are police organizations that can be merged into a national force to prevent panic and to insure care for the injured and the redistribution of bombed out inhabitants. Public utilities, railways, urban and interurban transportation systems, with little if any changes, can cooperate. It is comparatively simple for power companies to supply light and power to adjacent areas in emergencies. Railways are accustomed to restoring tracks. Salvage companies are prepared to clear harbors and fairways and to raise sunken ships. It is a commonplace for big corporations to start to rebuild huge plants destroyed by fire before their ashes are cooled.

The Todt Construction Corps in Germany showed that modern organization and machinery could rebuild faster than Anglo-American planes could destroy German cities as long as the Germans had radar stations in French and Belgian territory between them and England to warn their fighter squadrons. German armament production increased by almost two thirds from 1942 to 1943. A further increase occurred in 1944 so that, in spite of all that the bombers could do, armaments output in 1944 was double that of 1942. The United States will have three oceans between it and Russia and greatly improved means of defense. Americans are alert, intelligent, accustomed to local self-government, and decentralized authority. Certainly, they are as courageous as the Chinese, Japanese, Russian, British, and German people who lived in the cellars of bombed out cities and continued to fight. They certainly will carry on if proper preparations are made to intercept enemy attacks, to minimize the damage from airplanes that do get through, and to provide reasonable shelter, food, and medical attention for bombed-out civilians.

The most important improvement in weapons, since World War II, is the production of smaller "A" bombs, that formerly could only be delivered by very heavy, long-range, high-speed bombers. Today, "A" bombs can be delivered by carrier-based planes, by mobile heavy guns of the field army, by coast defense batteries, by guns on surface ships and, eventually, by torpedoes from submarines. Thus a weapon first employed to attack civilians and cities can now be used to defend them. The little brother of the "A" bomb that was hailed as the destroyer of all fleets can now be used to protect naval task forces, to assist fleets to control the sea, and to extend their power still further inland over continental land masses. Perhaps the most important effect of reducing the size of "A" bombs will be to divert them from attacks on civilians and cities to attacks on widely deployed enemy armed forces.

The same is true of the flying missile, Hitler's last secret weapon, designed especially to destroy London and break the will of the British to continue the war. It has been improved in the United States and will be employed in the defense of citizens, cities, and industrial areas against hostile air attacks. Simultaneously, improvement of radar and other electronic instruments has greatly increased the efficiency of all defensive weapons.

Radar was as necessary in the defense of England as fighter planes and flak. Little has been recorded of its vital importance in the Battle for Britain, but the whole world has been told that, by using radar, long-range bombers could attack cities through fogs, clouds, and darkness. Americans are reminded every morning that increased range, speed, and ceiling of airplanes have brought their cities and industrial areas within a one-way trip of Soviet planes that can launch "A" and "H" bombs. Little, if any, reference has been made to the increased capabilities of fighter planes, antiaircraft weapons, electronics, and radar.

A comparison of the claims made for new weapons prior to World War II and their subsequent performance during six years of combat will show that these new weapons fell far short of their predicted effect upon the morale and endurance of the Chinese, the Japanese, and the people of the European nations. The record will also show that every weapon so far invented can be used to protect as well as to menace noncombatants, their homes and property. Americans in particular can calmly consider their situation, decide upon a course of action, and not be frightened into hasty decisions. Undoubtedly, we are living in a critical era; but the world has always been a dangerous dwelling place and we are still masters of our fate.

It *is* imperative to strengthen the nation's defenses and to prepare the minds of Americans for the situations we are likely to encounter in a future war. The first step toward these two objectives is to consider the limitations as well as the powers of new and improved weapons; and the measures already taken by the government to protect its citizens and industry. Secretary Dulles has publicly recognized that the ultimate survival of the nation depends upon the armed forces. Since the first "A" bomb was exploded, all three branches have been studying methods of using the new weapons to defend ourselves and our allies as well as to attack the enemy.

The powers and limitations of weapons employed in World War II and the results they attained are already a matter of record; official statements by the Department of Defense of the improvements made in the United States and its estimate of those made by possible enemies are also available. Americans should appraise the limitations of new weapons and the defensive capabilities of these weapons and auxiliary instruments, before they accept the somber conclusion that their armed forces can destroy other nations but cannot protect their own territory and citizens.

Nuclear weapons have been used only on two cities, and thus there is little actual experience to guide us. It is definitely known that present "A" bombs are much more powerful than those used in Japan. The Nagasaki and Hiroshima bombs were approximately equivalent to 20,000 tons of TNT, that is, each was equivalent to several 1,000 airplane raids in the European war. Before the "A" bombs were dropped, the Yokohama-Tokyo area had been thoroughly devastated by block-busting explosives and incendiary bombs; more time was required, but the end result was the same. Present-day "A" bombs may have around five times the power of the first two bombs. The "H" bomb may have 50 to 200 times the power of the "A" bombs; that is, 5 to 20 million tons of TNT equivalent. They have been tested in the Pacific Ocean. According to President Eisenhower, the development of the "H" bomb has reached its useful limit. Bombs with greater power can be developed, but so much of their power would be dissipated upward that they would not be more efficient.

Nuclear bombs have reached the stage at which they can be considered as "city-busters" as compared to the TNT "block-busters" of World War II. *If* they can be delivered to the target, the results attained in World War II in destroying cities by large-scale and repeated air raids can now be equaled in one small raid. Against an opponent possessing neither an effective active military defense nor a comprehensive and well-organized civil defense organization, atomic weapons easily could be decisive; just as the first blitz air and tank attacks of World War II were decisive against the continental European armies and nations in 1939-40. But against a well-prepared, virile nation, the number of atomic bombs that can be delivered to their targets will be small; and the damage and loss of life, although enormous, will be minimized and bearable and should not cause the country to surrender. If the fate of Poland under Nazi and Communist occupation and of France and French prisoners after the French surrender is remembered, it will be evident to all that it is better to have many cities destroyed than to yield. It is better still to have adequate defenses that can inflict unbearable losses on attacking planes.

In June 1944, immediately after Eisenhower's landing in France, Hitler unveiled his last secret weapons and unleashed the V-I on London. This small pilotless plane, resembling an aerial torpedo with wings, flew noisily at high speed on a determined course, unless its journey was interrupted, until its mechanism halted its flight at the target area. It then dove for the earth and its heavy load of explosive exploded on contact, with a terrific blast effect. When first exposed to this weapon, Londoners found them more nerve-racking than the old and familiar "blitz." For a time, at Churchill's request, the fastest fighting planes were withdrawn from Eisenhower's invasion force to intercept these aerial torpedoes. They proved to be harder on the nerves than on lives, the average bomb only killing one person. They were too inaccurate to interfere with the steady flow of supplies from the Southhampton area to Normandy. During the last half of June, 2,000 V-I's were launched from the Calais area aimed at London; 660 of these were intercepted, barely 1,000 reaching the city. In a short time, Churchill told Eisenhower not to divert planes needed in the Normandy battle for the defense of London.

Germany's V-2, a free missile, was a huge rocket. It shot to a great altitude and fell at such a high speed that it could not be seen, heard, or intercepted before it struck. It carried an enormous explosive charge in its head that detonated on impact. When it fell in vacant ground it buried itself deeply; consequently its explosive effect was limited to the air immediately overhead. If it struck a building its demolition effect was instantaneous and obliterating. Traveling faster than its own sound, its noise resembled thunder; when you heard it you knew you had escaped. It did not cause the nervous strain of the V-1.

When General Eisenhower broke out of his Normandy bridgehead, the launching sites of the V-weapons were withdrawn to the Netherlands; and when the Allies occupied Antwerp, that city was in easy range. Almost 6,000 landed within eight miles of the center of the city but only about 300 fell within the limits of the port. One ship was sunk, sixteen damaged, one drydock placed out of commission for three weeks; 682 casualties were inflicted upon the armed forces while 3,470 civilians were killed. When the Allies occupied Holland, the V-bomb sites were abandoned.

The British obtained information that V-bombs were being designed in November 1939. Not until the spring of 1943 was the threat considered serious enough to bomb Peenemünde, the place of manufacture. Nearly 2,000 tons of explosives and incendiaries were dropped; 700 workers, mainly Allied prisoners of war, were killed. The factories of the V-bombs were dispersed, which added to British difficulties, but the damage done to original installations probably delayed the completion of bombs by three months. In the meanwhile, launching sites built by the Nazis were noted along the French coast from Calais to Cherbourg. During the fall and early winter of 1943 intermittent bombing attacks were made on launching sites. These were intensified late in November, and thereafter attacks on these sites caused a decided diversion of Anglo-American bombers from other enemy targets. The principal military advantage secured by Hitler's last secret weapon was the absorption by these launching sites of Anglo-American air blows that otherwise would have fallen on German cities and industries. On the other hand, if the time and labor required to construct the V-weapons had been utilized in constructing jet fighters, the Nazis might have wrested control of the air from the Allies.

While noting the comparative ineffectiveness of V-bombs, the inability of Anglo-American bombers to destroy or neutralize the launching sites just across the Channel from the air bases in England should not be overlooked. Both failures reveal a distinct limitation on offensive air strikes, and create considerable doubt about the wisdom of depending upon a fierce and instant retaliation, unless an extremely effective defensive system is provided. The *U.S. Official Air Forces History* * states that it is apparent that the Germans had made their improvised modified launching sites impervious to conventional attacks by heavy bombers. The Germans could build new ones faster than they could be destroyed. The authors conclude that ". . . (Air) operations during the critical period were a failure." The record supports this conclusion; between June 12 and the first of September, 6,716 V-1's were plotted in flight, despite the magnitude of Allied efforts to neutralize the sites by offensive air action. The Royal Air Force had previously found it impossible to destroy the 'concrete pens' built by Hitler at Brest to protect Nazi U-boats.

Since World War II, the army, navy, and air forces have all developed both free and guided rockets that are improvements on the V-weapons. The Nike, the army's guided missile, is reported to be very accurate. It is expected to be effective against planes flying faster than sound, with a ceiling higher than any known bomber can fly; and outranges by many miles any antiaircraft battery. Another army favorite is Honest John, a preaimed rocket that cannot be jammed or diverted from its course. For low level attacks, multiple-mount machine guns and very high-speed rockets will be used. For medium ranges, these are supplemented by the army's Skysweeper, a fully automatic antiaircraft gun effective against high-speed planes at medium alti-

* Vol. 3, p. 540.

tude. World War II 90- and 120-millimeter guns equipped with necessary radar are also provided. Army chiefs are so pleased with the Nike, which is already in production, that they are equipping antiaircraft batteries with them. General Bradley, the former Chairman of the Joint Chiefs of Staff, made the wise recommendation of arming National Guard batteries with Nikes, and training their personnel to protect their own cities where their knowledge of local highways, railways, and traffic bottlenecks would add to their efficiency. Brigaded with Nikes would be Skysweepers and other antiaircraft batteries.

The navy has three, temporary, relatively inexpensive types of flying missiles that are modifications of World War II weapons, and these will be presently available if required. It also has high priority air defense missiles, Terrier 1 and Sparrow, that will soon be operational. The Regulus, a surface-to-surface guided missile, is in production and, according to General Bradley, can be launched from a submarine or surface ship; its range of a few hundred miles will add greatly to the navy's offensive power. Research is continuing on three other types of flying missiles. These missiles will be employed against planes attempting to attack naval task forces, American cities, and industrial areas.

General Bradley, in two articles in *The Saturday Evening Post*, gave a bird's-eye view of the defense system designed to protect Canada and the United States from enemy attacks: the United States and Canadian air forces already have in operation a radar chain of completely self-contained installations that will give about one hour's warnings. This is sufficient to ensure that some enemy planes will be shot down before they reach critical target areas. This radar chain will be reinforced by trained civilian observers at presently existing 'gaps' and it will be extended into the Atlantic and Pacific by naval ships. The navy will provide specially equipped radar planes which will operate at sea to increase the range of discovery. Northern cities, such as Bangor, Portland, Boston, Cleveland, Chicago, Minneapolis, Seattle, Spokane and Portland, Oregon, will be able to save many lives with even five minutes' warning. And, equally necessary from a national point of view, industrial plants will suffer less damage.

An arctic picket line would be disrupted at times by aurora borealis, and telephone lines are difficult to maintain in Canadian tundra. But with the "H"-bomb menace now present, an arctic picket line is being established. Around vital target areas, such as Chicago, squadrons of interceptors and Nike batteries are already on guard, while naval units operating along Atlantic or Pacific coasts will use both radar and interceptor planes to extend the defensive line through which hostile planes must fly.

Defensive measures in the United States have lagged. But today they are fairly effective and can be steadily improved. Naturally, this can be so with the defenses of other nations. Air defenses around Moscow were more effective than those around London in the summer of 1941, according to Harry Hopkins who visited both cities during that season. Stalin, with a Chief of Staff and a few aides, directed three huge armies from the Kremlin when Moscow was partly encircled by Nazi troops and in easy range of their bombers. The late General Hoyt S. Vandenberg, former Chief of the Air Force, in his last appearance before a House Sub-Committee on Appropriations, made the following significant comments on air force weapons. For offensive use, the inter-continental bomber, B-36, a combination propeller and jet-driven plane presently in use, is considered too slow; it cannot be refueled in the air but can be at bases in Alaska, Okinawa, and Greenland. The present ideal of the air force is a fleet of inter-continental supersonic planes capable of delivering "A" or "H" bombs to any targets in the world from bases within the United States. The B-52, just emerging from experimental status, is a huge all-jet intercontinental high-speed bomber that can be refueled in the air.

There can be no doubt of the value to the United States of such an airfleet as visualized by the air force; its cost would be immense, but it would free the nation from relying on overseas air bases in countries that in time of war might prefer to remain neutral or be overrun by an enemy, as were Poland and France. Supplemented by carrier-based planes, it would be the most powerful offensive and defensive force in the world. Heavy, very long-range bombers will always be expensive and few in number. Even heavy bombers can operate more effectively the nearer their bases are to their targets. The more numerous and less expensive medium bombers, B-29, B-50, and B-47, can reach Russian targets from bases in Alaska, Japan, Okinawa, England, and North Africa. These overseas bases make possible the employment of medium bombers to supplement the heavy bombers that operate at very high speeds and high altitudes.

Both the British and American heavy bombers discovered during World War II that they could not accept the heavy losses inflicted by flak and fighter planes on unescorted squadrons of bombers. If Soviet defenses inflict unacceptable losses on our heavy bombers, again they will have to be escorted by fighters.

During four-day attacks by the 8th Air Force in October 1942 on Bremen, Danzig-Munster, and Schweinfurt, 1,344 planes were dispatched; 1,174 made attacks; 148 were lost, 11 per cent of those dispatched, 12 per cent of those attacking. The heaviest losses were suffered in the attack on Schweinfurt, 320 bombers participated; 229 reached target area; 60 did not return; of those returning 17 suffered irreparable damage, 121 reparable damage. The attack on Munster was led by the 100th Bombardment Group; it was jumped by Nazi fighters "who flew parallel—out of range, in groups of 20 to 40, stacked in echelon down. They peeled off singly or in pairs in quick succession to attack the lowest elements of the bombers." In two minutes the bomber formation was broken, in seven minutes the entire group had been dispersed or destroyed. Not a plane of this group returned; and 29 out of 119 of the Third Division were lost. Only superb courage and determination enabled bomber pilots to reach their targets, and there they encountered more effective antiaircraft fire and more fighters.

Between February 4 and October 31, 1943, the over-all loss of the United States 8th Air Force doing day bombing was 4.4 per cent; during the same period British night bomber losses were 3.9 per cent. General Spaatz suspended American attacks deep into Germany in October. The British continued night attacks until February 1944, when their over-all losses reached 7.7 per cent due to improvement in Nazi night-fighter tactics. Air

Marshal Harris then suspended night attacks and completely revised his attack tactics. General Arnold, Chief of Army Air Force, did not realize the effectiveness of German defenses because, just as the 8th Air Force returned from its defeat over Schweinfurt, he cabled General Baker that "evidence in Washington indicated that the German Air Force was on the verge of collapse"!

Both bombers and fighters have been greatly improved since 1943, but airplanes designed primarily for fighting will always have a great advantage over the heavily loaded and less maneuverable bomber, particularly toward the end of an intercontinental flight as they near the targets, where fighters, stacked overhead, and radar-controlled antiaircraft batteries await them. Both British and American bombers found by sad experience that unescorted bombers were in the words of Air Marshal Harris "dead ducks" for fighters. Today bombers and fighters fly at supersonic speed, use instruments to aim and fire at targets that they pass so quickly they never see. But elementally one is still a fighter and the other a bomber; and fighters can usually shoot down bombers. Even when escorted by fighters, bombers may not be able to get through in sufficient numbers to justify their losses. In a conversation with Secretary Forrestal in July 1948, General Vandenberg said that it was very difficult to predict what weapons would become obsolete within five years, that development in the field of antiaircraft weapons "might make the heavy bomber as obsolete as the battleship." In 1954 the sub-chairman of the Atomic Energy Committee of Congress reported that developments in electronic devices would soon enable defense forces to protect cities and strategic areas from planes carrying nuclear weapons. Vandenberg's prediction may be confirmed.

Moreover, in discussing the problem of defending the United States from enemy bombers, General Vandenberg pointed out that it would be unnecessary to shoot down every enemy plane. He doubted if any enemy air force could sustain 25 per cent of losses and continue an effective air bombardment. In light of the experience of the German attacks on England in 1940-41, and the Anglo-American attacks on Germany in 1943, this estimate is probably correct. In short, the first four or five intercontinental strikes will be by far the heaviest. If these attacks are pushed home, bomber losses will be enormous; more important, the 'first team' of bombardiers will be badly depleted, and a longer time will be required to train another first team than for the factories to replace the bombers.

Probably no nation had a better 'first team' of naval aviators in 1942 than Japan, whose rapid conquests in the western Pacific and Indian oceans were due primarily to mobile groups of land-based naval planes plus a striking force of eight heavy carriers with trained fighters, torpedo, and dive bombers. These skillful aviation teams were disrupted in the battle of Midway in June 1942, and, despite persistent efforts of the Japanese navy to replace their 'carrier pilots,' they never succeeded. Under the direction of the present Chairman of the Joint Chiefs of Staff, Admiral A. W. Radford, then in the Naval Bureau of Aeronautics, our carrier pilot replacement system furnished trained pilots to each carrier as it was completed, although in the first five months of the war our carrier losses exceeded the Japanese. Again, in the very last phase of the war, Japanese suicide attacks placed a critical strain on our pilot replacement program, but Radford's system met the test. After the war, Admiral Nagano, Chief of the Naval General Staff, attributed the rapid collapse of the navy after its early victories to its inability to replace its 'first team' of naval aviators.

Since World War II, the limited war in Korea, where Communist air forces *did not attack our bases in Japan* and our forces refrained from attacking Communist bases in Manchuria, has defined more distinctly the powers and limitations of aircraft. Enemy antiaircraft batteries in Korea, known to airmen as 'flak,' made it unprofitable for American B-26s to venture very far by day. After October 1950, four months after the war began, ⅘, 80 per cent, of more than 53,000 sorties of B-26s were made at night, presumably on account of losses that enemy flak and a few fighters inflicted during day attacks. Bomber losses received during night attacks were light; but so was the damage they inflicted, although crews flew regularly over the same routes. According to Captain G. F. Wolfe, one of the most successful United States pilots in Korea, to new crews a convoy of trucks appeared an easy target as they turned on lights to pick their way along the pock-marked roads at night. But by the time B-26s were in the groove to attack, the lights were off and the convoy pulled off the road in complete darkness. Then, there was apt to be a will-of-the-wisp string of lights along a cliff into which unwary bombers might crash.

In spite of bomber attacks, to the very end of the war North Korean trains still ran on schedule from their sanctuary in Manchuria, and bombers still found it very difficult to hit a fast moving train. Even when trains were derailed and track cut in two or more places, on the very next night trains would be running on schedule.

As previously mentioned, the German Todt Construction organization during World War II boasted that it could repair damages inflicted by air attacks faster than they could be made and demonstrated its ability as late as the summer of 1944 by keeping the V-bomb launching sites in operation despite repeated attacks. Not until ground troops occupied these sites did the menace cease. A similar but more classic example can be offered. During Sherman's advance through Tennessee and Georgia, Confederate cavalry and guerrilla bands repeatedly destroyed sections of the long railway line from Ohio that supplied his army. Very soon, Union repair crews with small escorts could repair the railway faster than Confederate raiders could wreck them.

Douhet, one of the prophets of air power, and his followers predicted that air power would win World War II before the ground troops in Europe could mobilize. The war lasted six years and was essentially a war of attrition. Young air officers, skillful, courageous, and justly proud of their intercontinental bombers, are sincerely convinced that strategic air power could win World War III. General Vandenberg was equally convinced "that the first 6 or 8 days will be decisive." Gallant young airmen are unquestionably overestimating their weapons. Their conviction should not be shaken; without confidence in their planes and bombs they would not operate them fearlessly. Their leaders should certainly be the last to impair this faith; but in planning they should give due weight to previous experience. The first six or eight days probably will not be decisive of the war; but properly utilized they will give one side or the other a tremendous advantage, the effect of which would be cumulative and might decide the war at a later date.

The air force is still placing emphasis on 'the strategic air arm' plus that part of the tactical force stationed in striking range of Soviet airdromes, for it considers that combination America's greatest defensive and offensive weapon. The strategic air force is still convinced it can reach its selected targets and deliver bombs with acceptable losses. Unquestionably, gallant officers, inspired by the air force tradition of never turning back before reaching the target, would accept heavy losses. But not until this theory is proved under war conditions can it be accepted as the basis for the defense of the United States. Remember that General Spaatz, who before his experience in World War II, was as positive as General Vandenberg that bombing of enemy cities and industry alone would win the war, admitted after the war was over that the struggle in the Pacific was essentially a naval war supported by air forces and the war in Europe was essentially an army war supported by air forces.

In a recent interview with the *U.S. News and World Report*, Admiral Radford described the functions of the U.S. High Command as follows: The President and the National Security Council determine the national policy; the Congress, if it agrees, makes appropriations. The Joint Chiefs of Staff recommend the military plans and programs to support this policy; when the President approves them, the Joint Chiefs determine the land, sea, and air forces best adapted to protect the United States and to assist their allies, and thus to meet the many commitments made under the United Nations and regional associations such as the American Republics and the North Atlantic Treaty Organization set up under provisions of the United Nations Charter. When the Korean War occurred, the Department of Defense was obliged to generate military strength as quickly as possible. The forces were pointed toward a peak for 1954.

The change inaugurated by President Eisenhower looks forward to a sturdy military posture to be maintained over an extended period of time, with emphasis on modern national air power. In this are included the aviation of the air force, of the navy and marine corps, and the aircraft industry and civilian air transport system. All branches of the service realize that air power is a primary requirement on the offense, defense and in support of land and sea forces. The other arms are not to be neglected for each has a vital role to perform. The aim is to increase the effectiveness of army, navy, and marine corps with better equipment, new weapons, and a reserve component more quickly available for service.

The government's policy is that any proposal for disarmament cannot be limited to atomic weapons; naturally, countries with huge populations whose ground troops are easily provided would like to abolish all nuclear weapons, while we base our strategy on the assumption that nuclear weapons give us a great capacity to counter instantly by means and at places of our own choosing. But the United States is not depending entirely upon air power and nuclear weapons. We will maintain the world's largest navy and an army of over a million men. While we believe that Soviet Russia does not desire an open war now, the Kremlin is maintaining armed forces greatly exceeding those needed for her own defense and they might inadvertently precipitate a shooting war. The present tension may continue for years, according to Admiral Radford, but we must keep ready, for "it would not be possible for the United States to initiate a war." We must provide armed forces sufficient for the security of our country and so organized that they complement those of our prospective allies. We must do this over a period of years without unduly straining our national economy. With this background, the Joint Chiefs of Staff have recommended land, sea, and air forces that in their judgment will give the nation a reasonable degree of security and that can be maintained indefinitely at that level with continuous qualitative improvement without jeopardizing our economic structure.

Within a period of a few weeks, General Bradley, General Ridgway, former Commander, and General Gruenther, present

Commander of NATO's armed forces in Europe, published, al-
most simultaneously, accounts of the present military situation.
These, together with reports from the Defense Department to
Congressional Committees, give an authoritative view of the
American and NATO High Command and the resources at their
disposal, as well as their estimate of Soviet strength.

In explaining the monetary needs of the armed forces to Congress, the U.S. High Command is obliged to disclose its fundamental strategy and the tasks of the land, sea, and air forces. This
publicity makes it impossible to gain a strategic surprise over the
enemy. But a tactical surprise is always possible provided the
armed forces are not required, as they were in December 1941,
to wait until the enemy has struck the first blow. With information presently available, and it is difficult to obtain reliable information of the Red air force, it is estimated that 2 per cent of Red
long-range bombers are capable of making a 'one-way attack' on
the continental United States with "A" or "H" bombs; the Reds
also have practically an unlimited number of medium-range
bombers capable of striking European and English cities and our
air bases in those countries.

If Europe cannot be protected, many of our overseas bases will
be jeopardized. Van Fleet and Gruenther *have set up an efficient
command organization* in Europe through which Gruenther, the
present Commander, can control the forces now on hand. The
Northern Flank is commanded through a Norwegian Commander
at Oslo; the Center Force under a French Commander at Fon-
tainebleau; an American Admiral at Naples commands the U.S.
6th Fleet; a British Admiral at Malta is responsible for maintaining communications in the Mediterranean; while the Admiral
commanding the Atlantic Fleet is responsible for controlling the
Atlantic and maintaining a flow of supplies from the United States.
An American General of the air force is Deputy for Air to the
Supreme Commander (Gruenther). The French Commander
controls the Coastal Navy; the Basic Tactical Air is controlled
by the Supreme Commander through his Deputy for Air, who
also is integrated with the U.S. Strategic Air Command and U.S.
Air Bases in Europe. The organization is necessarily complex,

but trained officer personnel are operating together in peacetime. The transition to war should be smooth, provided the enemy is not given a free hand to disrupt it by a surprise attack, and if the ground troop commanders are supplied with sufficient combat-trained divisions.

The Turkish-Greek Headquarters are in Thrace and are not yet formally integrated in NATO, but they are ready to resist any thrust toward the Mediterranean from the Black Sea.

NATO is numerically inferior in ground troops. Compared with thirty Red Divisions in Europe and one hundred and fifty in Russia besides troops from satellite states, NATO can dispose of approximately eighty divisions, including Greco-Turkish Divisions. Of these, six are United States Divisions, and the President recently announced they would not be reduced. NATO has actual naval superiority and potential air superiority, but there are an estimated three hundred plus Red submarines and 20,000 operational aircraft that can operate with Red troops or attack European cities and installations. Still General Gruenther is confident that he can and he intends "to defend western Europe" for the enemy divisions would have many difficulties to surmount in launching a major attack.*

General Ridgway, after conferring with leaders of fourteen NATO states, found everyone convinced that the recent change of leaders in the Kremlin had not altered the basic Red policy of expansion by force and by underground. He agreed with them. He considers that the greatest problem is the danger that these NATO nations will, on account of their meager standard of living, tire of maintaining their present large though inadequate forces. His real hope is in rearming western Germany, but the prospect is dimmed by the dread of Germany still deep-seated in the minds of the French people, who fear the Germans more than they do the Reds. Soon after the liberation of France, General deGaulle renewed the former Franco-Russian alliance. Reliable reports indicate that at present a majority of French people are opposed to German rehabilitation. The refusal of France to enter the

* France and Italy had not joined the European Defense Community in August 1954.

European Defense Community, which she had proposed, led Anthony Eden to propose the revival of the Brussels Pact of 1948 that provided for military, economic, and cultural cooperation of Britain, France, Belgium, the Netherlands, and Luxembourg as the simplest means of reconciling French opinion to restoring west German sovereignty and recreating her army. In September 1954, Secretary Dulles assured Chancellor Adenauer that the President, the Congress, and American people shared his views that sovereignty should no longer be withheld from west Germany, nor could she be longer denied the inherent right of individual and collective self-defense.*

French critics assert that the Anglo-American governments are determined to rearm west Germany with or without the approval of France, primarily because they consider twelve well-trained German divisions are absolutely essential to protect western Europe, including France, from a Red invasion. Traditional and persistent European rivalries such as those between Germany and France, Germany and Russia, Austria and Russia have a direct effect on the defense of the United States for, as a member of NATO, she is pledged to go to the aid of many of them if attacked. The almost insoluble problem confronting the Security Council is how to meet our responsibilities to quasi allies and simultaneously provide protection for the United States, other American Republics, their citizens and interests abroad.

The present plan assigns the following tasks to the army, navy, and air force. The Army's mission is to provide the land forces necessary to defend the United States and the Western Hemisphere; to protect our national interests in the Far East, and to supply America's share of the defense of Europe. It must also defend the United States from enemy lodgment, sabotage, or riots, and support the Civil Air Defense. While a large part of the army must still be committed abroad to be ready to help in the defense of Europe and our other bases overseas, must of the army as a strategic reserve is to be kept in the United States. The more it is possible to assign the initial defense of the countries

* *New York Times*, September 19, 1954.

and bases surrounding the Soviet bloc to locally-raised forces, the greater strategic reserve will it be possible to have and the greater will be the efficiency of the whole defense system.

The objectives of the air force are: to provide all possible protection for the people, military forces and vital installations and industries of the United States; to provide all possible aid and protection to our allies; and, by carefully coordinated attacks of strategically deployed long-range bombers, to strike the most vital enemy installations.

The tactical arm, which has been neglected by all independent air forces, has been directed to prepare to establish local air superiority except in areas of naval operations. This important exception was made because experience in World War II demonstrated that ship-based and naval land-based planes were better fitted to control the air over the sea. The mission of the tactical arm recently reaffirmed: "is to take its part in deterring Soviet aggression" and, in the event of war, assuring the survival of its impact upon the United States, and the *protection* (italics supplied) of the United States industrial and military capacity to secure ultimate victory."

The strategic arm of the air force is to prepare to destroy an enemy's capacity to wage war, including the production of all raw material, strategic stockpiles, essential agricultural regions, communication and industrial systems. During the Normandy landings the strategic bombers under orders of General Eisenhower discovered that they could give effective tactical aid to ground troops. Recently, Sir John Slessor, Chief of Air Staff 1952-53, reminded his countrymen and the Royal air forces of the flexibility of heavy bombers that could be switched from long-range bombing to defending the United Kingdom, her shipping, to laying mines in enemy waters, and to giving support to an army in the field. United States long-range bombers possess the same capabilities.

Today, the B-36 is the only American intercontinental bomber that can reach Russian targets from the United States. In a few years, the air force expects to have jet powered B-52s with equal capabilities. These heavy bombers are very expensive, and their numbers will always be limited. They all have to approach their targets from the north after long trips. So the air force plans to launch its medium bombers, the bulk of its strategic force, from its world-wide system of air bases. In peacetime, the bulk of heavy and light bombers are based in the United States with enough at the foreign bases to insure that the fields are operating. Experience of U.S. 8th Bomber Command and British night bombers in World War II indicates that reinforcements of carrier-based planes will be required to supplement the retaliatory attacks of the strategic air force and also to furnish escort fighters to protect the bombers from hostile interceptor planes. General Bradley and Admiral Fechteler, former Chief of Naval Operations, agree that naval support of the strategic air force will probably be necessary in World War III.

An objection has been made to the fact that the strategic air force depends upon naval aircraft whose primary mission is to control the sea. But carriers can steam 700 sea miles per day; they are very difficult targets for the enemy to locate; in addition, carrier task forces wherever they go are guarded by the very powerful combination of fighter and flak defenses. The defensive powers and mobility of carrier task forces will permit them to furnish escort to long-range bombers and to supplement the retaliatory attacks of the Strategic Air Command without neglecting their major task of controlling the sea. Sir John Slessor very properly emphasized the flexibility of long-range bombers. Carrier-based bombers and fighters possess this same flexibility, to which is added the mobility of carriers. One of the unexpected results of combat aviation and its prompt integration in the battleships, cruisers, and carriers of the United States fleet during World War II was the great increase in the power of fleets to intervene in battles ashore and to exercise direct control over the land. With nuclear powered submarines and surface ships capable of delivering nuclear bombs, the combat navy can intervene more decisively in battles ashore and assist in direct control of the land.

General Bradley only recently reached the opinion that "the primary mission of the big carriers is shifting toward strategic air attack." Naval experts long have been convinced that carrier planes can greatly assist the strategic air force and still do their part in controlling the sea.

In 1948, the Navy Department was directed by the President to organize, train, and equip the navy and marine corps to conduct prompt and sustained operations at sea, including the operations of sea-based planes and their land-based components. In time of war, the navy was charged with gaining and maintaining general sea supremacy with the definite addition of establishing local superiority, including air superiority in areas of naval operations. Air superiority must be sufficient to enable naval operations at a selected time over a particular area without being interrupted by hostile aircraft.

In recent testimony before Congress, the Assistant Secretary for Air restated the navy's mission substantially as given in 1948. He emphasized that only the navy could control the sea and thus assure a continuing flow of raw materials to our factories to sustain the industrial productivity on which our war effort depended. Thus, the navy's mission does not duplicate or compete with any other service. He emphasized also that the naval aircraft "is today the basic instrument of naval power," "the principal weapon for the conduct of naval operations," and naval campaigns and for the fulfillment of the navy's mission. This means that the gradual improvement in engines and design, lighter-weight material, and more powerful fuel have increased the capabilities of carrier-borne planes. But the increased weight and speed of planes has demanded corresponding increase in size of aircraft carriers from the *Essex* class, of which we have twenty-four, to the three larger *Midways*, and to the super-carriers, still under construction, the three *Forrestals*, the first of which will join the fleet in 1955, and one authorized by the 83d Congress.

It would be well here to reiterate that carrier planes must equal in performance land-based fighters and bombers. Otherwise the carriers cannot control the air over the sea in range of land-based planes.

Carrier losses occurred in the first year of World War II, largely due to inability to control fires, resulting from explosions by bomb or torpedo hits. Many measures have been adopted to improve fire fighting, the interior compartmentation has been modernized, the landing deck strengthened. In spite of kamikaze attacks and many hits, not one of the big carriers was sunk in the last half of World War II. This improvement was due mainly to the protection of its own fighting planes, the antiaircraft fire of its own and escort ships' guns. Since the war, three *Midways* have been improved as well as several of the *Essex* class of twenty-four. But only the *Forrestal* class will be able to handle the latest type planes in the same smart fashion in which squadrons of smaller planes were launched and recovered during World War II.

Control of the sea has been the determining factor in gaining our independence, in preserving the Union, and in keeping war from our country in the last two world wars. The navy can still protect friendly and suppress hostile shipping if it is given carriers that can house, maintain, launch, and recover planes equal in performance to contemporary land-based planes. At present, the navy is prepared with its own planes to protect from air attack its own task forces; to reduce to acceptable losses attacks from modern U-boats on transports, supply ships and combat ships. As long as the navy has these capabilities it can also supplement the retaliatory action of our bombers, can escort and land expeditionary forces on enemy soil, and can reduce all threats to the United States to those from the air. Carrier planes have extended the direct effect of the navy deep into continental land areas and did facilitate amphibious landings in World War II.

Fiascos at the Dardanelles and in Mesopotamia in World War I caused many observers to believe that weapons of that day had made amphibious operations impossible. United States marines refused to accept this doctrine. In 1923 one of their most brilliant Commandants, General Lejeune, announced that "the most important duty of the Corps" was the maintenance of "an expeditionary force—in instant readiness to support the fleet." Under his leadership officers at Quantico began to adapt new weapons to amphibious operations. They developed artillery, tanks, and aviation expressly to land marines from ships on hostile shores.*

A decade later Admiral A. W. Johnson began and Admiral E. J. King furthered the training by embarking the Fleet Expeditionary Force and landing it on various islands in the Caribbean. About the same time the Pacific Fleet exercised army regiments in landings in California and the island of Oahu. At the beginning of World War II, training commenced on a huge scale. Two marine training centers, one on the Atlantic and one on the Pacific, and several army training centers concentrated on amphibious training, while General MacArthur and Admiral Barbey trained divisions of General Kruger's 6th Army until it could stage amphibious landings as readily as jumping off from a shore position.

"Triphibious" defines more accurately than "amphibious" the landing operations in World War II, for without control of the air over the landing area and its sea approaches, no landings could have been made. The loss of four Japanese major carriers at Midway prevented the Japanese invasion of Midway and made possible the seizure of Guadalcanal. A few months later Admiral Kent Hewitt landed General Patton's army in Morocco. From that time the American war effort was a succession of triphibious invasions. In June 1944, almost at the same time, Anglo-Americans invaded Normandy and seized Saipan.

Triphibious operations could not be standardized because of very different terrain conditions, but they gradually assumed a general pattern. They could succeed if the following conditions were met: control of the sea and the air over the seas adjacent to the objective; and sufficient properly trained ground troops. These troops must be transported to the vicinity of the invasion and protected from attack en route. Thanks to the mobility of ships, troops were concentrated on Leyte from widely separated bases; all converged on the battle area simultaneously. While troops were brought to the landing place, carrier planes softened up the landing beaches and kept adjacent enemy air fields covered. Mine sweepers and underwater demolition parties sent

* For details, see two essays by Colonel D. W. Weller, USMC, in *Naval Institute Proceedings*, August and September, 1954.

ahead of the troops were covered by aircraft and bombardments of battleships and heavy cruisers.

Special types of ships were provided to carry combat troops, tanks, and various types of landing craft. Ships loaded with combat teams carried their own landing craft, which were hoisted out about five to eight miles from the landing. They were preceded to the beach by gunboats and picket boats carrying howitzers and machine guns. Many small boats were equipped with machine guns to repel low flying planes.

In Normandy the air force isolated the combat area and prevented enemy counterattacks. In the Pacific, aircraft kept adjacent enemy air fields covered while the fleet kept off any hostile surface attacks. This panoramic formation could put men ashore with bearable losses. Ships' artillery and aircraft would continue attacks ahead of the advancing troops. In many islands the ground troops would have to use their flame throwers to kill or rout Japanese hiding in caves and tunnels. Under almost impossible conditions, culminating at Okinawa when supporting ships were under continuous suicidal attacks by kamikaze planes, one successful landing after another was executed. Japanese weapons and techniques improved, yet Americans succeeded in every landing.

The question now is, can landings on well defended positions be successful if the enemy employs nuclear weapons? The marines are confident they can be, and have designed an 80-ton flying boat that lands on the water and taxies to the shore, drops a ramp and unloads twenty-four tons of vehicles and other cargo, including troops, if desired. By reversing propellors it backs off the beach and within thirty seconds can take off the water. They are still concentrating on their classical problem of spearheading a 'ship to shore landing.'

Simultaneously naval task forces are cruising in more widely deployed formations; oceans are broad, means of communication are increasing ships in task forces, task forces in fleets can be spaced farther and farther apart and yet be tactically concentrated. The navy can keep open our overseas communications and escort expeditionary forces. They can control the seas as long as their carriers can launch fighter planes equal in performance to those that take off the land. In the light of the experience of World War II and the present state of nuclear weapons, there is good reason to believe that the triphibious forces of the United States can land troops on a hostile shore in the nuclear era. The task will be increasingly difficult and complicated. Landings must be made more promptly, which requires accepting heavy losses, but they can be made. At the end of World War II we possessed all the outposts in the Pacific we needed; to retake any of them will require the entire attention of the armed forces. Common sense dictates that the United States retain the islands still in its possession and recover from the United Nations those placed in trust.

The general pattern of American grand strategy has been very clearly stated by General Bradley; he assumes two national objectives, the first "to defend America"; the second "to prevent another world war." To accomplish them he proposes to maintain such forces as will (a) deter any sane aggressor from attacking, and (b) enable us to defeat an insane aggressor. In addition to the United States armed forces, Bradley requires sufficient allies (1) to avert sudden disaster such as a surprise atomic attack on America that would cripple or prostrate the nation, and (2) to avert installment-plan disaster such as the sudden conquest of an exposed ally. Simultaneously, we must be prepared to deliver instant, terrible, and sustained retaliatory attacks on the aggressor's military forces and productive capacity and be prepared with our mobilized industry and manpower to generate the power to defeat the enemy. We must be prepared to do all of these things and then await the enemy attack because if we attacked first—no matter how extreme the provocation—we "would be deep into the very war we are seeking to prevent."

General Vandenberg has given a preview of the opening phase of this all-out air war. Heavy and medium bombers already at overseas bases would make the first attacks on enemy targets; simultaneously, the bulk of our heavy and medium bombers would take off from bases in the United States for the overseas bases and the attack. Naturally, the enemy would be counterattacking our overseas bases and probably making one-way suicidal attacks on

American cities and bases. These air battles would merge into one great world-wide air struggle. To direct the air battles and give them form will require a communication system that will permit the Air Command to coordinate the widely-deployed forces. General Vandenberg has told the Congress that the air force has many apprehensions concerning the rapid increase by Russia of its atomic weapons and the planes available to deliver them. As the enemy will undoubtedly endeavor to destroy the overseas bases and interrupt our communications, Vandenberg was convinced that the first six or eight days may be decisive.

It is obvious that voluntarily giving the enemy a free hand to deliver the first blow is giving him a great advantage and would make it difficult to deliver instant, terrible, and sustained atomic retaliation against the enemy. Bradley's main dependence is on our atomic arsenal and the means to deliver varied and sustained attacks for he admits that we have not accomplished the goal of forces and alliances (both Gruenther and Van Fleet confirm the statement concerning our allies) that would "avert sudden disaster, such as a surprise atomic attack on America. . . ." Bradley says, "One of the enemy's first major efforts . . . might be to destroy our retaliatory power by knocking out the air bases from which our atomic planes can take off." Bradley also is aware that the location of these overseas bases from which the Strategic Air Force expects to reach its targets with medium bombers are well known to all the world and are in easy bombing distance of Russia's medium bombers.

The strategy of basing all on atomic retaliation but giving the enemy the first blow, which blow would undoubtedly be designed to destroy or cripple our retaliatory power, is, therefore, essentially self-defeating. Pursuing this policy means that the hope— probably in any case illusory—of winning World War III quickly and relatively cheaply has no real basis at all. There are several alternatives.*

* Apparently Secretary Dulles is beginning to realize the limitations of instant retaliation. Undersecretary of State Robert Murphy recently stated "the capacity for retaliation . . . is not enough"; he admitted that the capacity itself might "be overpowered" and even if maintained was "not necessarily the complete answer." *U.S. News and World Report*, September 3, 1954.

In order to make atomic retaliation effective as a deterrent to aggression, we must decide now and prepare to strike first whenever we have positive evidence that an attack is being mounted against the United States. Such a policy does not contemplate a preventive war or a sneak attack. We would only strike if the prospective enemy did not cease preparing to attack us or our allies by a certain time. It involves only a modification of the plan proposed by Bradley, but a necessary one. To depend on either policy means that a certain number of our heavy long-range bombers with their crews at hand must be ready at all times, that air patrols must be on station, that radar stations be manned night and day, and that a certain proportion of antiaircraft guns, flying missiles, and associated arms be on the alert. All these measures will have to be carried out under Bradley's plan of 'instant retaliation' after waiting for the enemy to deliver the first nuclear attacks.

The following additional measures will have to be taken to permit us to strike first. We should announce now that in future any unidentified plane approaching certain areas will be shot down; a similar precaution was taken many years ago, by declaring that if unidentified ships entered certain strategic or tactical areas they would be in danger of submerged mines or attack by patrol vessels. We would have to accept similar restrictions by other nations on our planes; we have already permitted both Russia and Yugoslavia to shoot down our planes with only half-hearted protests. In the era of nuclear weapons and long-range bombers International Law or custom should permit any nation to deny certain air areas to any but identified planes.

If the government had positive evidence that a nation was deploying its planes or ships in such a way that they could launch a heavy nuclear attack, it should immediately man all our planes and batteries, deploy our ships in readiness to launch an attack or protect our own territory, and then give the potential enemy notice that if he did not dismount his attack within twelve or twenty-four hours we would feel free to attack at once. The prospective enemy would then either have to launch his attack or comply. If he launched his attack we would be ready to oppose him and simultaneously attack. We would get at least an even break. If he still remained in a menacing position, we could attack and gain the initial advantage.

A specific application of this doctrine would have met the situation envisaged by Secretary Dulles in the spring of 1954. He announced that Red China had come perilously close to intervening in the Indo-China war and that this action might justify the application of instant and stern retaliation with weapons and in places of our own choosing. Vice-President Nixon stated subsequently that, if the French withdrew their troops from Indo-China, it might be necessary for the United States to send troops to prevent the conquest of Indo-China and eventually southeast Asia by the Chinese Reds. This presented to the American public a choice of another land struggle similar to the one in Korea or an application of the Dulles policy of "retaliation with weapons and in places of our own choosing." From the combat point of view the Dulles plan is obviously better, provided the Administration realizes it is not restricted to either a preventive war or to conceding the enemy the first blow. We could deploy our land, sea, and air forces in a posture of defense against Russian air attacks, place the greatest portion of our strategic bombers, including carrier-based bombers and fighters, where they could strike the heaviest blows at Russia, and station enough of these in the Far East to strike heavy blows at Peking and Mukden and other Red Chinese cities. Then when we were in all respects ready, we could inform Red China that if she did not in twenty-four hours cease her aid to the Communists attacking Indo-China, Peking and Mukden would be obliterated. If Moscow attempted to come to the rescue of her ally, our offensive and defensive forces would all be in position to act.

There is nothing immoral or illegal in such a procedure. At Argentia, Roosevelt, upon the request of Churchill, sent a formal note to Japan stating that the United States would be free to take any and all measures it thought necessary if the Japanese continued the advance southward. The advance continued. About a month before the attack on Pearl Harbor, Secretary Stimson, familiar with domestic and international law, advised the President that this note issued in August was sufficient basis for going to Congress in November and asking for a declaration of war against Japan. At San Francisco in 1945 we agreed to place at the disposition of the Security Council a contingent of land, sea, and air forces that it could employ, without reference to Congress, to avert or suppress war. Shall we take more effective measures for the United Nations than for the United States? Shall we let one President, who had tied his own hands in a political speech, establish a precedent that will certainly give a future enemy an immense initial advantage? Shall we accept the dismal prophecies of scientists like Einstein and Oppenheimer, who know nothing of the science of war, that the hydrogen bomb will destroy us as well as our enemy and then give our 'know-how' to the prospective enemy to placate him? Military members of our Joint Chiefs of Staff should reconsider their policy of attempted 'retaliation' upon an enemy privileged to deliver the first blow. If they do not, some future historian will record how citizens of the United States, when the country was in the prime of life, misled by some scientists and deluded by their political and military leaders, committed national suicide.

The risk to the nation's existence, voluntarily accepted by President Roosevelt on December 6, 1941, increases with every improvement in weapons. In the opinion of Sir John Slessor and General Doolittle, very long-range bombers will soon be rendered obsolete by intercontinental or transoceanic guided missiles or rockets. V-2s sped across the Channel to London at five times the speed of sound; to obtain a range of 4,000 miles a speed of thirteen times the speed of sound is required. Sooner or later nuclear power plants will provide the power from uranium, possibly from one pound that only occupies $2\frac{1}{2}$ cubic inches of space. When missiles of this range attain reasonable accuracy it would be fatal to await an enemy attack. Other nations besides the United States are striving to improve these weapons. It is not too soon for the United States Senate to resolve that never again shall American armed forces be ordered to allow an enemy the first blow.

Chapter 6

Leadership and Its Effect on the Conduct and Consequences of World War II

In the first three chapters the theory of the use of force as an instrument of national policy; the application of force by a preponderant land, sea, or air power; and the responsibilities of statesmen, generals, admirals, and air marshals in the employment of force were discussed. Chapter 4 contrasted their different concepts of the theory prevailing in Japan and the United States and the consequent different approach to, and conduct of, World War II. Chapter 5 described new and improved weapons and endeavored to anticipate their probable effects in a future war. Chapter 6 analyzes the effects of important decisions made by the heads of the most powerful belligerent nations of World War II. Chapter 7 relates the efforts of civilized nations from 1899 through 1945 to limit armaments and to avert or suppress war. Chapters 4, 6, and 7 utilize decisions of the same leaders, sometimes at the same conference, to define their efforts to win one war and then to avert or suppress another. While using the same carefully collected material a determined effort has been made to avoid unnecessary repetition.

The United States, Japan, China, and five European Powers—France, Germany, Great Britain, Italy, and Russia—took the lead-

ing parts in World War II. Two—France and the United States
—were republics; two were insular empires—Japan, governed
by an autocratic government, Great Britain, by a Parliamentary
cabinet; and four—Germany, Italy, Russia, and China—were
one-party states whose party leader ruled through a dominant
party, Nazi, Fascist, Communist, or Kuomintang. Every variety
of government was thus subjected to the test of war. Each state
began hostilities with more or less well-trained land, sea, and air
forces, and had made provision for recruiting, training, mobiliz-
ing, and directing each branch of these forces by a General Staff
with a Chief of Staff at the head. Unity of action of the armed
forces was provided by joint committees of representatives of each
branch. Some had a Supreme War Council, including at least
the foreign, finance, and defense ministers and headed by the
Chief of Government, directly responsible for averting war or
providing the necessary forces to win it.

France collapsed after six weeks of German attacks. In Japan,
after war began, operations were directed by the general staffs of
the army and navy; in China, whose navy was negligible, by
Generalissimo Chiang Kai-shek who had received a military education in Japan. In the United States, President Roosevelt; in
Great Britain, Prime Minister Churchill; in the Soviet Republics,
Prime Minister, later Generalissimo, Joseph Stalin; in Germany,
Chancellor Hitler, as Commander of the Wehrmacht; and in
Italy, Il Duce Benito Mussolini dominated the Chiefs of the
Armed Forces, made policy and major strategic decisions that
shaped military operations. During a war of six years, that en-
compassed large areas of the world, studded with land, sea, and
air battles, abounding in triphibious operations, numerous admirals, generals, and air marshals proved their skill in battle and
their ability to reap the military fruits of victories. But except
in China and Japan, these commanders conformed to the directives of heads of governments. World War II was conducted by
"amateurs."

Mussolini was the first of the wartime Chiefs of Government to
attain supreme authority. He seized power in October 1922.
Stalin, one of a triumvirate with Lenin and Trotsky, overthrew

Kerensky in 1918; on Lenin's death, he outmaneuvred Trotsky, and by 1929 was the second of the wartime chiefs to attain supreme power; he had considerable experience in raising and equipping armies and some combat experience during revolutionary civil wars and the war with Poland in 1921-22. Roosevelt and Hitler came to power almost simultaneously early in 1933. Churchill, who had held Cabinet posts in World War I and became Chancellor of the Exchequer, was the last to attain power, returning to the Admiralty as First Lord in September 1939 and becoming Prime Minister in June 1940.

In China, Chiang Kai-shek, after a series of campaigns between 1924-28 in which he defeated several provincial war lords, was made President of the Chinese Republic and Commander-in-Chief of the Army and Navy by the Central Committee of his party, the Kuomintang. From 1931 to 1945, he was continuously at war with Japan.

All of these leaders had participated in World War I; they had witnessed its consequences and the futile attempts to preserve the peace by the League of Nations and by international agreements. Each of them had obtained political control in his own country and was familiar with the organization of his government. In attaining power at home these leaders had gained experience in dealing with political opponents and colleagues that should have prepared them for diplomatic maneuvres with enemy and allied leaders. All were orators accustomed to arousing and directing public opinion among citizens or subjects. Radio networks provided a convenient method of appealing to their countrymen and of broadcasting propaganda to other nations.

Stalin and Hitler were the first two to match their adroitness as colleagues. Both had risen to power by ruthless methods. Traditional rivalry between their nations, added to the difference between Communist and Nazi ideologies, made them natural antagonists. Stalin was familiar with party management and the intricate government of the polyglot, Eurasian peoples under Red dominion. Naturally astute, with rare self-control, years in the underground had taught him caution without depriving him of a native willingness to make immediate and dangerous decisions during emergencies. To natural cunning he added dissimulation. Prepared to hold his own with the most accomplished European diplomats, he was the best qualified Russian leader to carry on the party program and to protect his nation's interests.

In April 1933, shortly after Hitler and Roosevelt rose to power, Stalin expelled one third of the members of the Communist Party. In November of the same year his Red regime was recognized by President Roosevelt; within a few months Roosevelt was involved in a controversy with Stalin's Ambassador Litvinov in which the Red envoy flatly contradicted the President. In their first verbal skirmish with the President, the Reds had the last word. In 1934 Stalin signed a nonaggression pact with Poland and the Baltic States, and negotiated treaties with Czechoslovakia and Rumania, recognizing the latter's annexation of Bessarabia. He was welcomed into the League of Nations and celebrated the occasion two months later by a new purge. Stalin's ruthlessness created no official unfriendliness among foreign countries. Later the Spanish Republic gladly accepted his assistance in its civil war.

In June 1934, Hitler adopted Stalin's methods of ridding himself of party rivals; not to be outdone, young Japanese officers revolted and assassinated two Cabinet officers. The world-wide depression had added to the resentments among defeated nations and the unsatisfied victorious nations of World War I. Hitler's first attempt in 1934 to seize Austria was foiled by the prompt action of Mussolini, who despatched two army corps to the Brenner Pass. The subsequent failure of Great Britain and France to fulfill their pledges to support Italy's aspirations in Africa alienated Mussolini. Soon after, he assisted Hitler in consolidating his authority in Germany, in rearming the Reich, and in annexing Austria.*

Between 1933 and 1938, Hitler kept the army busy and happy increasing its strength; he made General Halder Chief of Staff in place of General Beck who had opposed the invasion of Czechoslovakia. He gained the support of the navy by promising Ad-

* For details, see *Goebbels Diaries*, Doubleday, Page & Co., p. 461.

miral Raeder it would no longer be subordinated to the Army General Staff. Air Marshal Herman Goering was a devoted Nazi follower. In five years Hitler had secured dependable Chiefs of the Armed Forces, and he accepted their advice to reach an understanding with Stalin before invading Poland; which he easily obtained by offering Stalin more than England and France could give him plus the prospect of peace with Germany. Ribbentrop and Molotov arranged the details of the nonaggression pact in September 1939.

The Hitler-Stalin love feast quickly climaxed as Red troops occupied East Poland, Esthonia, Latvia, and Lithuania. Later when Stalin invaded Finland he warily watched Hitler, but by April 1940 his hands were again free; and Hitler looked over his shoulder nervously at Stalin, as the Nazis invaded western Europe. The sudden collapse of France in June 1940 increased the self-assurance of Hitler and revived the fears of Stalin, who redoubled his efforts to reorganize the Red army. He made Timoshenko, his most successful combat General, Commander-in-Chief, allowed him to reduce the indoctrination of recruits in communism and to give them more training in the use of arms.

The cumulative effect of recurring European crises on President Roosevelt and Prime Ministers Baldwin, MacDonald, and Churchill was discussed in Chapter IV. In September 1939, Chamberlain returned Churchill to the Admiralty and as First Lord he began a correspondence with the President that continued until his death. In May 1940, Churchill became Prime Minister and promptly wrote Stalin assuring him that Great Britain was determined "to save herself from German domination" and then to free Europe. He asked Stalin to consider how German hegemony in Europe would affect Russian interests. His statesmanlike appeal was buttressed by the successful British resistance of the Nazis that gave Stalin another breathing spell. Stalin, always fearful of German designs on the small states lying between the Baltic and Black seas, received Sir Stafford Cripps, the British Ambassador, personally—an unusual compliment. Simultaneously, the Red leader strove to persuade Hitler that he was convinced that the triumph of the Nazis was assured while he ordered

Red envoys abroad to encourage resistance to Germany. Hitler, equally suspicious of Stalin, sent German troops into Finland and Rumania and, when Stalin protested, blandly replied that Nazi troops were only intended to resist projected British invasions.

After September 1940, when Hitler abandoned his half-hearted intention to invade England, he had been compelled to contemplate hostilities with Russia for he knew, while he was expending sea and air forces attacking the British Islands and commerce, that Stalin was busily strengthening his armed forces and stubbornly insisting upon a larger share of the spoils of war. Before resorting to arms, Hitler invited Stalin to join Germany, Italy, and Japan in long-range plans to dismember and divide the British Empire. Stalin accepted tentatively but suggested that he and Hitler first apportion among themselves territory already acquired or at their mercy in Europe; he proposed that the Nazis withdraw from Finland and Rumania, recognize that Bulgaria was within Russia's sphere of influence, assist the Kremlin to obtain bases in Turkey and an outlet to the Mediterranean, and then discuss dividing the remaining Balkan territory between Russia and Germany. Stalin's huge demands enraged Hitler. In November he began to squeeze the Reds out of the Balkans and, on December 18, he began "preparations to crush Soviet Russia in a quick campaign before the end of the war with England."

In January 1941, Stalin protested Hitler's actions in the Balkans; on April 4, he concluded a treaty with Yugoslavia just before the Nazi invasion. Matsuoka arrived in Berlin soon afterward to reaffirm Japan's allegiance to the Axis. Hints dropped by Hitler and Ribbentrop of the imminent invasion of Russia did not prevent Matsuoka from stopping at Moscow on his return to negotiate a Japanese-Russian accord. Relations between Japan and the United States worsened just as tension between Russia and Germany increased, facilitating a bargain that relieved Russia and Japan from the danger of a war on two fronts (described more fully on pp. 84-86).

Stalin apparently persuaded himself that he could preserve peace with Germany—his first major mistake. He knew that Churchill would obstruct his attempt to conciliate Hitler; but felt confident that in England's desperate situation the Prime Minister would be compelled to assist Russia if attacked by Germany. When the British Ambassador warned the Soviet Government of the impending Nazi attack, Stalin publicly accused the British Government of attempting to bring on a Russo-German conflict. The invasion surprised Stalin; but he had anticipated Churchill's reaction correctly because the Prime Minister immediately ranged Britain by the side of Russia and sent the Right Honorable Anthony Eden, the British Foreign Minister, to Moscow to ascertain Russian needs.

Stalin had secured his Pacific frontier by his treaty with Matsuoka; he increased the number of recruits, male and female, for the army, and accelerated and modernized their training. He converted factories to war production, and constructed new ones designed primarily to supply the army. Throughout the war, these factories furnished practically all the Red guns, rifles, and ammunition; the United States and Great Britain supplied trucks, motorized equipment, boots, shoes, and petroleum products. The Allies provided the mobility, Russian workers and factories the fire power of the Red army.

Hitler and Stalin offer a perfect example of two shrewd, unscrupulous heads of government each seeking to overreach the other. Churchill's action in dispatching Cripps to Moscow as Ambassador to detach Stalin from Hitler reveals the measures any European minister will take when his country is in need. Likewise Roosevelt, instead of asking Congress to increase the armed forces, had sought British aid to resist Japan in 1938. After the collapse of France, Roosevelt established closer ties with Churchill. Relations between the Anglo-American leaders were on a higher level than those between Hitler and Stalin, or Stalin and Matsuoka; but Churchill strove as earnestly to involve the United States in the war as Hitler did to persuade Japan to attack either Vladivostok or Singapore. International intrigues invariably precede and accompany global wars. However, it is rarely possible for one nation to persuade another nation to supply aid in a war without paying more than it would cost to provide their own armed forces.

While the United States was still nominally neutral, Roosevelt joined Churchill in rushing aid to Stalin, who subsequently used the same methods with them that he had employed in negotiating with Hitler. Roosevelt and Churchill decisively influenced Anglo-American policy and strategy. They typify the civilian leadership Anglo-American citizens can expect in a future war. Their concepts of policy and strategy and their methods of conducting diplomacy and war are apt to prevail in a third World War, unless American and British voters insist that their political leaders pay more attention to the causes, conduct, and consequences of war.

Churchill, having been dropped from the Admiralty by Asquith for overruling his professional adviser, Admiral Fisher, was reinstated in the Cabinet by Lloyd George in 1917. During the remainder of the war he supported Lloyd George's strategy of dispersing British divisions in Salonika, Mesopotamia, and Palestine. Lord Beaverbrook attributed Churchill's actions in World War I to "his assurance and self-confidence. He was honestly convinced that only by his advice and methods could it (the Empire) be saved." From 1924 to 1929 he served in Baldwin's Cabinet. According to Captain Grenfell he did little to strengthen the armed forces. For the next decade he was in Parliament but not in the government. He opposed Baldwin's foreign policies and criticized failure to support the armed forces (see Chapter 4). When, as he had predicted, Hitler struck in 1939, public opinion demanded his return to the Admiralty, where his vigorous action in establishing convoys and adopting other anti-submarine measures reduced submarine losses in the first months of the war.

Roosevelt and Churchill had met in London in the latter part of World War I when Roosevelt was Assistant Secretary of the Navy. Soon after Churchill's return to the Admiralty he received a personal letter from the President inviting him and Prime Minister Chamberlain to forward any information they desired him to have. Churchill accepted and began a correspondence that continued throughout the war. As First Lord of the Admiralty, Churchill, still rueful over his expulsion from the Cabinet in 1915 and its subsequent handicap to his political career, accepted some professional advice from his First Sea Lord, Admiral Sir Dudley Pound; notably so when Churchill, although he agreed with Admiral Sir Roger Keyes that the Royal Navy should intervene in the Norwegian campaign, nevertheless informed the House of Commons that he would accept the advice of the First Sea Lord to oppose intervention.*

When Churchill became Prime Minister he exulted in becoming Great Britain's "accepted leader"; he was confident that he knew what "orders should be given." Familiar with parliamentary-cabinet government, by a simple device he took direct command of the armed forces. He created a new office, the Ministry of Defense, and became its Chief. He thus consolidated the direction of the war in his own hands and his action met the approval of the Crown and the Parliament. Thereafter, subject only to the approval of the War Cabinet and House of Commons, Churchill ran the war. Members of the War Cabinet were his appointees; they could be dropped if they did not approve his plans. The Prime Minister, a veteran of Parliament and a sincere believer in parliamentary government, knew how to appeal to the House. In the darkest hours of the war he could always get a vote of confidence. Churchill's system of directing the armed forces closely paralleled that adopted by Roosevelt when he placed the Joint Army-Navy Board directly under his orders. In both countries civilian secretaries of military departments were by-passed. The Prime Minister and President had legislative and constitutional authority for their action. And the similarity of the systems facilitated the subsequent establishment of the Combined Chiefs of Staff.

The President's senior naval adviser, Admiral Harold R. Stark, became Chief of Naval Operations in September 1939 just as Hitler invaded Poland, and Roosevelt declared a limited national emergency. Stark's army colleague, General George C. Marshall, had been chosen Chief of the War Department General Staff in

---

* But even at this time, the British official naval history (*The War at Sea*, by Captain S. W. Roshill) notes difficulties and confusion caused by Churchill's frequent direct interventions in fleet operations.

1938 after serving as Assistant Chief. According to Sherwood,* Marshall attributed his appointment to the Honorable Harry Hopkins and stated that during their subsequent long and intimate association he had only one serious disagreement with Hopkins; and that concerned General Stilwell's relations with Chiang Kai-shek. Stark had served as Chief of the Bureau of Ordnance and as Aide to Secretary of the Navy, the Honorable Claude Swanson. Both officers were familiar with the organizations of the two departments, knew their way around Washington, and had often appeared before Congressional Committees. Throughout their service they worked together harmoniously.

In a letter to Admiral T. C. Hart, Commander-in-Chief of the Asiatic Fleet, written in February 1940, Stark promised to keep him informed of actions "contemplated by the State Department and to support him in a firm policy." About the same time Stark wrote Admiral J. O. Richardson, Commander-in-Chief of the U.S. Fleet, repeating Hart's opinion that 1940 might "prove critical in the Far East" and his own view that what happened in the western Pacific might be more important to the United States than "troubles in Europe." This was the general opinion in Washington as 1940 opened. The French army reinforced by the British Expeditionary Force was comfortably deployed in the Maginot Line which the War Department was convinced the Nazis could not break; the War Office in London held the same view, and Liddell Hart, the *London Times* military expert, told his readers that French defenses were impregnable.

Probably at the suggestion of the State Department, the President ordered the United States fleet to remain at Honolulu after the spring maneuvers in 1940. Later, after the Germans crashed through Anglo-French armies, Churchill was made Prime Minister and, among other requests, immediately asked the President to restrain Japan. In reply Roosevelt pointed to the fleet in Honolulu. Admiral Richardson did not think that the fleet's presence in the Hawaiian Islands without tankers or supply ships would deter the Japanese Government. He was also convinced that the

* *Roosevelt and Hopkins,* by R. E. Sherwood, Harper & Brothers.

paramount interest of the United States was the security of the Western Hemisphere and that war in the Far East should be avoided. He and Stark were intimate friends: he took the liberty of reminding the Chief of Naval Operations that the latter was the President's Senior Naval Adviser and that if he did not tell the President the facts concerning the naval situation, no one else would.

Richardson practiced what he preached. On October 8, 1940, at a luncheon with the President and Admiral W. D. Leahy, former Chief of Naval Operations and subsequently the President's Chief of Staff, Richardson restated his views to Roosevelt who just as positively replied that he knew "that our fleet has had and is now having a restraining influence upon Japan's actions." Richardson sturdily maintained his position, adding, "I know our fleet is disadvantageously disposed for preparing or initiating war operations." He also told the President the fleet was not ready for war, a statement that embarrassed Leahy who, as Chief of Naval Operations, previously had advised Roosevelt that the navy was ready for war. In January 1941, the President quietly relieved Richardson of his command a year short of the usual tenure of office. His successor, Admiral H. E. Kimmel, later corroborated Richardson's views. Testifying to the Congressional Committee investigating the disaster at Pearl Harbor, Kimmel said that he knew "the fleet at Pearl Harbor was vulnerable . . . that he thought the Navy Department also realized that fact . . . that the Administration insisted upon the fleet remaining there . . . that he [I] had the choice of refusing the Command or accepting it under prescribed conditions . . . later he [I] wished that he [I] had declined the appointment."

During 1940-41 Stark did his utmost to increase the navy and prepare it for war; after June 1940 Congress gave him ample appropriations. But the Presidential campaign was on; Roosevelt, candidate for a third term, was plagued by differences between Democratic leaders whom he did not wish to offend. Also he had promised labor leaders that shifting industry from consumer goods to munitions would not reduce benefits labor had obtained under the New Deal. Accordingly he ignored the recommendations of a Board he had appointed to facilitate the transition of industry to war production. Output of munitions lagged and convinced Admiral Stark that Americans would not produce bullets instead of butter until they were drawn into war. He also believed that unless the United States did help England she would be defeated and then the United States would face Germany and Japan alone and still unprepared.

Stark may have reached this conclusion independently, but he was very loyal to the President and this was the view of the Administration. Stark's loyalty limited his efforts in thwarting State Department strategists and restraining the President's own impulsive naval strategy. One example will suffice: on February 11, 1941, after giving sound professional reasons for opposing a strategic deployment of the Pacific Fleet proposed by Roosevelt, Stark added ". . . I will defer to your better judgment with a cheerful 'Aye, Aye, Sir'. . . ." On a technical problem, such as a fleet deployment, Stark's professional views were supposed to be accepted by the President or, if he had lost confidence in Stark, he should have relieved him. Stark's answers encouraged Roosevelt to make other strategic suggestions or to pass on some from his correspondent, Winston Churchill, who was also 'brimful' of strategic plans.

Before and after our entry into the war the President was given some very poor professional advice by Stark and Marshall. He could have selected other advisers; instead he became more receptive to suggestions from the State Department, from Harry Hopkins, and ever more willing to follow his own impulses.

The President's service as Assistant Secretary of the Navy had familiarized him with departmental procedures and their inevitable delays and added to an innate aversion to using official channels. Important orders were sent directly to Sumner Welles or bureau chiefs in the navy on a White House memorandum pad with the formidable initials, "FDR."

Early in the New Deal era, Harry Hopkins had gained Roosevelt's confidence. Mrs. Roosevelt explained that her husband found "companionship and loyalty" in Hopkins who, she said, would give his opinions honestly, but she added that Hopkins frequently agreed with the President "regardless of his own opinion" or would wait for an "auspicious moment" to broach a subject, for he soon learned that Roosevelt "did not like opposition too well. . . ." Members of the Cabinet and the Chiefs of Staff, as well as Hopkins, soon learned that the President did not enjoy opposition. Some used Hopkins to learn Roosevelt's ideas in advance or to gain his approval of their plans. The rest usually waited to be told what to do. Mrs. Roosevelt credited her husband with educating Hopkins in world politics and grand strategy, after he moved into the White House in May 1940. Certainly Hopkins made himself indispensable and did not restrict his activities to world politics for, at the Democratic convention, he took charge of the delegates who nominated the President for a third term.

After the election, Hopkins helped the President to formulate lend-lease legislation. In January 1941, he was sent to London as Roosevelt's emissary to discuss with Churchill measures for increasing American aid to Great Britain and immediately reported that Britain "needs our help now—with everything we can give them." The President accepted this advice and appointed Hopkins as his representative on lend-lease. Thereafter, Hopkins decided the distribution of munitions produced in the United States. Hopkins was favorably impressed by Churchill, whose main concern was obtaining war material for his hard-pressed country. The Prime Minister maintained direct communication with Hopkins, leaving other diplomatic matters to be handled by Foreign Minister Anthony Eden, through Ambassador Winant with Secretary Hull. Soon after his return, Hopkins sent the Honorable Averell Harriman to London as his personal representative to manage lend-lease directly with the Prime Minister, and obtained the President's consent to assign Mr. C. E. Bohlen as liaison officer between the State Department and White House.

In July 1941, the President sent Hopkins to London to arrange the agenda for the Argentia Conference with Churchill. At this conference, upon the request of Roosevelt, the Prime Minister prepared the first draft of the Atlantic Charter. According to Churchill, the purpose of the charter was to persuade Americans to accept closer ties with England, and he considered it astonishing that the President "of the United States still technically neutral" joined "with a belligerent power in making such a declaration. . . ." The inclusion in the declaration of the hope of the two nations to create a better world "after the destruction of Nazi tyranny" Churchill thought implied a challenge that Hitler was too wise to pick up. So what pleased him most was Roosevelt's promise "definitely to use hard language" to Japan. Churchill correctly anticipated that the State Department would "tone it down"; but, even as read by the President to Nomura soon after and sent to Tokyo, the message convinced the Japanese Ambassador that if Japan attacked either British or Dutch possessions in the Far East the United States would enter the war. Nomura reported his opinion to his government who accepted it and reached their subsequent decisions on his assumption. This policy caused their navy to strike simultaneously at British, Dutch, and American forces when they began the war.

It was while Hopkins was in London arranging the meeting at Argentia that Roosevelt sent him to Moscow to assure Stalin of American aid. On Hopkins' recommendation, Roosevelt began direct communication with Stalin. Hopkins with rare tact soon became the confidant of Roosevelt, Churchill, and Stalin. The reactions of the President, Secretary Stimson, Secretary Knox, Admiral Stark, and General Marshall to the invasion of Russia have been given (Chapter 4, pages 86-88). The advice given the President by his senior professional advisers may explain and certainly partially justifies Roosevelt turning to Hopkins. In any event, after Hopkins' visit to Moscow his activities and influence increased rapidly. Except for seven months in 1944 when he was in the hospital, Hopkins was the regular intermediary between the Big Three. He assisted the President in preparing for Allied conferences and sat at his elbow during them. At Teheran and Yalta, important suggestions made by him were accepted by Roosevelt.

In addition to representing the President in lend-lease, Hopkins was chairman of the committee that controlled the disposition of strategic materials. No one in the war or navy departments could ignore him. He began dropping in uninvited to meetings of the Joint Army-Navy Board and no member dared to object. Stimson and Marshall expressed a high regard for him that was not fully reciprocated; Hopkins said that Stimson "is obviously unhappy because he is not consulted about the strategy of the war, and I think he feels that I could be more helpful in relating him and Marshall to the President." On another occasion, Hopkins slightingly remarked that Stimson and Marshall "feel we cannot win without getting in the war, but they have no idea how that (getting in the war) is going to be accomplished." Admiral Stark openly expressed the same conviction that we could not win unless we entered the war. He and Marshall rarely disagreed, so Hopkins' estimate of Marshall's and Stimson's views was probably correct.

On several occasions in 1940-41, Stark unsuccessfully endeavored to get definite answers from the President about his policies. Roosevelt replied on one such occasion that when he was in doubt about the right course of action he generally did nothing. On another occasion he told Stark to quit asking him what he would do if the Japanese continued their advance southward. Sherwood observed Roosevelt's reluctance to limit his future freedom of action by making commitments in advance. Any White House correspondent could vouch for his refusal to answer "iffy" questions.

Relations between Churchill and Stalin quickly drew closer after Hitler invaded Russia. Der Fuehrer's occupation of the Sudetenland without opposition, his quick conquest of Poland and France had finally convinced the German General Staff that Hitler was "an untutored genius of war." The army accepted his leadership because of his land victories; the navy, for his invasion of Norway and his pledge to construct a fleet. His repulse in the battle for Britain did not dim the luster of his European victories. Elated by successes, he willingly assumed control of the armies and accompanied them in the field, still convinced that his inner consciousness was a surer guide to success than advice of the General Staff. Hitler's generals acquiesced in his plan to destroy Red armies in a brisk, summer campaign. They were so confident of success that they did not provide winter clothing for troops and made no arrangements to operate motorized transport in sub-zero temperature.

Like Churchill, Stalin was Minister of Defense; he also directed Russia's foreign policy and acted as Quartermaster-General. He never visited the front but ran the war and governed Russia from the Kremlin. He solicited the views of Field Commanders, insisted on positive answers to questions but allowed time for careful consideration of the situation. When Field Commanders disagreed, he informed them of their different recommendations and asked them to reconsider. Then he made the final decision. When the invasion began in June 1941 the opposing forces were arrayed as follows:

Reds	*Post*	*Nazis*
Stalin (in Kremlin)	Commander-in-Chief	Hitler (in the field)
Shaposhinkov	Chief of Staff	Brauchitsch
Voroshilov	Northern Army	Leeb
Timoshenko	Central Army	Bock
Budenny	Southern Army	Rundstedt

The territorial objective of the Nazi northern army was Leningrad; of the central army, Moscow; of the southern army, Kiev. The tactical objective was the destruction of Red armies west of the Dniester River before winter began, because the roads eastward would not thereafter be fit for motorized warfare. The Nazi army commanders were the same leaders who had crushed Poland and western Europe.* They employed the same grand tactics that had succeeded in Poland and France. They strove to encircle Red armies in a double envelopment; the inner enveloping force of two groups of motorized infantry moved on opposite semi-circumferences of the smaller inner circle; the outer enveloping forces led by Panzer Divisions moved parallel but in much wider semi-circumferences. If claws of the inner and outer forces

---

* After the war Brauchitsch, Halder, and Rundstedt claimed they opposed the invasion; undoubtedly Rundstedt did, but all three made preparations as ordered and none of them provided winter clothes for the army, so they must have expected victory in a summer campaign.

could close almost simultaneously, the opposing Reds would be caught in a double bag and their destruction insured.

Stalin's purpose was "to drive Hitler's armies out of the Soviet Union." His strategy was to trade land, beginning with the provinces recently given him by Hitler, for time to complete the training of sufficient divisions to eject the invaders. As Red armies retreated, the earth would be scorched and irregular troops trained in guerrilla tactics would be left behind. Inhabitants must evacuate or remain to starve. About 75 per cent of Russian factories were around or west of a line running through Leningrad, Moscow, and Stalingrad. As armies retreated, Stalin evacuated factories of machines, workers and their families, repeating on a larger scale Chiang Kai-shek's removal of Chinese factories ahead of Japanese invaders.

Had Stalin been given all details of Hitler's plan, he could not have devised a better defense. Only once did the Nazi double envelopment tactics work as planned. Near Kiev, Rundstedt surrounded, killed, or captured almost 600,000 Red troops, but only after being held up for two months and with the aid of General Bock's central army. In September, Timoshenko with fifty divisions launched a counterattack that forced the Nazis to retreat almost to Smolensk and saved Moscow temporarily.

Along the high road to Moscow, Bock nearly succeeded first at Slonim, next at Smolensk. Thousands of Red soldiers were killed or captured, Minsk was taken, but the bulk of the Red army crossed the Dniester in good order and were regularly reinforced as they fell back.

At Smolensk the Nazis were 200 miles inside Russia, as far as they had planned to go to destroy Red armies, but the Red armies had not been destroyed. Hitler, cheered by the victory on September 26 at Kiev, in the following month ordered the advance on Moscow resumed. Bock was still confident he could surround and destroy the opposing armies in the neighborhood of Moscow, as Rundstedt cleared the Black sea coast of Red troops and advanced into the Caucasus.

In World War I, Field Marshal von Falkenhayn had warned Hindenburg and Ludendorf that tactical envelopment would not succeed against Russian armies on account of their numerical supremacy and the huge area of the country which enabled them to withdraw repeatedly without abandoning vital areas. Except for Rundstedt's success at Kiev, the experience of Hitler proved that Falkenhayn was correct. Again and again, superior Nazi leadership, personnel, and equipment enabled them to encircle some and to destroy or to capture many Red divisions. But more divisions withdrew from the noose, and their formations were refilled. The Red armies, reinforced by reserve divisions, formed new lines in the rear compelling the invaders to mount other attacks which required time and more supplies, particularly gasoline, for as the Nazis advanced they stretched their line of communications.

It is reported that General Guderian, Commander of Bock's Panzer Corps, realized that encircling tactics could not destroy the Russian army; he proposed to drive straight for Moscow with his tank divisions to keep the Russians on the run. He might have reached that vicinity sooner, but Russian reserves coming from the east, north, and south could still have anticipated his arrival in front of Moscow. Red commanders were not panic-stricken when tank columns crashed through their lines. They re-formed on either flank of the enemy and counterattacked. It was impossible with Hitler's forces to overrun or destroy the numerically superior Red armies as long as they followed Fabian tactics and adhered to the scorched earth strategy of Stalin, whose nonaggression pact with Matsuoka enabled him to reinforce his European armies with one half of the Siberian army.

By the end of the Argentia Conference, leaders of two still unacknowledged opposing Alliances were in charge. Roosevelt, a benevolent neutral, Churchill, Stalin, and Chiang Kai-shek, with General deGaulle representing the Free French and the representatives of occupied governments of Poland, the Netherlands, Norway, and Belgium, confronted Hitler, Mussolini, Franco, representatives of the Nazi satellite states of the Balkans and Finland with Japan pledged to join. Churchill and Roosevelt sent Stalin a message prepared by Harry Hopkins and Stafford Cripps saying they had consulted "together . . . how best . . . to help your country . . . against the Nazi attack." In addition, Roosevelt had agreed at Churchill's request to send a stiff warning to Japan.

Hitler's armies were still advancing in Russia and sustaining Mussolini's reeling armies in the Mediterranean area, when the press release subsequently known as the Atlantic Charter was issued. It associated the United States, a nominal neutral, with belligerent Britain in an effort to destroy Nazi tyranny, to disarm aggressor nations, and then to reduce world armaments. The charter was an obvious appeal to world and domestic public opinion; Roosevelt and Churchill disclaimed territorial gains, vetoed such changes without consent of inhabitants, guaranteed free passage of the seas and access to raw materials. These promises were broken in the same month when British and Red forces, with no objection from Roosevelt, invaded Persia to gain direct communications between their countries.

In October, Harriman and Lord Beaverbrook were sent to Moscow to arrange for delivery of supplies from Great Britain and the United States. Churchill delayed the meeting to learn "where the Russian front would lie in the winter." Churchill dealt more charily with Stalin than did Roosevelt. Early in November he ignored a rude note from Stalin who, three weeks later, apologized. Roosevelt relied more upon soothing words and large contributions. Stalin, even when Nazi armies surrounded Moscow, treated Churchill and Roosevelt brusquely and failed to fulfill pledges.

Tactical discussions by American and British staff officers at Argentia revealed Churchill's determination that British troops should never become involved in "a war of vast armies firing immense masses of shells at each other." British Chiefs of Staff accordingly were preparing to invade France with "small forces, chiefly armored, that with their power of hard-hitting . . . would be able to quickly win a decisive victory." This was a faithful reflection of Churchill's views reached in July 1940, when he admitted that Britain had no continental army that could defeat the Nazis. He also assumed the blockade was broken, for Hitler could draw supplies from Asia and Africa.

Churchill concluded that the only way to bring Hitler down was by ". . . an absolutely, devastating, exterminating attack by very heavy bombers from England upon Germany . . ." He asked the Air Secretary, ". . . When can air mastery [over Germany] be obtained?" Three days later he complained to the Secretary that losses in the bomber command "seem unduly heavy" and directed that "the long-range bombing of Germany be conducted with a desire to save the machines and personnel as much as possible, while keeping up a steady attack." After another four days he asked the Secretary, "Why have we not been able to obtain better [bombing] results in the Kiel canal?" and demanded to know, "How many raids, how many bombs, what kinds of bombs, and [why] the canal still works?" Within the same week, Churchill ordered the air force to win the war alone with heavy bombers, next complained of losses trying to carry out his orders, and then sternly commanded that a steady attack be maintained on Germany and simultaneously that they build up the bomber force.

Churchill then turned to the army. On the same day he instructed them on how to emplace a 14" gun, the kind of steel girder to use and the sand bags to provide protection, how it should be camouflaged, the number of rounds it should fire before being relined, and finally reminded the General that it would be necessary to remove the structure while relining the guns. Copies of Churchill's minutes to the land, sea, and air forces fill appendices of his volumes. They indicate a complete lack of confidence on the part of the Minister of Defense in his professional assistants. Yet he retained practically all of them during the war and at its end paid them deserved praise.

Churchill's respect for the Wehrmacht, verging on fear, was confirmed by the repulse of the British attack on Dieppe in August 1942 and continued until Eisenhower landed in Normandy. Obviously Great Britain in 1940 could not hope to invade Europe. She had difficulty in maintaining the sea and air forces that were essential for her own defense. Even after Russia and the United States had entered the war, Churchill was convinced they could not meet the Nazi armies; he extended his distrust of newly raised American troops to their aviators and urged Roosevelt to send bombing planes to England to be flown by the Royal Air

Force. Churchill was at *his* best before a microphone, stimulating his indomitable countrymen who are at *their* best in adversity. The broadcasts of this undaunted spokesman of the British Commonwealth also had a profound effect on public opinion in the United States.

In October 1941, Lord Beaverbrook said the British Chiefs of Staff considered the European "continent to be out of bounds to British troops." Their opinion reflected exactly the views of Churchill. While timid about fighting in France, the Prime Minister was continually urging both the navy in the Mediterranean and the troops in North Africa to accept all risks. On a moment's notice Churchill could cite reasons for an expedition to Persia, to the Caucasus, to Burma, to Java, to Crete, to Murmansk; anywhere except to the principal theater to fight against Nazis who had to be defeated before eventual victory could be obtained. The total of the losses accepted in minor theaters might have brought victory sooner in western Europe.

On October 30 President Roosevelt cabled Stalin approving all the material promised by Harriman, adding that supplies worth one billion dollars would be provided by lend-lease; payments for additional supplies would not begin until five years after the war, no interest would be charged, and the Reds would have an additional ten years to complete payment.

Stalin had already directed General Zhukov to hold Moscow at all cost, when Hitler ordered that the city be taken and the Kremlin destroyed. In late November, General Bock, massing for the final attack, forced powerful spearheads eastward both north and south of the city. In the first week of December, Bock called upon commanders of the spearheads to complete the encirclement. The southern group crashed through; the northern group was repulsed by reserves, some of them brought from Siberia. Having committed all his reserves, Zhukov ordered a counterattack all along the line on December 6. Favored by heavy snow and subzero temperatures, Zhukov saved Moscow. Hitler, having prematurely announced the capture of the Red capital, held Brauchitsch responsible for the failure and took direct command of the field armies. Rundstedt resigned his command. Hitler ordered army commanders to hold their positions at all costs and soldiers to die rather than surrender. Thereafter, massive Nazi armies were directed by Hitler's inner consciousness and the numerically superior Red armies by Stalin whose military training was acquired during the Red Revolution and who was guided by advice of his generals. On December 6, General Zhukov launched the first great Red counterattack. The following day Japanese forces attacked British, Dutch, and American forces and possessions in the Pacific.

President Roosevelt, by branding December 7 a "day of infamy," turned initial mortification of most Americans with their armed forces into righteous indignation against Japan. Naval officers generally continued to writhe with shame that the Pacific Fleet had been completely surprised. They were relieved when they learned that Admiral E. J. King, Commander-in-Chief of the Atlantic Fleet, was summoned immediately to the Navy Department and their morale rose when shortly after Secretary Knox announced Admiral King's appointment as Commander-in-Chief of the U.S. Fleet and directly responsible to the President. They knew that the navy had at last been entrusted to the officer best fitted to command it.

On December 22, 1941, Churchill, accompanied by civil and military advisers, arrived in Washington for the Arcadia Conference, fearful that the disasters in the Pacific might cause the American High Command to divert forces from the Atlantic. However, Marshall and Stark had recommended, and Roosevelt had approved adherence to, Rainbow Five which gave priority to the Atlantic theater. This sound decision, and the most important military decision of the war, naturally pleased Churchill.

General Marshall followed it with a proposal to establish "unity of command" over the land, sea, and air forces of America, Britain, Holland, and Australia in the ABDA area under the euphonious title ABDA. To support this innovation Marshall cited the action of the Allies in 1918 when they gave Foch command of ground troops on the almost continuous land front of France and Italy. Marshall failed to consider the difference between directing only army troops in an almost unbroken line of trenches and controlling the operations of land, sea, and air forces, deployed from India to Australia, with three great archipelagoes —Philippine, Malaysia, and Bismarck—intervening. Churchill was surprised when he first heard Marshall's proposal, but Hopkins persuaded him not to reject it until he learned who would be given command, and he agreed when told that Wavell was to have the baton. To complete his catastrophic idea Marshall had recommended for the Supreme Command, Field Marshal Wavell, whom previously Churchill had gently pushed upstairs as Viceroy of India because he had considered Marshall's candidate a "tired, old man" unequal to commanding the British army in North Africa. British Staff Officers were astonished at the fantastic plan and unjustly suspected Marshall of seeking a scapegoat for the disaster they knew was imminent.

The ABDA forces would have been defeated in any event. Marshall's plan only hastened and increased the disaster. Wavell did not appreciate that Japanese control of the air over Malaysia rendered Singapore as well as Manila useless as operational bases. With traditional army courage he dispatched reinforcements in a vain attempt to hold Singapore. Troop-loaded transports and their escorting ships were attacked by planes as they approached the harbor, as they hastily disembarked doomed soldiers, and as they attempted, often in vain, to depart. Japanese aviators had an air man's holiday; for ABDA's ships, sailors, and soldiers, it was a holocaust. On February 14, Wavell was succeeded as Supreme Commander by the civilian Governor General Van Mook. Marshall's theory of unity of command was being carried to its logical conclusion. If an army officer can command land, sea, and air forces, why cannot a brilliant civilian like Van Mook? If professional training is unnecessary in two of the great military branches, why is it necessary for the third?

Van Mook's situation was more desperate than Wavell's. But his Naval Commander, Admiral C. E. L. Helfrich, who had succeeded Admiral Hart, was still convinced that Java could be held. The hopeless struggle continued until March 1. Rear Admiral Doorman, Royal Netherlands Navy, commanding ABDA naval forces in a last gallant effort, attacked the superior Japanese fleet on February 27. The remnants of his defeated force were finally ordered by Helfrich to escape if possible. The *USS Houston* under Captain A. H. Rooks, U.S. Navy, and *HMAS Perth* under the equally intrepid Captain H. M. L. Waller, RN, were the last cruisers sacrificed on Marshall's altar. They were sunk on the night of March 1st.

Admiral King participated in the Arcadia Conference and accepted Marshall's plan for that particular occasion; he disapproved of its general application. Unity of command was the product of the army generals who convinced themselves, President Roosevelt, and Harry Hopkins that, if Marshal Foch was able to command French, British, and American troops, any Flag officer can command land, sea, and air forces. King gained the impression that high ranking army officers for many years had been seeking to make the Chief of Staff of the Army the Supreme Commander of the Army and Navy.

General MacArthur commanded in the Philippines. He had decided he could hold the southern islands as well as Luzon with thirty-five bombers and his Filipino army. Marshall exempted MacArthur from Wavell's command. But on his recommendation, Admiral Hart with the remainder of his Asiatic Fleet was subordinated to Wavell.

In Chapter 4 the debacle in Luzon has already been described. A few decisions by President Roosevelt and Generals Marshall and MacArthur are cited to show that Marshall's doctrine of unity of command is not applicable even to widely deployed armies if separated by long stretches of the ocean. On February 8, as Singapore was breathing its last, President Quezon proposed that the United States grant immediate independence to the Philippines; they would be neutralized; American and Japanese forces would be withdrawn; the Filipino army disbanded. With Quezon's proposal MacArthur sent to the President his own estimate of the situation, stating that his divisions had been reduced to regiments; his regiments to battalions; the men were "battle worn and needed rest." Warning that his command might be completely destroyed at any time, he added that the Filipinos, whose stamina he previously had greatly over-estimated, violently resented the situation and he suggested to the President that Quezon's plan might be "the best possible solution of what is about to be a disastrous debacle." As MacArthur was only continuing the fight to gain time, he pointed out to Roosevelt and Marshall that the Quezon plan would "secure at least equal delay" as resistance by the army.*

The President replied authorizing MacArthur to surrender Filipino soldiers but forbidding the surrender of American troops, "so long as there remains any possibility of resistance," and closed by requesting the General "to make your resistance as effective as circumstance will permit and as prolonged as humanly possible." On February 22, the President ordered MacArthur to Mindanao to stiffen the defenses there and then proceed to Australia where, like Wavel, he was to be given Supreme Command of land, sea, and air forces in another huge oceanic area where air and sea forces would decide the outcome. At MacArthur's request the President left the time of his departure and details of method including command arrangements to the General. On March 12, Mac-Arthur and his party left Manila, spent a day in Mindanao and arrived in Darwin, Australia, on March 17.

Until his departure MacArthur had done much to maintain morale by optimistic references in his Orders to prospective reinforcements. On leaving he emphasized that he was only going to expedite relief personally. Theoretically he was still in command of the Philippines, so he left a member of his staff at Corregidor to control the distribution of supplies and ammunition. He gave command of the field armies and Corregidor to General Wainwright with the President's order not to surrender. Wainwright passed this order along to General King, commanding forces in Luzon, and to General Sharp commanding those in Mindanao. The attempt of MacArthur to command the forces in the Philippines from Australia created so much confusion that Marshall was obliged to obtain the President's approval to give the command in the Philippines to Wainwright who, besieged in Cor-

* *U. S. Army in World War II, War in the Pacific, Fall of the Philippines,* Government Printing Office, Chapter V, pp. 77-97.

regidor, theoretically still commanded field armies in Luzon and Mindanao.

As General King's forces were driven back in the Bataan Peninsula, Wainwright in accordance with Roosevelt's order refused to permit him to surrender. King, when his forces were cut into small groups and all his field hospitals under enemy field artillery fire that could not be returned, disobeyed the order to prevent further useless slaughter of his helpless men. Later Wainwright underwent a more humiliating experience. MacArthur had ordered him to destroy the guns of Corregidor and blow up the ammunition if compelled to yield, so the guns could not be used to prevent MacArthur's return. The night before he offered to surrender, Wainwright disabled the heavy guns, broke the rifles and exploded the ammunition. The next day General Homma refused to accept the surrender of Corregidor unless Wainwright included the United States armies in the Philippines. Technically Homma was correct, for Wainwright had signed his correspondence as Commander, U.S. Army Forces in the Philippines. Having executed MacArthur's orders to destroy the fortress guns of Corregidor, Wainwright was literally helpless. Also, MacArthur had permitted many women and children to take refuge in Corregidor, who would be killed along with combatants if he attempted to resist. Wainwright, thanks to the army system of extending commands over vast areas, felt obliged to comply with Homma's demand to include the surrender of Sharp's forces in the other islands although they were fully armed, well organized, and had been trained to carry on guerrilla war. American forces in the Philippines were compelled to suffer every humiliation known to brave men, and largely as a result of orders of the High Command in Washington, compounded by MacArthur in his dual capacity as Field Marshal of the Filipino Army and Commander of the American Armed Forces in the Far East.

An Anglo-American Joint Committee set up during the Arcadia Conference developed into the Anglo-American Combined Chiefs of Staff that sat in Washington during the war. General Marshall, General Arnold, and Admiral Stark were the original

American members, Admiral King participated in discussions after he became Commander-in-Chief of the U.S. Fleet on December 18; on December 30 King was relieved of command of Atlantic Fleet by Admiral R. E. Ingersol. Admiral King's first official order to Admiral Nimitz, who had relieved Admiral Kimmel, was to hold the Hawaii-Midway line and its communications with the Pacific Coast and thus to maintain communications with Australia; and the Fiji Islands were to be occupied at the earliest possible date. On March 26, King relieved Stark as Chief of Naval Operations and thereafter filled both offices with Admiral F. J. Horne as Vice Chief of Naval Operations. King then became the sole naval representative on the Joint Chiefs of Staff and Combined Chiefs of Staff until the President in July appointed Admiral W. D. Leahy as Chief of Staff of the Commander-in-Chief of the Army and Navy.

Leahy considered his "job to pass on to the Joint Chiefs of Staff the basic thinking of the President on all war plans and strategy." In turn he brought back to the President from the Joint Chiefs "a consensus of their thinking." The U.S. Joint Chiefs gradually took over the former duties of the Joint Army-Navy Board and represented the President on the Combined Chiefs of Staff. The British members of the Combined Chiefs of Staff in 1942 were Lt. General G. N. McReady who represented Churchill as Minister of Defense, Admiral Sir Andrew Cunningham representing the First Sea Lord, Air Marshal D. C. S. Evill representing the Air Chief Marshal, Field Marshal Sir John Dill representing the Chief of the Army General Staff. During the war only a few changes were made in the British personnel and none in the American. British and American members frequently disagreed on strategic decisions and then the problem was referred to the Prime Minister and President for final settlement. American members sometimes disagreed among themselves; usually the President would return the question and direct them to try again to reach a unanimous decision. They usually did. By common consent even when individual members disagreed they signed the joint report. Some important disagreements will be related. Speaking generally, the Combined Chiefs of Staff functioned efficiently and provided the necessary military mechanism to coordinate and command land, sea, and air forces of two Great Powers. A common language and, in most cases, a common acceptance of fundamental concepts of waging war facilitated their planning.

When Admiral King became Commander-in-Chief and Chief of Naval Operations, U-boats were sinking tankers in sight of Atlantic coastal cities, they were combining with Nazi planes to take heavy toll of convoys steaming toward Murmansk, and on May 6, 1942, Wainwright was compelled to surrender the Philippines. Two naval victories occurred in the next thirty days—the first, at Coral Sea, blunted the enemy thrust toward Australia; the second, off Midway Island, dealt a vital blow to Japanese carriers and, more important, destroyed the first team of Japanese carrier pilots. Then Admiral King justified the faith of his brother officers. Realizing that the victory at Midway put the enemy fleet off balance, he determined to keep it off balance. He insisted that Ghormley and Vandergrift seize Guadalcanal early in August although they reported, and he knew, that they had not completed their preparations; nor had the Japanese. King's determination brought on a succession of land, sea, and air battles in the Solomon Islands where the enemy was fighting three fourths as far from his base as were Americans. King's insistence on maintaining unremitting pressure on the enemy kept them off balance.

King's determination involved heavy losses, for many new ships had barely completed shake-down cruises before going into action. Officers and men had much to learn about night fighting and were taught by the Japanese the hard way. At one time only one American carrier was fit for combat in the Pacific. King sent all ships he could get to Admiral Halsey, Admiral Ghormley's successor; Halsey kept them fighting. Today around Savo Island the hulls of many ships entomb many brave sailors who supported the marines while they enlarged their beachhead and held Guadalcanal. The line of communication to Australasia was unbroken.

The military decisions made in Washington in January 1942 that affected Russia were: to increase all possible material aid to the Red armies; to intensify the naval blockade and assist underground troops in Nazi-occupied countries. It was not considered feasible to land an expeditionary force in France during 1942, but a diversionary landing would be made if the Reds were sorely pressed; any evidence of a Nazi collapse would be exploited; and if invited by the Vichy Government an Anglo-American Force would be landed in Africa. None of these contingencies arose, but troops held in the United Kingdom for these undertakings prove Anglo-American good faith.

On January 22, 1942, a week after Churchill had left Washington predicting British victory in North Africa, Rommel launched a successful offensive against the British 8th Army. On March 15, 1942, Stalin's winter offensive was halted by the Nazis, leaving them free to prepare the summer campaign and causing the President great anxiety about the Russian front. On April 4, he sent Hopkins and Marshall to London to propose an invasion of the continent, and a few days later asked Stalin to send "Molotov and a General on whom you can rely to Washington" to advise upon "the strategic course of our common military action."

At the President's request Stalin sent Molotov to Washington, where Roosevelt assured him that the defeat of Germany was the first objective. Molotov emphasized the advantages of opening a second front in 1942, because if an Anglo-American invasion were made soon, it might draw forty German divisions from the Russian front and thus might end the war in 1942.

Before Molotov left, Marshall told him that "we are preparing for a second front," and the President confirmed Marshall's statement. Molotov had pressed the Kremlin's view vigorously but, when leaving, he pledged the Red armies to do their best, warning his listeners to reckon fully with the danger of a Russian defeat.

Churchill with military and naval staff was again in Washington before Molotov left. The military situation went from bad to worse. The Nazi armies were besieging Sevastopol and menacing the Caucasus; in North Africa, Rommel was driving the British eastward. In the Atlantic, U-boats still were operating in the coastal waters of the United States and, assisted by German planes operating from northern Norway, were taking heavy toll of lend-lease ships bound for Murmansk. For example, of eighty-four ships with over one-half million tons of stores that left United States ports, forty-four with 300,000 tons got through; twenty-three ships were lost; seventeen were compelled to discharge cargo in Scotland.

On June 21, 1942, Rommel took Tobruk with 25,000 prisoners, after destroying the British Armored Forces. This disaster caused Churchill and Roosevelt to lay aside long-range plans. Tanks, planes, and motor vehicles were rushed around South Africa to Cairo to re-equip the 8th Army, under its new commander General Montgomery. Stalin loyally agreed to Roosevelt's proposal to divert forty light bombers from the Red to the British army, although the Germans were opening their summer offensive.

After the escape of the Scharnhorst and Gneisenau from Brest and the fall of Singapore, the Prime Minister demanded and was given a vote of confidence in the House of Commons because he had involved the United States in the war. Churchill admitted many military mistakes but claimed credit for realizing from the beginning that it was necessary to get the United States to enter the war and that he had persistently followed a policy that achieved his objective. Never before had a head of government so frankly boasted that he had lured another nation into war.

The shock of the British defeat in Cyrenaica and the determination of the President and Chief of Staff to give American troops battle experience in 1942 renewed the discussion of a possible Anglo-American landing in Northwest Africa; it was finally approved in July after Hopkins, Marshall, and Admiral King had conferred with Churchill in London.

As Churchill had violently opposed any landing in Europe in 1942, the President suggested that he and Harriman go to Moscow to explain why the landing could not be made. At the first meeting Stalin was surly and rude but softened at the second and gave them a banquet. After the banquet he and Churchill discussed until daylight ways to win the war. Stalin had some reason for being irritable; the Nazis were advancing in the Caucasus and toward the Volga. He was obliged to recall more Siberian troops to Europe, and they were only able to halt the invasion in October. But the oil fields in Baku were saved and the road to the Persian Gulf denied the Germans.

By the middle of August 1942, operations in Russia were dominated by the struggle for Stalingrad. Two Nazi armies, under General Bock's direction, were across the Don ready to converge in three great columns on Stalingrad some forty miles distant. In 1812 Marshal Kutusov burned Moscow to deny shelter to Napoleon. Stalin in 1942 used Stalingrad to trap Nazi armies. He ordered General Chuikov to hold the city and General Zhukov to surround the besiegers. On November 23, the German 6th Army was encircled. General Paulus, its commander, was not unduly alarmed; he organized the conventional hedge-hog defense, received supplies by air and waited to be relieved. But the army sent to his relief was decisively defeated. Hitler ordered Paulus not to surrender and, by exhausting the air force in a fruitless effort to supply the army, dealt it a vital injury. Nazi ground troops were ground to pieces between Chuikov's army inside and Rokossovky's outside Stalingrad. Paulus was captured February 2, 1943, with more than 200,000 troops, 6,700 guns, and 1,500 tanks.

By March 1943, Red armies had retaken Rzhev, Velikie Luki, and Vyazma. Under Stalin's directives, the Red military chieftains had secured jumping off places for their first summer offensive. Outstanding was Zhukov, defender of Moscow, savior of Stalingrad, and future conqueror of Berlin. Others included Timoshenko, Chuikov, Rokossovky, and Vorenov. In the summer of 1943, Stalin could take pride in his generals; he had selected them, fired the incompetent and promoted the competent. Simultaneously he redisciplined the men by subordinating political commissars to military officers. In November 1942, the Kremlin announced through Pravda that "the soldier has no socialistic obligations whatever, his job was simply to serve the fatherland as his forebears had done." Red army regulations were remodeled after those of Peter the Great. Guard regiments and divisions were created with names reminiscent of Imperial Russia.

The military orders of the great Czarist generals, Suvorov and Kutusov, were revived. The Cossack formations once despised as symbols of oppression were reinstituted.

During the last three months of 1942, Anglo-American forces also had been successful. In October, General Montgomery began his advance from El Alamein; in November, Anglo-American armies under General Eisenhower landed in North Africa. Admiral King was steadily clearing Atlantic coastal waters of U-boats; Halsey and Vandergrift were forcing the Japanese out of Guadalcanal; and MacArthur was strengthening his grip on New Guinea.

In January 1943, in conference at Casablanca, the President and Prime Minister agreed upon the following military objectives for the calendar year: first, control of the sea without which neither ground nor air troops could be transported overseas; second, assistance to Russia, qualified by the phrase "in relation to other commitments," which reduced its importance; third, the assault on Sicily, tentatively set for July; fourth, American forces in the United Kingdom would be increased, with a view to operations against the Channel Islands and a landing on the Cotentin Peninsula on August 1; in the Pacific operations were planned from Midway Islands toward Truk and Guam and to reconquer Burma.

At this conference the President demanded the "unconditional surrender" of enemy states as the price of peace. Roosevelt subsequently insisted on fulfilling the formula and Churchill loyally agreed. On its conclusion, messages were cabled to Chiang and Stalin. The latter replied, "It is my understanding that . . . you have set yourselves the task of crushing Germany by opening a second front in Europe *in 1943*" (italics supplied) and requested further information of the proposed operations and their schedule. He added that the Red armies will do their utmost to maintain the campaign against Germany but "our troops are now tired . . . and will be unable to continue the offensive beyond the middle of February."

In mid-February 1943, just as the Red army offensive ground

to a very successful close, United States troops in Tunisia were defeated at Faïd and Kasserine Pass and yielded some hard-won terrain. Hitler was reinforcing the Germans in Tunisia, and the Nazis recaptured Kharkov in the Ukraine. Stalin asked Churchill and Roosevelt embarrassing questions. The President again assured the Red Prime Minister that the American forces would be sent to Europe as soon as possible "to reduce the Axis forces opposing your heroic army." On March 8, Admiral Standley informed American correspondents in Moscow that while Russia was getting large quantities of American supplies, the Kremlin was telling Russians that they were fighting the war unassisted. In White House circles Standley's statement was considered in bad taste; he was summoned to Washington for consultation. Yet at that very time in London, Maisky, the Russian Ambassador, was complaining to American correspondents of the inadequacy of our aid. From London, Harriman reported that many of his friends, British and American, felt that Standley's action was well taken. They were convinced that there would be trouble in the future if Americans allowed themselves to be kicked around by Russians.

In the spring of 1943 when it was evident that the invasion of Europe could not be undertaken until 1944, the U.S. Chiefs of Staff suggested the over-all strategy should be changed from "To defeat Germany first and then Japan" to: to bring the war to a successful conclusion at the earliest date practicable by concentrating "first on Germany and then Japan." Admiral King insisted that some of the air forces assigned to Europe on the assumption of its invasion in 1943, now postponed, be sent to the hard-pressed American forces in the Pacific. The British, until their hold on the Indian Ocean was threatened, had urged that "no U.S. forces should be sent to the Pacific" above a bare minimum to hold the positions then occupied. Admiral King insisted that enough forces be provided to "maintain unremitting pressure against the Japanese." King's view eventually prevailed in spite of determined efforts of the British Staff, spurred by Churchill to extend operations in the Mediterranean and postpone the cross-channel invasion. This difference of opinion prevailed throughout the war.

On May 11, 1943, the day before von Arnim surrendered in Tunisia, Churchill, accompanied by 100 advisers, arrived in Washington. During a two-week conference Anglo-American leaders decided that during 1943 they would increase the air-bombardment of Germany, invade Italy, occupy the Azores, destroy the Ploesti oil wells in Rumania, and prepare for a cross-channel invasion *in May 1944*. In the Pacific area they proposed to expel the Japanese from the Aleutian, Marshall, Caroline, and Solomon islands and the Bismarck Archipelago, while carrier task forces and submarines operated against enemy sea communications.

The operations of Admiral Nimitz and General MacArthur had been subordinated to those in the Atlantic in order to insure the safety of the British Isles and assist the Red army. They could have begun their offensive earlier if they had been given the additional ships, planes, tanks, and ground troops that were being sent to Europe. American military chiefs had disagreed with the British estimate of the comparative importance of the Near East and Far East before our entry into the war but had been compelled to yield to Churchill.

Roosevelt, disturbed by the growing rift with Stalin, arranged a personal conference alone with the Red Prime Minister, hoping he could settle many troublesome problems. Churchill resented the President's action, although he and Stalin had met together without Roosevelt. When Stalin received the report of the Anglo-American plans for 1943 he was incensed at the delay of the cross-channel invasion until 1944, and questioned the good faith of the western Allies in a dispatch to Churchill, who sent a stinging reply. Whereupon Stalin recalled Soviet Ambassadors from London and Washington and canceled his meeting with Roosevelt.

The breach between Russia and the Anglo-Americans widened when an Italian general brought informal offers of surrender of Italy. Stalin was immediately informed of the proposals but could not rid his mind of suspicion that the western powers were ready to make a separate peace with Germany.

Stalin had no reason for suspicion but some reason for irritation. While the situation of the Red armies was better in the early summer of 1943 than in the autumn of 1941, they had only retaken territory lost in the summer of 1942, and not a British or American soldier had been landed in Europe. There was a fundamental cause for Stalin's suspicion and the eventual breach between Russia and the western powers. The Anglo-American-Russian agreements were based solely on their fears of the Nazis; as the Wehrmacht weakened so did this unnatural alliance.

When the Prime Minister and President with a caravan of advisers met in Quebec in mid-summer 1943 the long battle against the U-boats in the Atlantic had been won; American shipyards were launching an unprecedented tonnage. Italy had surrendered. Portugal had agreed to lend bases in the Azores. Beginning in July the Red armies in a succession of victories over the Nazis had liberated an area 700 miles long and in many places 180 miles deep. Red armies were still more numerous than the German; but even more important, their High Command had greatly improved and was capable of directing mechanized and motorized armies, and equaled if not excelled the Nazis in the employment of massed artillery. The Axis Powers were visibly weakening. Hitler had loyally assisted Mussolini in his vain effort to hold Italian North Africa by sending him Rommel with Panzer Divisions and Stuka Bombers. After Mussolini was displaced by a palace coup d'etat in July 1943, Hitler rescued him from capture and established a shadow Fascist Government in North Italy. Anglo-American sea power prevented any military cooperation between Berlin and Tokyo. Some strategic material was exchanged by U-boats and armed merchantmen but the effort was too costly; Japan and Germany exchanged information but fought separate wars.

In June 1941 aid was rushed to Russia on account of her weakness just to keep her in the war. Manifestly that argument had no validity in August 1943. Hopkins and ranking officers in the army were ready with another argument taken "from a very high level United States military strategic estimate." This document was being passed around by Hopkins at Quebec when word was received from Moscow that Stalin had agreed to a meeting of American, British, and Russian Foreign Ministers in Moscow in October. According to Sherwood, this news was greeted enthusiastically "for it meant the *beginning* (italics supplied) of the long-desired collaboration between the Big Three." Sherwood's comment proves that for almost two years of war there had been no collaboration. This implication was overlooked in the hopes raised when Stalin kindly permitted Hull and Eden to come to Moscow. In the happy atmosphere thus created, Hopkins passed around among the delegates the memorandum extracted from a high level army estimate of the strategic situation.

Sherwood says this document was of great importance for it shaped the policy which guided American delegates making decisions at Teheran and Yalta. As these decisions had a profound effect on the course of the war and postwar conditions, the document is quoted in full.

Russia's Position in Europe

Russia's postwar position in Europe will be a dominant one. With Germany crushed, there is no power in Europe to oppose her tremendous military forces. It is true that Great Britain is building up a position in the Mediterranean vis-a-vis Russia that she may find useful in balancing power in Europe. However, even here she may not be able to oppose Russia unless she is otherwise supported.

The conclusions from the foregoing are obvious. Since Russia is the decisive factor in the war, she must be given every assistance and every effort must be made to obtain her friendship. Likewise, since without question she will dominate Europe on the defeat of the Axis, it is even more essential to develop and maintain the most friendly relations with Russia.

Finally, the most important factor the United States has to consider in relation to Russia is the prosecution of the war in the Pacific. With Russia as an ally in the war against Japan, the war can be terminated in less time and at less expense in life and resources than if the reverse were the case. Should the war in the Pacific have to be carried on with an unfriendly or a negative attitude on the part of Russia, the difficulties will be immeasurably increased and operations might become abortive.

General Marshall was present at this conference, where he was considered to be the prospective Commander of Overlord. He was on intimate terms with Hopkins; he must have been aware of the document and, if it did not represent the views of the War Department, he could have disavowed it. Apparently he said nothing, because Stettinius later corroborated Sherwood's assertion that the document foreshadowed the policy that guided American representatives at Teheran and Yalta.

The document was essentially defeatist. Experts in the War Department in July 1941 had predicted the collapse of Russia within six weeks; two years later they went to the other extreme and could only visualize Red armies astride a prostrate Asia and Europe. British authorities agreed. From South Africa, General Smuts warned Churchill in September 1943 that "in the postwar world Russia will be 'diplomatic master' of the world." Churchill replied in two days agreeing "that Russia will be the greatest land power in the world" after the war "which will have rid her" of Germany and Japan the military powers who "had previously defeated her." The Prime Minister hoped that fraternal association of Great Britain and the United States together with sea and air power "may put us on good terms, and in a friendly balance with Russia at least for the period of rebuilding." This letter shows that Churchill agreed with Hopkins' memorandum.

Influential army officers in Australia and Washington were convinced that the Japanese could only be defeated by first invading Japan and then destroying her armies in China and Manchuria. The failure of the army High Command in the Pentagon and General MacArthur to appreciate the vulnerability of Japan, an insular empire dependent upon supplies from overseas, added support to this almost unbelievable policy of appeasing Russia.

Many naval officers in Washington did not agree with Hopkins' document. Most of them were convinced that Russia needed the support of the United Nations more than they (the United Nations) needed that of Russia. The navy thought we had heard too much of Red contribution to victory and too little of the Anglo-American. They feared that if the Anglo-American representatives continued to extol Russia's effort and apologize for their own, Stalin would demand more and more concessions.

They proposed to tell the Kremlin that we would not attempt to impose on them but would not be stupid enough to let Russia impose upon us. At that time the Russians had reached the line of the Dnieper; when they reached the Dniester or raised the siege of Leningrad, many naval officers were convinced that if, at that time, Russia did not declare war on Japan the United States should divert all supplies going to Russia to west Europe or the Pacific.

Military decisions at Quebec in 1943 included reaffirmation of May 1, 1944, as the target date for the landing in Normandy with an American, presumably General Marshall, as Supreme Commander; the establishment of the Southwest Asia Command under Lord Mountbatten as Supreme Allied Commander with General Stilwell as Deputy SAC. Among the top heavy, complicated organizations that mushroomed under Marshall's sponsorship was that of General Stilwell, who was commanding the American troops in China, Chief of Staff for Chiang Kai-shek and deputy to Admiral Lord Louis Mountbatten who was Supreme Allied Commander. Marshall was never content until he had obtained the appointment of a Supreme Commander over land, sea, and air forces and he usually recommended a general for the post.

This is a convenient point to summarize Marshall's extension of the doctrine of unity of command until this military absurdity exploded. When General Eisenhower was given command of the Anglo-American forces in North Africa, Roosevelt and Churchill agreed that a British officer would command the invasion forces landing in France. As the operation was postponed the numbers of American troops available to participate increased until they exceeded the British shortly after landing. At Quebec Churchill generously suggested to the President that an American be chosen as supreme commander; Roosevelt agreed and Churchill assumed, as did most others, that it would be Marshall. Roosevelt did not commit himself.

Sometime later the U.S. Joint Chiefs of Staff sought to extend Marshall's unity of command doctrine so that the Supreme Commander of the landing in Normandy (the operation known as "Overlord") should also command the Mediterranean. It was Churchill's understanding that Roosevelt desired Marshall to command both theaters. On November 8, 1943, he cabled Field Marshal Dill to tell Leahy that he would not consent. Leahy replied that that would end the matter. According to Churchill, at Cairo on November 25 the American Chiefs of Staff still felt strongly that a Supreme Commander should be appointed to command all the United Nations operations *against Germany* from the Atlantic and Mediterranean. This would include all air and naval operations; both Churchill and the British Joint Chiefs of Staff gave excellent reasons for opposing such a plan.

Churchill pointed out that the Supreme Commander, British or American, would have to work under general directives prescribed by the Combined Chiefs of Staff and under political conditions fixed by the heads of government. He would be responsible for announcing decisions and then risk being disavowed. Churchill questioned "whether any single officer exists who would be capable of giving decisions over the vast range of problems now being dealt with by the British and American Governments assisted by the Combined Chiefs of Staff." This last observation alone should have terminated Marshall's endless arrangements for extensions of command.

As Marshall claimed he was animated by military reasons, it is well to add the objection offered by British Joint Chiefs of Staff, all highly competent military officers, with more experience as field commanders than Marshall. They reminded Marshall that his argument was based on his slender experience in war on the staff of General Pershing on the western front; then they stated "that there is no real analogy between the position of Marshal Foch and the position now contemplated for the Supreme Commander against Germany . . . Foch was only responsible for the western front and the Italian front. His authority did not extend to Saloniki, Palestine or Mesopotamia [or to the Allied fleets. W.D.P.]. Under the arrangement contemplated [by Marshall] the Supreme Commander will have . . . Overlord . . . the Italian Front . . . the Balkan Front . . . and the Turkish Front if it is opened." They then added "There must be some limit to the responsibilities which Allied Governments can delegate to a single soldier. . . ." *

Most who know Marshall agree that he is a modest gentleman. At the time the Joint Chiefs of Staff under his prodding made this recommendation, he was assumed to be the prospective Supreme Commander. In all probability his suggestion was not inspired by personal vanity or vaulting ambition, but was due to his unlimited confidence in the General Staff system. He was convinced that any outstanding general who could command ground troops could, with equal competence, command air and sea forces if he had representatives of these branches on his staff. Marshall had never commanded in the field in war; he had never experienced the difficulty a commanding general has in reaching decisions involving technical questions of which he has had no personal experience. So he blithely added sea and air problems, for he was honestly convinced that with a proper staff a competent general could command anything and everything. Like Archimedes, he felt he could move the world with a general as a fulcrum and a general staff as a lever if he could find a place for the fulcrum, and a long enough lever.

Churchill had accepted Marshall's suggestion in 1942 when he made Wavell Supreme Commander, but mainly to please Hopkins. At Cairo in November 1943, Churchill still had hopes of diverting troops, planes, and landing craft from the Normandy invasion to the eastern Mediterranean and the Prime Minister had no intention of yielding to Marshall who opposed such diversion. Be it said for the British Joint Staff that they objected both in Washington and in Cairo. Afterward Churchill attributed Roosevelt's final choice of Eisenhower instead of Marshall for the command to the President's feeling that command of the invasion of France alone was not important enough to justify Marshall's departure from Washington.

* *Closing the Ring*, by Sir Winston Churchill, Chapter 17, pp. 301-341.

Certainly the President had the highest regard for Marshall; to console him for not getting a field command, he told Marshall, "I could not sleep at night with you out of the country." Marshall undoubtedly had looked forward to leading in battle the army he had done so much to recruit and train for the relief of Europe from Hitler's domination. But he was loyal to the President; he would not say which position he preferred and insisted that the President make the decision and refused "to . . . estimate his own capabilities." Admiral King openly opposed Marshall's transfer from the Joint Chiefs of Staff, advising the President "not to break up a winning team."

King himself had been urged by some of his friends to take personal command of the United States fleet in the Pacific for he was the only naval officer whose rank and prestige compared with MacArthur's and that, therefore, only he could get proper consideration for naval factors in the Pacific. They also reminded him that his own future reputation as an Admiral demanded that he show his capacity to command a fleet in battle. He resisted both arguments saying that he had carefully considered the question and had decided his presence in Washington was more essential to victory than to command the United States fleet at sea. There was no question that King was needed in Washington, but he was badly needed in the Pacific to restrain MacArthur. It would have been well for the nation if the navy had had at its disposal two Admiral Kings.

Many naval officers completely disagreed with Marshall's idea of unity of command when it involved land, sea, and air forces engaged in overseas amphibious landings. They were convinced that command of mixed forces should pass back and forth, always keeping officers of 'paramount capability' and experience in command at each stage of operations, admirals at sea, and generals of the army or marines ashore. There was no permanent 'unity of command' in the Pacific; neither by the Japanese in their very successful offensives in the first six months of the war or in the subsequent American victories that regained control of the Pacific. In neither Japanese nor American joint operations did an admiral exercise command of soldiers ashore or a general of sailors afloat.

MacArthur was in operational command of the Southwest Pacific and Nimitz in operational command of the Central Pacific. An admiral commanded an amphibious force while the troops were embarked, during the landing, and until they were firmly established in their immediate and principal objectives along the shore. When the commander of the ground troops, a general of the army or marines, believed he could maintain his position, he took command ashore, and the admiral continued to be responsible for supplying the forces. For example, in the landing in Normandy a British admiral was in tactical command of the ships, a British air marshal of the planes, and, until General Eisenhower moved his headquarters in Normandy and took command of all the armies, General Montgomery was in tactical command of the ground troops. After General Eisenhower was securely established ashore, the Anglo-American fleets became responsible to the admiralty and to the American admiral in London for maintaining the sea communications of the armies ashore. Similarly in the invasion of Leyte, Admiral Kinkaid, not General MacArthur, was in command en route from the Bismarck Archipelago to Leyte of the amphibious movement and landing; of amphibious operations; and his command continued until the ground and air troops were established ashore.

No American landing was repulsed either in the Atlantic or Pacific. If one had been the command would have passed back to the admiral, who would have become responsible for re-embarking and evacuating the soldiers and escorting them safely to their base. Catch phrases and loose military terminology have left an erroneous impression on Americans of amphibious operations. Of all catch phrases, 'unity of command' has propagated the most dangerous ideas. It has led Americans to believe that their sons (and now also daughters) can safely be submitted to the orders of officers who are not technically qualified to estimate the situation and to reach sound military decisions.

The establishment of the Department of National Defense is the natural climax of this doctrinaire idea; and Marshall, the chief proponent of unity of command, was its indefatigable advocate. Forrestal, one of the ablest Secretaries of the Navy, has recorded in his diary that it required him two and one-half years to acquire a fractional knowledge of the Navy Department. By using misleading army slogans and by gagging naval officers, Congress was beguiled into arbitrarily merging three huge services and then expecting a President every three or four years to find a civilian, who at most could be partly acquainted with one branch, to direct this triphibious behemoth. A fly going around on a wagon wheel has as much control of the wagon as the ablest Secretary of Defense can ever have over the huge Department of Defense. Presidents or Chairmen of the Boards of Directors of our huge corporations usually have grown up with their organization from early manhood. Only by a ruthless policy of selection do they reach the top. Then they are surrounded by trained assistants, who have risen to the next lower echelon. They can decide from experience whether the advice they get from subordinates is sound. Under the former organization of the armed forces, in three departments a civilian Secretary was surrounded by officers fully acquainted with their own branch. Even then Forrestal found the task difficult and was frank and modest enough to say so. It is no reflection on the extremely capable heads of our vast and usually efficiently run corporations to say that it is as absurd to expect one of them to direct efficiently and economically the Department of Defense as it would be to expect a successful combat general, admiral or air marshal to direct the operations of Standard Oil of New Jersey or General Motors Corporation.

Once in 1942, twice in 1943, Stalin declined to participate in personal conferences with Roosevelt and Churchill. Finally Secretary Hull persuaded him to attend the Teheran Conference in November 1943. En route Churchill and Roosevelt conferred with Chiang Kai-shek at Cairo, but even at that late date the cautious Stalin refused to parley with Chiang for fear of offending Japan. On November 28, 1943, Stalin and the President met for the first time; for forty-five minutes they discussed military operations in Russia, the situation in France and the Far East, and British problems in India. After warning Stalin against discussing India with Churchill, the President told him that reform in India would have to start at the bottom; Stalin predicted that such procedure would lead to revolution.

At the suggestion of his colleagues, Roosevelt presided over their plenary sessions. Feeling that Stalin did not appreciate the American effort in the Pacific, Roosevelt first reviewed naval operations in that ocean after Pearl Harbor and gave a preview of Anglo-American plans to open the Burma Road and to continue aid to Chiang. Next he emphasized that together with Churchill he had been planning a second front in Europe and that the invasion of Normandy had been set for May 1944.

Stalin explained that Red forces in Siberia were only sufficient for defense but promised that after the defeat of the Germans they would be reinforced and then he would declare war on Japan. Churchill reverted to his plan for drawing Turkey into the war; his success in getting the United States in the war spurred him on, but Turkey was too wary. Roosevelt mentioned the possibility of assisting Tito's partisans in Yugoslavia. Stalin urged them to use all available forces in the Normandy invasion and to land an auxiliary army in south France as soon as Rome was captured.

Stalin had a clearer understanding of the strategic factors than either of his colleagues. He doubted Roosevelt's observation that Hitler was mentally unbalanced, asserting that only a very able leader could have solidified the German people. Obviously Stalin considered that Hitler's only irretrievable blunder was the invasion of Russia. In the conversation after dinner Stalin agreed with Roosevelt that free navigation through the approaches to the Baltic Sea were desirable but questioned the doctrine of 'unconditional surrender' because it would delay German capitulation.

On November 29, Stalin and Roosevelt had another forty-five-minute conversation. They discussed terms for Russian assistance against the Japanese, the use of Russian bases for American planes, and finally reached the subject most important to the President, the establishment of the United Nations. Their conversation is covered thoroughly in the next chapter, because it illuminates the means employed by the President and the arguments he offered to gain the adherence of Russia to the new organization.

It is only necessary here to record that, for his pledge to support the United Nations, Stalin was assured of an invasion of France that gave his armies a freer hand in the Balkans, of an increased American effort in the Pacific that insured the defeat of Japan, of the disarmament of both Germany and Japan, and the dismemberment of Germany which, by relieving Russia of two strong neighbors, assured her predominance in Europe during the postwar era.

All of these benefits were showered on Russia by Roosevelt to gain his consent to the formation of the United Nations. As a bonus Churchill and Roosevelt on November 30 added the port of Darien in Manchuria. Stalin accepted and later obtained the signatures of his colleagues to the bargain. In the final plenary session Stalin was given one third of the Italian fleet and a vague agreement on the frontiers of Poland, but views of the Big Three on German dismemberment could not be reconciled.

Fourteen months elapsed between the conference at Teheran and the one at Yalta in February 1945. During this time allied victories in Europe liberated countries previously occupied by Nazis creating new and difficult problems among the Allies just as the increasing prospect of victory continued to loosen the only bond holding them together. During this same period the presidential nomination and election and the effort to found the United Nations required much of the President's attention. After the Republicans nominated Governor Dewey, according to Sherwood,* Roosevelt "had to conduct a vigorous campaign" for the fourth term and he felt "it to his political disadvantage" to meet Stalin in Russia. Stalin refused to leave Russia, and the conference was postponed until after the election. The President, realizing that Harry Hopkins was a political liability, kept him under cover during the campaign; but after July 4, Hopkins was convalescing in his Georgetown home in easy reach when needed, and in close touch with intimate friends in the departments, bureaus, commissions, and agencies who had important roles in directing the war.

By June, MacArthur and Halsey had isolated Japanese forces

* *Roosevelt and Hopkins*, by Robert Sherwood, p. 844.

in the Bismarck and Solomon Islands. Eisenhower launched the cross-channel invasion of Normandy; Spruance landed General Smith in the Marianas. Stalin made good his pledge to synchronize his summer offensive. On June 27 Cherbourg surrendered. The rapid advance of Anglo-American armies and the attempted assassination of Hitler caused many Anglo-American officers to predict victory by Christmas. In an exact ratio as the Nazi control of Europe decreased, the Communist threat increased. Churchill had witnessed the revival of prewar rivalries between France and England when the German collapse in 1918 sundered the only tie that had held them together. Its recollection may have alerted him to critical situations that were bound to occur as the armed forces of the United Nations continued their victories.

As early as May 4, 1944, Churchill warned Eden that the Russian advance in the Balkans had raised the question whether Britain should acquiesce in the communization of the Balkans and perhaps Italy. Communist intrigues in Italy, Yugoslavia, and Greece were making a decision necessary; Churchill added that they must consult the United States first. Two weeks later at Eden's invitation, the Russian Ambassador discussed at the Foreign Office a British proposal that the Soviet consider Rumanian affairs as their concern and leave Greece to the British. The Russian envoy was agreeable but immediately inquired if the British had consulted the United States. Not until May 31 did the Prime Minister request the President's approval. The State Department expressed its dislike of creating spheres of influence in the Balkans. On June 11, Roosevelt replied directly to Churchill suggesting 'consultative machinery' to restrain the development of military agreements into permanent spheres of influence.

In spite of this objection, the President on June 13 agreed to Churchill's arrangements for "three months." With this encouragement, on June 23 in a long, persuasively worded message, Churchill pleaded that he and "Uncle Joe" be allowed to settle the fate of the Balkans, reminding the President that he had not informed Churchill of his conversations with Stalin about the Poles. Churchill reported that the Russians insisted on consulting the Americans directly, although in July the Prime Minister had informed Stalin that he had the President's approval for a three months' trial of a Russo-British dual arrangement for Rumania and Greece. In the same message he asked Stalin to consider the question of persuading Turkey to break relations with Germany, as the first step toward war. He offered these thoughts as his personal ideas. Stalin replied that the American Government had doubts concerning the Anglo-Russian arrangement for Rumania.

The American Joint Chiefs of Staff differed fundamentally on the most effective means of compelling Japan to surrender unconditionally. Navy members realized that Japan could be defeated by a sea blockade assisted by heavy air bombardments. The army members not only insisted upon an invasion of Japanese islands but were further convinced that Russian assistance was needed in order to defeat or contain the Japanese army in Manchuria. It is known now and was estimated then that Japan had withdrawn many troops and planes from China during the course of the war.

In July after securing the Democratic nomination, the President, accompanied by Admirals Leahy and Brown, sailed for Honolulu where he conferred with Admiral Nimitz and General MacArthur. The conference was strictly military and naval. Admiral King was easily available for this meeting, but the President knew he was in favor of by-passing Luzon and landing in Formosa. King was not invited to attend, although he was the President's senior naval adviser and the problem was preponderantly naval.

According to Leahy, "MacArthur was convinced that occupation of the Philippines was essential before any major attack in force should be made on Japanese-held territory north of Luzon." Nimitz disagreed and developed the navy's plan of by-passing the Philippines and attacking Formosa. Nor did Nimitz see that "Luzon, including Manila Bay, had advantages that were not possessed by other areas in the Philippines that could be taken for a base at less cost in lives and material." The President decided in favor of taking Luzon and occupying the Philippines. Not only did this decision cause unnecessary loss of American lives, but stubborn Japanese resistance to American reoccupation of

Luzon resulted in enormous destruction of property and lives of Filipino civilians.

At the *second* Quebec Conference in September 1944, the President and Churchill initialed the "Morgenthau Plan" for destroying future German war potential while the Combined Chiefs of Staff perfected plans for the invasion of Japan. The British and American Ambassadors reported these plans to Stalin on September 23. No reference had been made to Soviet participation in the attack on Japan; Stalin tartly informed the envoys that if the western allies preferred to defeat Japan unaided he was agreeable.

Roosevelt contemplated a second conference with Churchill and Stalin. On the military side it was necessary to agree upon the date and extent of Russian participation in the campaign against Japan. Political questions still unsettled were the postwar status of Germany, including the extent of reparations, zones of occupation, treatment of war criminals; the Polish government and frontiers; the place of France in Europe; and the voting procedure in the United Nations. But Roosevelt still thought it unwise to leave the country to confer with Stalin during a presidential campaign. Churchill, also a practical politician, appreciated Roosevelt's dilemma. He cabled the President that Red armies would not halt their advance until American ballots were counted; and on September 29, in another long, persuasive cable, he endeavored to divert Roosevelt's attention from his campaign to the increasingly critical situation in Europe. Advising the President that he and Eden were considering a visit to Moscow, he gave the following objectives: to clinch Red entry into the war against Japan which had already been pledged; and to settle the Polish problem amicably; apparently as an afterthought, Churchill added the most important point that while there they would discuss with Stalin points concerning Yugoslavia and Greece.

On October 3, Roosevelt had prepared a cable to Churchill implying his willingness to let Churchill speak for the President in his approaching conference with Stalin. When Hopkins heard of it, perhaps through his protégé Charles E. Bohlen, liaison officer between White House and State Department, he took the extraordinary liberty of stopping the dispatch. Then he went to the

President and persuaded him to alter the message entirely. The revised message said that the President would consider Churchill and Stalin's talks "as preliminary" to a meeting with all three as soon as the election was over. Then he asked that "Mr. Harriman be present." There was certain justification for Hopkins' recommendation and the President's action. Churchill always reserved full rights to talk on any subject directly to Stalin and already had stretched the President's reluctant acquiescence to deal directly with Stalin in the Balkans to include attempts to get Turkey in the war. Roosevelt's action left Stalin free to overrun eastern Europe. On the other hand, if Churchill had been permitted he would have dispersed forces all over the eastern Mediterranean.* In any event Harriman attended the meetings and Roosevelt's message gave Stalin much satisfaction as indicating a rift in Anglo-American relations.

The message corrected Stalin's impression "that Churchill had been authorized to speak for Roosevelt as well as himself." Stalin could have gained this opinion by a sentence in a message Churchill had sent on September 27 when, after long talks "with the President" at Quebec, he assured Stalin of their joint "intense conviction" that the hopes of the world depended on the agreement of the Big Three, that a conference of them was necessary and that the "President intended to visit" England immediately after his election, win or lose. Also after receiving Roosevelt's message that Harriman would be an observer, Churchill cabled back that he was sure the President would not object to private conversations "between me and Uncle Joe, or Anthony (Eden) and Molotov." As Roosevelt had made a special point of holding private conversations with Stalin at Teheran, in which he made some uncomplimentary remarks about Churchill, he was in no position to object.

The temerity of Hopkins in delaying a personal message from the President to Churchill shows that he still enjoyed Roosevelt's confidence and that his numerous friends in key positions kept him informed of current events. It also indicates that Hopkins pre-

* *Roosevelt and Hopkins,* by Robert Sherwood, Harper & Brothers, pp. 833-834.

ferred Stalin to Churchill and had succumbed entirely to the pro-Russian atmosphere in Washington that he himself had done much to create. In September 1944 Secretary of the Navy Forrestal wrote a friend that "if any American suggests that we act in accord with our own interests he is apt to be called a . . . fascist or imperialist, while if Uncle Joe suggests that he needs the Baltic provinces, half of Poland, all of Bessarabia and access to the Mediterranean, all hands in Washington agree that he is a fine, frank, candid and generally delightful fellow who is very easy to deal with because he is so explicit in what he wants." *

By October 1, 1944, onrushing Red armies occupied Bulgaria, most of Estonia, Lithuania, and Poland to the Vistula; they had entered Hungary, Yugoslavia, and reached the frontiers of Greece and Turkey. British troops had been landed in Greece. As British and Russian troops liberated inhabitants of these countries some confusion was inevitable. The disorder was increased by the traditional Anglo-Russian rivalry in the Balkans in spite of Churchill's efforts to reach agreements with Stalin. Stalin and Churchill had agreed that in Bulgaria, Hungary, and Rumania the Soviet Union would have 75 to 80 per cent, the British 25 to 20 per cent, predominance; in Yugoslavia they would share 50-50; and the British would have full control in Greece. European statesmen were all accustomed to delimiting spheres of influence and, regarded simply as an arrangement between two countries liberating other countries from enslavement, it was a fair division. Apparently it was agreeable to both participants because, before leaving, Churchill got Stalin to pledge that Russia would take the offensive against Japan in Manchuria, three months after the defeat of Germany, provided the "political aspects of Russia's participation were clarified"; which meant that the good old paymaster, Uncle Sam, would provide Russia with munitions and supplies.

Anglo-American troops had by Christmas liberated most of Italy, Belgium, and parts of Holland. In November, Stettinius thought the British officials in Greece, Italy, and Belgium were supporting the conservative elements in these countries and attrib-

* *Forrestal Diaries*, edited by Walter Mills and E. S. Duffield, Viking Press. Entry made on 2 September 1944.

uted their actions to Churchill's desire to preserve the limited constitutional monarchies that prevailed before the war. In December, Stettinius stated officially that "the composition of the Italian government was purely an Italian affair." As his remark was evidently addressed to British officials in Italy, Churchill was indignant and informed Roosevelt he would reply in the House of Commons. He did. Relations were further strained between Roosevelt and the Prime Minister. According to his son Elliott, the President was outraged because he thought British troops were killing "Greek guerrillas who had fought the Nazis for four years." Almost simultaneously in a speech in Commons explaining the situation in Poland, Churchill left the impression of "secret agreements" among the Big Three at Teheran. Roosevelt was being accused in Washington of making secret agreements with Stalin. Being vulnerable to this attack he was increasingly indignant with Churchill. Hopkins in a carefully worded cable mediated. Churchill flew to Athens and arranged a truce between the two Greek factions; better feeling then prevailed. In addition to other liaison activities immediately after Roosevelt's re-election, Hopkins began arranging with Ambassador Gromyko the long awaited conference between the Big Three which took place at Yalta.

Domestic problems occupied most of the President's time until his inaugural, at which his physical appearance frightened many observers including Mrs. Frances Perkins and Mrs. Henry Morgenthau. The following day Harry Hopkins left by plane for London for preliminary talks with Churchill; on January 23, the President with Mr. Byrnes, Admiral Leahy, and other advisers sailed for Malta where they were joined by Hopkins and the new Secretary of State, the Honorable Edward Stettinius. The most exact record of Yalta is by Byrnes who kept stenographic notes; accounts by Stettinius, Leahy, and Churchill are in substantial agreement. Mr. Byrnes confirms the President's poor physical condition that confined him to his cabin and only permitted him four or five discussions with Byrnes and Leahy on the voyage. Hopkins too was ill when he arrived in Malta from London and departed shortly after for Yalta. Byrnes in the few conferences with the President found he had made little preparation for his talks with Stalin and Churchill; not until after his arrival in Malta did Byrnes have access to the State Department's well-prepared agenda.

This lack of preparation did not affect Roosevelt's actions. His purpose at Yalta, as at Teheran, was to gain and to keep Stalin's support for the United Nations. If he had been fully briefed he would have made the same decisions. Byrnes stated only the rapid advance of our armies caused the President to give "urgent attention . . . to European military and political problems." Stettinius and Judge Sam Rosenman, editor of Roosevelt's papers and speeches, confirm Brynes' statement. The immediate objective of Roosevelt was to get Stalin to overrule the Soviet Delegation at Dumbarton Oaks and agree to the President's agreement fixing the voting procedure of the Security Council. Stalin had not read the proposal, but when he did he emphasized his interest saying, "all questions are decided by votes and we are interested in decisions not discussions."

Stalin was familiar with and had positive views on the composition of the Polish Government, the future frontiers of Germany, Poland, and Russia, and German reparations. Stalin made it clear that he would have nothing to do with the Polish Shadow Government that had fled to London after Russo-German occupation of Poland and maintained the war against Germany. Churchill felt very strongly that its members should participate in the new government. This question was shuffled over to the Foreign Ministers for further study; while they studied Stalin installed his committee to govern Poland.

Stalin indignantly refused the timid suggestions of Roosevelt and Churchill that Poland retain Lvov and its adjacent oil fields, asserting that he would not dare to return to Moscow if he agreed. He also displayed impatience when Roosevelt opposed his request for two extra votes in the General Assembly for Soviet Russia. Hopkins became alarmed and penciled a note to the President to "get this problem referred to the foreign ministers before there is trouble." Roosevelt did so. On the big question of reparations Stalin demanded 10 billion dollars. Churchill objected, pointing out that it had been impossible to obtain half that sum from Germany after World War I. Stalin contended that he could get that much "reparations in kind" by confiscating German factories, machine tools, railway rolling stock and investments in foreign countries. This argument continued throughout the conference. On the last day, Hopkins penciled another memorandum to Roosevelt saying, "Mr. President: The Russians have given in so much at this conference that I don't think we should let them down. Let the British disagree if they want to—and continue this disagreement at Moscow. Simply say it is all referred to the Reparations Committee with the minutes to show that the British disagree about any mention of 10 billion." Byrnes recorded Roosevelt's subsequent statement made at Hopkins' suggestion that the Reparations Committtee take "as a basis for discussion the suggestion of the Soviet Government, that the total sum of reparations should be 20 billion and that 50 per cent should go to the Soviet Union." Thus Hopkins and Roosevelt gave Stalin ample reason for asserting that he had been promised 10 billion dollars in reparations.

The problem of reparations rapidly became academic, for as the Red armies occupied Germany and her former conquered states they took reparations in kind. To understand the atmosphere at Yalta it is necessary to note that in important questions Hopkins often intervened and always on behalf of Stalin. Stettinius also asserted that Russia made important concessions; he later acknowledged she did not keep them. Byrnes himself hailed Yalta as the high tide of Big Three Unity.

This is Stalin's record. He kept three pledges: to permit nations that declared war on the Axis by March 1, 1945, to join the United Nations as charter members; to grant France an occupation zone carved from the Anglo-American zones and a seat on the Control Council; during the last few weeks of war in Europe he coordinated movements of Red armies with Anglo-American. He delayed making air fields in Russia available for American planes until they were unnecessary. His delegation at San Francisco refused to fulfill his promise to Roosevelt at Yalta until Hopkins personally intervened. Stalin broke his pledges: to admit members of the Polish shadow cabinet in London to the new government; to settle the Polish boundaries at a peace conference; and to permit peoples liberated from Nazi control by Red troops to elect their governments; instead army commanders installed Soviet regimes.

Stettinius defended the agreements reached at Yalta asserting it was Stalin's failure to keep his promises that caused the trouble. That raises another question: Why did Roosevelt, Stettinius, Byrnes, Hopkins, and others trust Stalin's promises? He had repeatedly failed to keep them before. Stettinius had no reason to trust any promises of Stalin. General Deane, army representative in Moscow, reported to Washington just prior to the Yalta Conference that a Russian agreement in principle means exactly nothing; they are generous "in giving such agreements." But even after his return from Yalta Stettinius reported to Secretaries Stimson and Forrestal that there was every evidence at Yalta of Russian desire to cooperate along all lines with the United States.

Robert Sherwood, a stout supporter of Roosevelt, attributes his cosigning with Churchill the pledge to Stalin that the "claims of the Soviet Union shall be unquestionably filled after the defeat of Japan," to the fatigue which made him anxious to "avoid further argument." After the President made his formal report to Congress, secret parts of his agreements began to leak out. Soon the word "Yalta" assumed a sinister significance to Americans.

Admirers of the President can offer in his defense the insistence of high army officers that Russia's assistance was necessary both to invade Japan and then to defeat Nipponese armies in Manchuria before Japan would surrender unconditionally. Even here the President was partly responsible, for "unconditional surrender" was his personal suggestion. Stalin was better informed on the Japanese situation than the President or his army advisers. Before the army's long-range bombers and the carrier-based navy bombers began their final attacks on Japan, and at least a month before the A-bomb had devastated Hiroshima, the Emperor of Japan had requested Stalin to intervene to end the war. He delayed a reply to Tokyo; continued to receive supplies from the United States for a three months' campaign of thirty divisions; reinforced his divisions in Manchuria, and finally waged a week's campaign of rear-guard actions with retreating Japanese. The United States paid an excessive price to Russia primarily because Roosevelt accepted the advice of MacArthur and Marshall in preference to that of King and Nimitz. These generals, like many other army commanders, including Napoleon, were convinced that the only way to defeat a nation, even an insular Empire, is with huge armies.

The President could blame only himself for the sacrifices he made to get Stalin's support for the United Nations. This project like unconditional surrender was peculiarly his own. Roosevelt had less reason than any American official to trust Stalin. After he recognized Russia in 1933, only a few weeks had passed before the Red Ambassador flatly questioned the President's veracity in his own capital city. Yet he never abandoned his confidence in his ability to handle Stalin. Had he trusted his political opponents in the United States as he did Stalin, he never would have been elected Governor or President. In domestic campaigns he never let down his guard; he recognized instantly any political stratagem, but again and again he accepted at full value promises made by Stalin.

Only a few weeks elapsed between the President's report to Congress and his death. During this time Stalin cabled Roosevelt that "his action" in supporting the American acceptance of a German emissary "creates ground for mistrust." As near as he dared Stalin was questioning the President's truthfulness. In a second reply Stalin contradicted the President. Finally in a cable Roosevelt resented these "vile misrepresentations of my actions or of those of my trusted subordinates." On April 7 Stalin made a partial apology to Roosevelt declaring he had never doubted the President's honesty and dependability. Five days later on the day of his death the President sent a message to Ambassador Harriman to consider the incident closed. That same day, in answer to a query from Churchill, he replied: "I would minimize the general Soviet problem as much as possible . . . We must be firm, however, and our course thus far has been correct." As long as he lived President Roosevelt remained convinced of the wisdom of his policies and the necessity of acting as intermediary between Stalin and Churchill.

Rarely have such an oddly mated trio headed a great alliance during a global war. Between Teheran and Yalta, fourteen months, Churchill repeatedly reminded Roosevelt of the Kremlin's ambitions. During an election year, Roosevelt would take no political risks; otherwise Churchill might have opened his eyes to "Uncle Joe." But even after Yalta, Roosevelt was as suspicious of Great Britain as of Russia, stating at a Cabinet meeting in semijocular manner "that the British were perfectly willing for the United States to have a war with Russia any time . . ." * While jocular, the remark is entirely in accord with his confidential statements to his son Elliott at Cairo that the biggest thing he had done at Teheran "was to make it clear to Stalin that the United States and Great Britain were not allied . . . against Russia." In the President's own opinion his job was "to act as referee, as intermediary between Russia and England." In familiar fatherly talks with Elliott in the White House, the President, after his return, said he was "going to make the British fall in line with American thinking about colonies." Roosevelt's phobia against British colonies was a perpetual barrier between him and Churchill.

But it was the President's desire, bordering upon a mania for the United Nations, that caused him to make most concessions to Stalin—that and perhaps a certain sympathy with some of the aspects of communism. These two facets of his character led Roosevelt to add to the huge Russian Empire that was mainly composed of conquered countries forcibly embodied in the Russian Empire and inherited by Stalin; while on the contrary he continuously endeavored to make Churchill begin liquidating the British Empire by granting India her independence and internationalizing Hong Kong. Compared with the Russian Asiatic provinces under the Czars, governed by retired generals and later by Red Commissars, the most wretched bit of the British Empire was a model of good government. Roosevelt, while bent on destroying the British Empire, was willing for a few small conces-

* *Forrestal Diaries*, p. 36.

sions from Stalin for his United Nations to re-establish Russia in Manchuria. There was nothing consistent in Roosevelt's attitude toward the two empires, unless changing the name of Russian Empire to Soviet Republics reconciled him to the Red Empire.

When the Honorable Harry S. Truman succeeded to the Presidency, he brought with him considerable information of the American military establishment gained by a very thorough investigation he had made as Chairman of a Senate Committee. As Captain of an efficient battery of Missouri Field Artillery he had become well acquainted with land operations in World War I. But Roosevelt had almost ostentatiously excluded him from the top level conferences where United States policy and strategy were determined. Time was needed for him to acquaint himself with the diplomatic and military situation. But he had a clear idea of the heavy responsibilities of his office; he had shown during World War I a natural willingness to accept responsibility and as a Senator he had familiarized himself with government organization. Unlike Roosevelt, he preferred to use government departments and to follow prescribed channels of authority to carry out his policies.

It is not within the scope of this book to evaluate Truman's abilities as a war President. Only a few incidental references will be made to his Presidential decisions.

In the American tradition, Truman's first act was to invite the Cabinet members to remain and to announce that he would carry out the policies of his predecessor. In this spirit he informed both Russia and China that he would fulfill the promises made to Russia by Roosevelt. In other less important matters Truman was bound to accept previously made decisions. He could not be fairly criticized for carrying out half completed policies of Roosevelt. But he promptly showed Stalin that there was a new pilot at the helm when he refused point blank to recognize the Red puppet governments set up in the Balkans. In March 1947, he obtained Congressional approval to give military and economic assistance to the government of Greece threatened by bands of terrorists led by Communists. This was a reversal of Roosevelt's policy of supporting these forces who claimed they had fought Hitler's army of occupation. For almost the first time Stalin found that he could not change American policy.

As victory approached in the Far East, President Truman faced the same problem in China that Roosevelt had faced in Greece. The Chinese Communists, who had been openly defying Chiang Kai-shek, claimed to be resisting the Japanese and only seeking to obtain representation in the Kuomintang, a solution of the land problem, and a democratic form of government. Roosevelt had sent General Patrick J. Hurley as Ambassador to Chunking in the vain hope of uniting the Chinese factions. In November 1945, Hurley, convinced that some members of his staff in the Embassy were too friendly with the Reds and that he was not being supported by the State Department, submitted his resignation.

President Truman selected General Marshall to undertake the task laid down by Hurley. While Marshall was spending his days explaining to a Congressional Committee the reasons for his actions leading to the disasters in the Pacific in the winter of 1941-42, he was being briefed for his mission to China by the State, War, and Navy Departments. The industrious, patriotic Chief of Staff loyally undertook an impossible task. He would deserve entire sympathy for his failure had he not been primarily responsible for many of the decisions that led to the debacle in China. In 1941 he had supported General MacArthur and General Arnold's plan to defend not only Luzon but the southern islands with 100 bombers; he nominated Field Marshal Wavell as supreme commander of ABDA forces in the Far East; he had insisted that Russian assistance was essential to defeat Japan; throughout the war he limited the forces in the Pacific to over-insure success in Europe; and at the very end of the war he was chosen by the President to repair the result of a series of blunders to which he had largely contributed. In 1941 Secretary Hull had refused to consider the modus vivendi with Japan for fear of causing Chiang Kai-shek's defeat; yet after winning a war Truman's administration let the Russian and Chinese Communists unite to expel Chiang and the Nationalist Government from China.

In estimating Roosevelt's ability as a war President fairly, it is only just to consider the professional advice he received. The Joint Board headed by General Marshall and Admiral Stark and later the Joint Chiefs of Staff on several important problems either badly advised the President or accepted his decisions aware of their unwisdom. The most important of these have been related. As the individual officers signed Joint Staff decisions that they did not approve, it is impossible in many cases to fix personal responsibility; but in one case Admiral King was so strongly opposed to the decision reached he expressed his opposition publicly (see page 163). Admiral Leahy has recorded the limitations he placed on his recommendations to the President which effectively confined his role to liaison officer between the President and the Joint Chiefs of Staff. That left Generals Arnold and Marshall and Admiral King. It is easy to infer from the decisions finally reached which the Generals supported and Admiral King opposed; for the strategic concepts of each of them are well known. Summarizing, Arnold was convinced that Germany and Japan could be defeated by air power alone; King was convinced that Japan could be defeated by blockade and her surrender hastened by air attacks. He realized that the defeat of Germany would require large armies. Marshall believed that only massive infantry attacks could defeat either Germany or Japan; further, Marshall apparently accepted, for he never opposed, the opinion of General MacArthur that the invasion of Japan by American troops could not succeed unless it was accompanied by a Russian invasion of Manchuria either to defeat or to contain the Japanese armies in Manchuria. With these different views, defenders of the President's conduct of the war can justify many of his decisions by quoting advice from some member of the Joint Chiefs of Staff.

In all probability each member of the Joint Chiefs sincerely held the opinions they gave the President. It will be the same in a future war. Experts always differ, particularly experts on the conduct of war. The civilian Chief Executive should have a general knowledge of the science and art of war, and then he could anticipate and allow for the tendency of each of his military advisers to depend more upon a particular branch of the armed forces. Certainly it would be unfair to criticize President Roosevelt for accepting professional advice of the Joint Board from September 1939 to June 1940. But when the Chief of Staff of the Army was absolutely wrong about the ability of France to resist the Germans, the President should have been more wary about accepting his estimates of the resistance that Russia could offer to the Nazi invasion. And when Stark could only suggest provoking a war with Germany as the first step to prepare the navy for war, he should certainly have looked around for another Chief of Naval Operations.

Roosevelt did not need to be a military expert; he only had to recall the experience of President Lincoln to realize that very often generals or admirals who reached the top in time of peace lacked the more rugged character essential in a war. There is every reason for being charitable in judging the decisions made by Roosevelt based on bad professional advice. But it should not be forgotten that he "did not like opposition too well," which means he preferred compliant advisers. It is impossible to justify his frequent strategic suggestions to Admirals Stark and Richardson that, if carried out, would have been disastrous; and it is to their credit that often they restrained the President. Like most Presidents, Roosevelt was elected in 1932 primarily on domestic issues. He entered the White House during a very severe depression which required drastic action that inevitably would have aroused bitter feeling among many citizens. Roosevelt made little effort to reduce domestic resentment; often he seemed to enjoy stirring up strife, not only against political opponents but against prominent and respected leaders in his own party. He paid little attention to foreign affairs until 1939, and by that time he had created opposition among many citizens that handicapped his efforts to unite the nation on a foreign policy. His decision to run for a third term further divided the nation, and his promise to leaders of Union labor that he would preserve their gains acquired under his peacetime administrations added to the delay in shifting industry to war production. The length of the war involved another presidential campaign during which much, if not most, of his thought was concentrated on his re-election. All of these factors help to explain, but do not justify, many of the decisions affecting the conduct of the war that he made on his own responsibility.

His fiat that only "unconditional surrender" of the Axis Powers would be accepted enabled Hitler to convince the great majority of Germans that they had to fight to the bitter end or see their country destroyed; it hardened the firm resolve of the Japanese to continue the struggle; it had little effect upon the Italians who generally were opposed to the war. Had the President reflected briefly he would have realized that a nation that merely lays down its arms is at the mercy of the victor. His remark caused unnecessary loss of American lives.

On several occasions, notably at the Argentia Conference, Roosevelt announced that the United States sought "no aggrandizement territorial or other"; as the war progressed, American forces captured or recaptured islands and archipelagoes very important strategically, but mostly scantily inhabited and of little commercial value. Both the Navy and War Secretaries realized their value as outposts and wished to retain them. In June 1944, Forrestal asked Stettinius if the President was committed to the new theory of multiple ownership of captured territory by the United Nations. Apparently Roosevelt was, for he was determined to make the British, French, and Dutch follow the American treatment of the Philippines.* The action of the United States at the San Francisco Conference where this theory of multiple ownership was adopted is treated at greater length in Chapter 7. It is related here mainly to indicate how personal ideas, even whims, of Roosevelt profoundly affected American policy. His greatest mistake was made on the eve of American entry into the war as an announced belligerent.

About 9:30 P.M. on December 6, 1941, Commander L. R. Schulz delivered thirteen sections of an intercepted Japanese message to the President; he, after reading it, turned it over to Hopkins saying substantially, "This means war." After Hopkins had read the message he told the President it was too bad we could not strike the first blow and prevent any sort of surprise. Roose-

* *As He Saw It*, by Elliott Roosevelt, Little, Brown & Co., pp. 224-225.

velt replied, "No, we can't do that. We are a democracy and a peaceful people." The immediate effect of this pronouncement was cruel enough; the unnecessary losses entailed in Hawaii and the Philippines have been described. Since that time some high American officials have attempted to fasten that decision on the country as a national policy.

Apparently President Truman approved this policy, for his Secretary of State, Dean Acheson, and his Chairman of the Joint Chiefs of Staff, General Bradley, have made similar statements. Acheson said the United States can only fight a war like the one in Korea—that is, by remaining on the defensive and meeting Communist offensives wherever they occur with conventional weapons —because otherwise we would plunge the country "into the unspeakable disaster of a world war." Bradley does not quite agree with Acheson. He would not "wage a preventive war"; he would deter an aggressor nation by awaiting his atomic attack and then resorting "to instant, terrible and sustained atomic retaliation" against the aggressor. The unnecessary perils this policy would entail have been fully covered in Chapter 5; it is well to add here that Roosevelt had no historical basis for the fatal limitation his weird policy would place upon democracies.

The first democracies were the small city-states of Greece. The Roman Republic, then the Republic of Venice, also arose in the Mediterranean. Not one of them would have survived wars with autocratic states if they had awaited enemy attacks. Under John Adams and Thomas Jefferson our navy did not hesitate to attack French and Turkish men-of-war, privateers, or pirates in the Mediterranean and Caribbean. There is nothing in the history of the Greek, Roman, Venetian or American democracies that requires the United States to give the enemy the initiative. Hopkins realized that fact.

H. A. L. Fisher, one of England's most reflective historians, finished his history of Europe most impressed "with the impact of the unexpected" on each succeeding generation of man. Anyone hoping to anticipate the future by the past, therefore, must expect the unexpected. This is particularly true in war, because it is pure chance whether a nation, no matter if it is governed by one person, a few persons, or by all the people, will be efficiently led. Our own history since 1912 will illustrate the part chance plays in our destiny.

Both of our war Presidents felt the need of a personal confidant. Nothing indicates their different personalities so much as their selections as advisers. Wilson chose Colonel E. M. House, a quiet, refined, conservative, almost gentle southerner; Roosevelt picked Harry Hopkins, an invalid, a radical, with raucous voice, whose pastimes were night clubs and horse racing. To these two men, two war Presidents confided their inmost thoughts. And in the preparation for and the conduct of war, Wilson and Roosevelt followed similar patterns. Both were slow in preparing the armed forces; once involved, Wilson urged "the use of force without stint"; Roosevelt demanded the enemy's "unconditional surrender." Wilson insisted on changing the frontiers of Europe to accord with his doctrine of self-determination of people and to give to some land-locked nations access to the sea; Roosevelt permitted Stalin to alter the frontiers of neighboring states to get his support for the United Nations and demanded that Churchill relinquish some British possessions. Both were equally indifferent to the material interests of the United States or its citizens, but burning with zeal to create a new and wonderful warless world. They not only refused accession of territory in their time but proclaimed that the United States would never add to its territory. These two Presidents were elected when the nation was at peace and Americans were primarily concerned with domestic issues, yet they were required to make decisions involving present and future wars. It is evident that "the impact of the unexpected" has already had a great effect on the United States.

Chapter 7

Averting War by Means of Force

In this chapter the efforts of civilized states to limit or abolish the use of force as an instrument of statecraft will be discussed, beginning with the First Hague Conference in 1899 and continuing through the San Francisco Conference in 1945 where the charter of the United Nations was promulgated.

When the American delegation left for the Hague, the United States had been at peace since 1865, except for three months of war with Spain. An adult American generation had never been at war; successful arbitration of long standing disputes with Great Britain had convinced many of them that they would always be at peace. Satisfied with their possessions, busily and happily developing the heart of North America, they had acquired a condescending, almost unctuous, attitude toward quarrelsome Europe with its large conscript armies and its modern navies. Among the American delegates was Captain A. T. Mahan, a member of the Navy Board of Strategy, who, together with Assistant Secretary of State John Bassett Moore, had coordinated policy and naval strategy during the Spanish War.

The agenda of the Hague Conference included limitation of armaments and prohibition of the use of new weapons such as lethal gas and submarines. It later developed that the Foreign Ministers of Great Britain and Germany had agreed in advance to "wreck" the Conference; these statesmen did not believe the government of any great power would submit questions of national honor or vital interest to arbitration. They were unwilling to delay the opening of hostilities to allow attempts at mediation because at that time the Royal Navy and the Kaiser's army were kept ready for war. British admirals and German generals did not propose to forfeit this advantage to possible enemies, particularly to their traditional rivals Russia and France. (See p. 33.)

Captain Mahan agreed with Anglo-German leaders that great powers would not submit questions of national honor or vital interest to arbitration and was convinced that the United States should never submit questions arising under the Monroe Doctrine to arbitration, for it was a unilateral declaration with no legal basis in International Law. He also opposed any effort to outlaw lethal gas, because he questioned whether it inflicted more suffering than bullets or drowning at sea. Russian army officers opposed any decrease in their army; the United States army was so tiny our delegation refused to consider its reduction, and our navy was smaller than that of any large maritime country. The only useful accomplishment of the Conference was to reveal the practical difficulties of limiting armaments or of extending arbitration. Many optimistic Americans and a few foreigners ignored the obvious obstacles.

British and American citizens were more interested in preserving than increasing their territories and their foreign offices had successfully arbitrated many disputes not involving national honor or vital interest. Canada often complained that her interests had been sacrificed for the benefit of the Empire; and the United States Senate found it necessary to study these settlements, for the State Department, too eager to reach agreement, often sacrificed national interest. John Hay, for example, agreed to the British suggestion that the Panama Canal should not be fortified.

During the Spanish War the United States discovered that it was without friends in Europe; during the Boer War the British Government made the same discovery. European hostility caused them to draw closer together and they sponsored the Open Door Policy in China. Anglo-American relations continued friendly, and in 1912 Sir Edward Grey proposed to President Taft that the two nations agree to submit *all* future disputes to arbitration. When a treaty to this effect was submitted to the Senate, the Honorable Henry Cabot Lodge offered an amendment, which was adopted, that excluded questions "involving national honor or vital interest." During the ensuing nation-wide debate, ex-President Theodore Roosevelt and Admiral Mahan took the lead in supporting the amendment for, like Lodge, they were convinced that diplomacy was unequal to solving all international problems. Mahan cited our Revolutionary War and our Civil War to show that force had been necessary to attain our independence and to preserve the Union.*

These arguments foreshadowed those later offered for and against United States entry into the League of Nations. It was evident then that many Americans were in favor of arbitration. And the speeches of Senator Lodge indicate that his subsequent opposition to the League of Nations was based on life-long convictions.

President Wilson permitted his Secretary of State, the Honorable William Jennings Bryan, to negotiate numerous "cooling-off treaties" with various nations that provided for a year's delay in resorting to the use of force. Bryan believed tempers would cool and negotiations could prevent war; later he resigned rather than face the possibility of resorting to the use of force against Germany. When war occurred in Europe, Wilson proclaimed neutrality of the United States and asked Americans, most of whom sympathized with Belgium, to remain neutral in word, thought, and deed.

Sinking of merchant ships by U-boats without warning led Wilson to make many protests to Berlin. The belligerents refused his tender of the good offices of the United States to end the war late in 1916. When unrestricted U-boat warfare was resumed in 1917, he asked Congress to recognize that a state of war with Germany existed. Once in the war Wilson became spokesman for the associated powers and his summary in 14 points of their ob-

* For details see *Armament and Arbitration*, by A. T. Mahan, Harper & Brothers, 1912.

jectives became the basis of the Versailles Treaty and the League of Nations. At Paris in 1919 he wove the League and the Treaty so firmly together that when the Senate rejected the League the United States could only end war with Germany by a separate peace treaty.

In 1920 opponents of the League of Nations in the Senate were able to prevent ratification of the Versailles Treaty primarily because Article 10 of the League's charter pledged its members "to respect and preserve against external aggression the territorial integrity and the existing political independence of all members of the League." In the ensuing national election Democratic candidates, the Honorable J. M. Cox and the Honorable F. D. Roosevelt, who advocated entry into the League were decisively beaten. Their defeat was regarded as a rejection by American voters of the League. President Warren G. Harding announced that the United States would not enter the League.

Although Harding accepted his election as a mandate to boycott the League, many Republicans favored entry. To placate them and to reduce expenditures on the navy, he invited four other naval powers to Washington in 1921 to confer on naval limitations and Far Eastern policies. The consequences of this conference had a direct influence on Japanese-American relations and have been described in Chapter 4. Its immediate effect on the American public was to increase their confidence in international conferences. The subsequent advantage of its provisions taken by other naval powers and the failure of powerful nations to reduce land armaments created distrust among many Americans of all international pledges. A reaction followed that strengthened the American determination to avoid foreign entanglements.

The abstention of the United States did not prevent other nations from using the League; a few, in sincere efforts to promote world peace; others employed the League as a forum for propaganda and its machinery to promote their own interests. Prime Minister Ramsay MacDonald of Great Britain had advocated the extension of limitations on capital ships as already discussed in Chapter 4. At the 5th Session of the League of Nations he submitted the Geneva Protocol that pledged all signatories to settle disputes either by judicial decision of the World Court, by an arbitral award, or in accord with a report of the Council of the League. In addition, all signatories would promise to declare war against any other nation that failed to accept the Council's decision. It should be noted that MacDonald, who had opposed the entry of Great Britain into World War I to support British interests, advocated the use of force by his country as a member of an Alliance to preserve the peace. This willingness to use force for an international organization but not for their own country prevailed among many supporters of the League of Nations.

France and some other nations signed the Geneva Protocol; but before it was approved by the British Parliament, MacDonald's Cabinet had resigned. Austen Chamberlain, Foreign Minister in the Conservative Government of Prime Minister Baldwin, refused to sign the Protocol. Instead, he sponsored the Locarno Pact that was signed by Germany, Great Britain, France, Italy, and Belgium in the autumn of 1925.

By its terms the signatories mutually guaranteed German-Belgian and French-German boundaries as given in the Versailles Treaty. Also, arbitration treaties were signed by Germany, France, Belgium; and by Germany, Poland, and Czechoslovakia. The essential factor in these various treaties was the promise of Great Britain to intervene with military force against Germany or France if either one attacked the other. The Conservative Government definitely accepted this heavy responsibility as Britain's contribution to Europe's peace. The Senate had refused to ratify a similar pledge made by Wilson in 1919 to go to the aid of France if attacked by Germany.

Austen Chamberlain, Briand, and Stresemann were mainly responsible for the Locarno treaties that engendered good will throughout western Europe, led to German entry into the League and to French evacuation of the Rhineland. In the autumn of 1926 European nations came nearest to meeting their obligations as members of the League, and there was an undercurrent of hope that these agreements would be followed by a reduction in European armies.

President Coolidge had made several attempts to get the limitations already applied by the United States to its navy extended to the armies of Europe. The Versailles Treaty provided that, after the disarmament of Germany had been accomplished, all European nations would reduce their armaments. France, under the leadership of Raymond Poincaré, was determined to retain her preponderant position on the continent; she steadily refused to reduce her armies and had modified the provisions of the naval disarmament treaty by insisting upon retaining and increasing her submarine force. Her Foreign Minister, Aristide Briand, usually an advocate of arbitration, conformed to French opinion and refused Coolidge's proposal to extend naval limitations to land armaments. For various reasons, including a desire to soften his rebuff to the President, in 1927 Briand announced in the Associated Press the "willingness of France to subscribe publicly with the United States to any mutual engagement tending to outlaw war . . . between these two countries." And then inferentially chided President Coolidge by claiming that members of the League of Nations, signatories of the Locarno Pact, had already renounced war as an instrument of national policy.*

State Department officials quickly realized that Briand's plan, if accepted, might be regarded abroad as a French-American alliance and it would guarantee the neutrality of the United States, at least, should the ambitions of France plunge her into a European war. To avoid that liability they proposed that other nations be invited to join. Exactly a year after Briand had submitted his proposal to the United States, Secretary Kellogg, on June 23, 1928, submitted an American draft to 14 nations.

When the United States proposed to extend the pact, Briand lost interest, but he had committed France too openly to reject its extension. Much discussion continued in French and American journals. Many societies, particularly the wealthy Carnegie Endowment For Peace energized by a President of Columbia University, Dr. Nicholas Murray Butler, an advocate of all international organizations, ardently supported the proposal. Americans, generally encouraged by successful Anglo-American arbitration,

* See page 72, Chapter 4.

favored a World Court. In spite of the treaties limiting naval armaments negotiated by Hughes, the Republican Party was under sporadic attacks for failure to cooperate in international affairs. Another Presidential campaign was in the offing. Eventually the cautious Secretary of State, the Honorable F. B. Kellogg, after attaching certain explanations supported the treaty.

The British Foreign Office rushed to his aid: first, by explaining that a nation's right of self-defense could be taken for granted and need not be referred to in the Pact; second, by assuring him that the Pact would not conflict with the provisions of the League of Nations or the Locarno Pact that required certain European nations to take up arms to punish aggression because a violation of either the League Covenant or Locarno Pact by one member automatically released other members from that obligation.

Senator Borah also came to Kellogg's assistance. Although he had opposed American entry into the League, Borah was a veteran advocate of arbitration and conciliation. As Chairman of the Foreign Affairs Committee he publicly announced that "The effect of the Kellogg proposal is a solemn pledge (by the United States) . . . to let the arbitration treaties, conciliation treaties, Hague Tribunal, peace machinery of the League and Locarno work." Then the Senate Foreign Affairs Committee announced that "the United States regards the Monroe Doctrine as a part of its national security and self-defense." These declarations dispelled fears of many Americans that they might be dragged again into Europe's wars.

Secretary Kellogg also assured other powers that each one of them was the sole judge of what constituted self-defense and that the Pact could not be construed to impair existing treaty obligations, like those of the Locarno Pact and League of Nations. To be doubly sure, the British Cabinet also reserved freedom of action in certain, unspecified regions of the world in which it claimed special and vital interest. The explanations and reservations necessary to get the Pact approved nullified its value. Few Americans troubled themselves to read the attached memoranda. Peace societies hailed the Pact as a new triumph and proclaimed that its first article in which the signatory nations "solemnly declare

. . . that they condemn recourse to war . . . and renounce it as an instrument of national policy . . ." banished war from the earth. A few years later Japan, alleging self-defense, cited the Pact to justify her invasion of Manchuria.

Among the many oddities accompanying the acceptance of the Pact of Paris banishing war was the use made by its advocates of the Locarno Pact, which was based upon a definite pledge made by Great Britain to give military aid to either France or Germany if attacked by the other. That is, all three nations envisaged war and provided for war in the treaties which buttressed the Pact that so solemnly banished war from the world.

Kellogg's explanation of the Pact itself invalidated its provisions in these words: "Every nation is free at all times and regardless of treaty provisions to defend its territory from attack or invasion, and it alone is competent to decide whether circumstances require recourse to war." This official interpretation, coupled with the statement of the Senate's Foreign Affairs Committee that "the United States regards the Monroe Doctrine as part of its national security and self defense," left the United States free to resort to war in its own defense or that of the Western Hemisphere. Loaded below the water line with nullifying explanations and reservations, the Pact was signed amid public acclamation in Paris in August 1928 and convinced many million American supporters of collective security that war had been banished from the earth.

Thus, between the refusal of the United States to enter the League of Nations in 1920 and the inauguration of Franklin D. Roosevelt in 1933, repeated attempts had been made to reduce armaments, and to substitute arbitration, World Court decisions and League Council awards for war by member nations of the League. Although not a member of the League, the United States took a major part in the most ambitious attempt of all, to banish war from the earth in the Pact of Paris. This queer assortment of treaties, accompanied by minor wars and threats of larger wars, further confused Americans. Some reverted to their former conviction, reached after a generation of peace, that wars were unnecessary and peacetime expenditures on armed forces a waste of taxpayers' money. Others were certain that the United States had been lured into World War I by Anglo-French propaganda and that if they resisted European snares they could avoid war. Still others were equally convinced that only by cooperating with foreign nations and the League could peace be maintained. But when Governor Franklin D. Roosevelt entered the White House, all groups were more concerned with the domestic economic depression than with foreign affairs.

Wilson, sponsor of the League of Nations, shaped its charter shortly before and during a peace conference, and one of its objectives was to carry out provisions of the proposed treaty that required time for their fulfillment. Roosevelt, sponsor of the United Nations, required longer time to launch his super-state. The term Atlantic Charter was first used at Argentia in August 1941, before the United States was formally at war, to describe eight principles upon which he and Churchill based their hopes for a better world. At Roosevelt's request Churchill prepared the first draft. The eighth principle asserted their belief that the world must come to the "abandonment of the use of force" but only after Nazi tyranny had been destroyed so that "all men in . . . all lands" could be freed from "fear and want." The original Atlantic Charter was only a press release authorized by Roosevelt and Churchill, and it was primarily camouflage to conceal the agreement reached on joint action by the United States and Great Britain against the Axis powers. Its most important immediate effect resulted from the note addressed by Roosevelt, at Churchill's request, warning Japan to end her movement to the south in the western Pacific. (See p. 88.)

The Atlantic Charter became important in January 1942 when Roosevelt insisted that the United States, Great Britain, Russia, China, and 22 other states, then at war with the Axis Powers, subscribe to it and then pledge themselves to employ their full resources against and not to make a separate armistice or treaty with the Tripartite States (Germany, Japan, and Italy). All states assisting the United Nations were invited to join, and some did from time to time.

At the very first meeting Stalin sought to have the embryo

organization guarantee the territory bestowed upon Russia by Hitler, but only with difficulty was he persuaded to permit his representative to agree to a clause in the Declaration by United Nations to defend "religious freedom." Stalin revealed his ideas at that early date. Roosevelt had fair warning of the Generalissimo's purposes but, with incorrigible optimism and a certain amount of sympathy for some parts of Stalin's domestic program, the President persuaded himself that he could act as mediator between Churchill and Stalin.

Churchill had denounced communism for over twenty years when he rushed to the aid of Stalin in June 1941. He publicly announced that he did not retract a single epithet he had applied to communism. Privately, he said he would welcome the devil if his Satanic majesty would fight Hitler and the Nazis. Stalin was glad to accept Churchill's friendship in those terms, for he would have acted similarly under the same circumstances. Roosevelt's New Deal followers included a fringe that sympathized with Red ideology, and in July 1941 he had sent his confidant Harry Hopkins to Moscow to assure Stalin of American aid.* Hopkins in January had visited Churchill in London and gained his confidence; similarly he gained as much of Stalin's confidence as the Generalissimo ever extended to a foreigner, and Hopkins became liaison officer between the triumvirate that controlled the policies of Russia, Great Britain, and the United States. The development of the United Nations between 1942 and 1945 will be easier to follow if it is clearly understood that it began in Washington as an alliance between Russia, Great Britain, and the United States, when Stalin, Churchill, and Roosevelt pledged their nations not to make a separate armistice or peace with Germany, Japan, and Italy; and that its three most powerful sponsors were held together primarily by fear and hatred of Germany and Japan.

In May 1943, Winston Churchill outlined to a group of Anglo-American officials in Washington his views on the United Nations. He was convinced that force would be required to preserve the

* See Chapter 6.

peace. To prevent future aggression by Japan and Germany, an association of Russia, Great Britain, and the United States was required, to which China could be added. Subsequently, at Churchill's suggestion, France was added to the powers on which would rest the responsibility for peace. The Big Four thus became the Big Five. Together with certain other powers they would form a Supreme World Council; subordinate to this Council would be three Regional Councils, one each for Europe, the American Hemisphere, and the Pacific. Churchill agreed to a suggestion of Vice President Wallace that temporary members could be elected to the Council. To enforce the peace, the armed forces of each nation would be divided into two parts, one contingent for their national needs, the other to serve in the International Armed Forces. Even with this organization Churchill could see small hope for the world unless the United States and Great Britain worked together in the future. The Prime Minister agreed with a previous suggestion of the President that the Combined Chiefs of Staff be retained after the peace and went further in proposing a joint form of citizenship that would permit Anglo-American citizens to settle and trade with freedom and equal rights in the territories of both nations. Churchill's remarks on the United Nations are in accord with the views he had expressed in a letter to Prime Minister Smuts that the only way Great Britain could prevent Russia dominating the Eurasian continent after the war would be a close union with the United States; the Prime Minister realized more clearly than the President that the unconditional surrender of Germany and Japan would automatically elevate the Soviet Republics to the dominant power in Europe.

In spite of the generous contribution of scarce munitions made by both Great Britain and the United States, Stalin took umbrage because they did not immediately open a second front in France in 1942. His truculence increased when the invasion of France was postponed until 1944. In the autumn of 1943 Foreign Ministers Hull and Eden were sent to Moscow to soothe the Red Dictator. They secured Stalin's permission for Foreign Minister Molotov to join them and the Chinese Ambassador in a pledge to even "closer collaboration" in the prosecution of the war, the setting of the terms of the surrender and the disarmament of the enemy nations. At the urging of Hull, these four envoys then agreed upon the principles of a system of "international security and cooperation" and promised that the international organization "would be open to all peace-loving nations."

In September 1943, before the meeting in Moscow, the House of Representatives had passed a resolution favoring the creation of an international organization with "power to establish and maintain a just and lasting peace"; in October, the Senate approved Hull's action at Moscow by recognizing the necessity "of establishing . . . an international organization to maintain peace and security. . . ." Roosevelt and Hull easily gained the approval of Congress to transform an Alliance to wage war into an international organization to banish war from the earth, for the public generally approved the pleasing prospect of a warless world. The Locarno Pact had reconciled many Americans to the idea of intervening in wars of other nations; the Kellogg-Briand Pact had offered two rainbows, somewhat contradictory, a warless world but one in which the United States could use force to defend itself and the Western Hemisphere. At Teheran in December 1943 other nations and leaders began to mold the international organization.

Stalin and Roosevelt had begun a personal correspondence at the suggestion of Harry Hopkins after his first visit to Moscow in the summer of 1941.* In January 1942, Roosevelt refused Stalin's request that the United Nations guarantee Russia's acquisitions secured during his alliance with Hitler. During 1942 and 1943, Roosevelt learned from personal experience that Stalin could be very stubborn, but his natural optimism led him to believe that they could, in a personal interview, reach an agreement. He took the initiative in arranging the Teheran Conference during which he and Churchill openly wooed the Red Dictator; Churchill, welcoming Russia to the Mediterranean, and Roosevelt to the western Pacific. Both offered to provide the nucleus of a Red merchant marine at the end of the war.

* See Chapter 6.

Stalin proved less tractable than Roosevelt anticipated, at times being cynical and forceful in language. He made his points against the United Nations by implication; Roosevelt apparently missed some of them, due to faulty translation, or to perennial optimism. Stalin, after listening patiently to Roosevelt's long explanation of its charter, asked if small states would have the same rights as large, implying that they never had had, and he reminded Roosevelt that small states had often caused big wars.

Stalin's main point, also was well taken; he informed Roosevelt that if Great Britain, Russia, and the United States "wanted to keep the world at peace they had . . . power to do it and did not need the help of other nations." Roosevelt admitted the need of force to maintain peace and proposed that the enforcing agency should be "The Four Policemen": Russia, China, Britain, and the United States.

Stalin doubted the ability of Chinese armies as enforcing agencies and made the practical comment that European nations would object to being policed by Asiatics; Roosevelt said he was looking forward a long time and wanted 400 million Chinese as friends. Stalin then suggested regional agencies, one for Europe, one for the Far East. In previous discussions with Roosevelt, Churchill had suggested that three regional agencies be established, one each for Europe, the Far East, and the Americas. Roosevelt doubted if Congress would permit a President to send United States troops to Europe, saying that only the attack on Pearl Harbor persuaded Americans to send their sons to Europe. When Stalin pointed out that if the world organization were effected it might be necessary for the United States to send troops to Europe, Roosevelt rejoined that he had only anticipated sending naval and air forces to Europe, and presumed that Russia and Great Britain would provide ground forces. The President added that he expected only two types of threats to world peace: a minor menace like a boundary dispute between two small nations that could be halted by closing their frontiers or imposing embargoes; and a major threat on the part of a larger power that could be averted or suppressed by the Four Policemen.

Stalin showed keen interest in measures to prevent the future revival of Germany and Japan; he insisted that an organization or committee to maintain the peace must have continued military occupation of bases inside of Germany. Roosevelt agreed entirely with the Generalissimo on that point. Stalin shrewdly surmised that Congress would not agree to accept as binding decisions made by an Executive Committee of the new organization, and Roosevelt also realized that Congress could not under the constitution part with that much of its authority; he said the Committee could make recommendations that he hoped nations concerned would accept. During their conversations at Teheran, Roosevelt and Stalin deliberately or unwittingly avoided the most difficult problem of all. What could the United Nations do when one of the Four Policemen menaced the peace?

The Congressional endorsement of the Moscow Agreement entirely justified Roosevelt in negotiating an agreement with Stalin at Teheran, concerning an international organization to maintain peace. And at its conclusion, Stalin and Churchill joined him in a declaration, saying among other things, "We have concerted our plans for the destruction of the German forces . . . we recognize fully the supreme responsibility resting upon us and all the United Nations to make a peace . . . that will banish the scourge and terror of war for many generations . . . We will welcome . . . all nations . . . into a world family of Democratic Nations." Roosevelt had obtained Stalin's consent to his world organization, and in his elation he apparently did not observe how little real interest or trust the Red Dictator showed in the enterprise. Roosevelt *did* realize a fact that has subsequently been forgotten; that is, if the United States is required to assist the United Nations in averting or suppressing war by force, her contribution should be limited to sea and air forces.

In return for his passive consent to the creation of a super State, Stalin obtained assurance of the Anglo-American cross-channel invasion in 1944 that assured Red armies of continuous victories over and ultimate defeat of Germany; of increased American effort in the Pacific that relieved him of any fear of Japan. He accepted reluctantly Roosevelt's insistence on "unconditional surrender" of Germany and Japan, knowing that it would prolong the war. But he was heartily pleased when Roosevelt and Churchill agreed to dismember Germany and disarm Japan, for that decision would relieve Russia of strong neighbors and would permit her to dominate the Eurasian continent in the postwar era. To all these concessions Roosevelt added a warm water port in the western Pacific. Stalin obtained these desiderata by agreeing to enter the United Nations; by reaffirming a former promise to enter the war three months after the surrender of Germany; and making a new one, later broken, to permit American aviators to use Russian air bases.

With Stalin's blessings and Congressional approval, Roosevelt invited delegates from Great Britain, Russia, and China to meet with American colleagues at Dumbarton Oaks, where, between August 21 and October 7, 1944, they agreed upon recommendations that became the basis for the charter of the United Nations formulated at San Francisco in the next year.

Congress again approved the action of Roosevelt when he reported that preliminary conversations at Dumbarton Oaks promised the development of a "fully integrated world-security system." The President concealed the skeleton in the closet, the question of what should be done if one of his "Four Policemen" menaced the peace. It had popped out at Dumbarton Oaks. The delegates could not agree on the thorny problem, so the question was postponed to the next meeting of the Big Three; but throughout the Conference at Dumbarton Oaks the British and American views on the "Veto power" of the "Four Policemen" (Five when France was admitted) were identical and substantially as follows: any of four major powers could veto any proposal that might involve war. Russia went further and wanted the power to veto consideration by the Council of such questions.

Between the Teheran and Yalta conferences, American, British, and Russian victories liberated conquered territory in Europe raising troublesome questions among the Big Three leaders while their prospective victory weakened the artificial ties uniting them: their reaction to these crises has been discussed in Chapter 6. Roosevelt for half of the same time was busily engaged in the Presidential campaign, and the time he could spare from domestic politics he first devoted to inventing a formula for voting in the Security Council of the proposed United Nations that would be satisfactory to Stalin. As a full account of the Yalta Conference is also given in Chapter 6, only decisions affecting the United Nations will be related here.

Harry Hopkins and Senator J. W. Byrnes told Stettinius that the President regarded Stalin's agreement to the formula for voting in the Security Council as the most important item on the agenda. By various concessions in other matters Roosevelt gained the Generalissimo's approval to except procedural matters from a unanimous vote of the Big Five. Roosevelt, Churchill, and Stalin then agreed that all other matters must have unanimous approval. In effect this gave each member a veto on any decision involving the employment of armed forces to avert or suppress war. This statesmanlike decision had been suggested by the British and American delegations at Dumbarton Oaks.

The President supported a "veto" because he realized the Senate would not approve the charter without it. Churchill said he would never consent "to the fumbling fingers of 40 or 50 nations prying into the life's existence of the British Empire." Stalin more forthrightly declared he would "never agree to having any action of any of the Great Powers submitted to the judgment of the small powers." He was convinced that the three Great Powers having borne the brunt of the war should be the ones to preserve the peace. While Roosevelt, Stalin, and Churchill agreed on the formula, each had a different reason for his approval—that boded ill for the embryo organization. Also, it is doubtful if either Parliament or the Senate would have approved the charter without reserving the veto; for, if any member of the Big Five opposed intervention by the armed forces to avert or suppress war sufficiently to exercise a veto, the same power might employ his own forces to oppose the action, thus turning a small war into a large one.

This wise action of Roosevelt's has become associated in the minds of many Americans with the secret concession he made to Stalin to get his unnecessary aid in the war against Japan. The President's action in forcing Chiang Kai-shek to cede Chinese territory to Stalin and thus re-establish Russia in Manchuria flooded the Far East in a series of misfortunes that led directly to the rise of the Red regime in China, the wars in Korea and Indo-China. However, unless the United States had the right to veto a decision on the Security Council it could be involved in a major war that its citizens opposed. To obtain a veto the United States was obliged to concede the same power to the other four members. Abuse of the veto power by the Soviet Government has brought it into disrepute, but it is essential if the United Nations is to function effectively.

The Soviet authorities were not content with the concessions obtained at Yalta. Before the San Francisco Conference opened, "the cordial spirit" of Yalta so glowingly described by Roosevelt and others had disappeared. Much concerned, President Truman discussed the problem with the Secretaries of State, War, and Navy Departments. At San Francisco the Russian delegation refused to accept the voting procedure approved by Stalin at Yalta. The surrender of Germany was not a week old when Molotov, head of the Soviet delegation, and Eden, head of the British, were flying eastward on their way home, as were Harriman and Bohlen, American representatives, who suggested to President Truman that he send Hopkins to Moscow to persuade Stalin to intervene. Hopkins was dispatched and after six meetings obtained the Generalissimo's approval.

Stalin himself may have directed the Red delegation to refuse to agree. He had several grievances with Washington, and was shrewd enough to know that if he held up the formation of the United Nations, he could probably get them redressed. At any rate, he did not intervene at San Francisco until these were settled to his satisfaction. Hopkins repeatedly told Stalin the United States only desired a Polish Government satisfactory to the people and *friendly* to Russia; that Truman would fulfill all the promises made by Roosevelt; and apologetically explained that lend-lease had been abruptly stopped because legislation required it to cease when the war ended. Harriman joined with Hopkins to tell why Argentina had been admitted to the United Nations. They assured Stalin that the United States would not insist on including

France on the reparations commission; that Russia should have her share of captured German ships; and in effect, they approved the unilateral action of Stalin in establishing the Lublin Committee as the government of Poland by nominating four members of the Polish exiled government in London to this committee of twenty members.

Besides these concessions, Hopkins told Stalin that Truman had not abandoned Roosevelt's idea of dismembering Germany; nor did he defend Churchill from Stalin's accusation of attempting to revive the "cordon sanitaire"; he did not remonstrate when the Red Dictator said the "four freedoms" of the Atlantic Charter could only be enjoyed in peace and then with limitations. Hopkins did make several efforts to free Polish representatives of the London Government but Stalin refused.

Stalin agreed to permit three representatives of the American Red Cross to supervise relief in Poland if the Lublin Committee did not object to their presence and if Hopkins would give his word that they would not engage in political activities. He made his only other concession after he had reminded Hopkins that he must have a good reason to give his people for going to war with Japan, a hint that he be paid in advance the price promised him by Roosevelt for declaring war on Japan. Hopkins could give the needed assurance, for Truman had pledged himself to meet these commitments. For this reassurance Stalin on the sixth and last day of their meetings ordered the Soviet representatives at San Francisco to fulfill his pledge by voting for the compromise agreed upon at Yalta.

Hopkins in his last negotiations with Stalin in 1945 as in his first in 1941 made concessions; Stalin accepted them. On both occasions administration circles considered the Hopkins mission a diplomatic triumph. In 1941, Hopkins urged assistance to Russia because she was weak and must be aided to resist Germany; in 1943, he recommended still more aid because Russia had become so strong the United States must retain her friendship at any cost. In 1945 he did not blame her for strengthening her frontiers by taking German and Polish territory; and if behind those extended frontiers she wanted to maintain what Hopkins called "a socialist regime" it was her own affair. On one or two occasions when Churchill differed with Stalin, Hopkins sided with Stalin; so far as the record shows Hopkins never disagreed with his friend "Uncle Joe."

Hopkins' success was hailed with jubilation at San Francisco. Under Stalin's orders the Red delegation accepted the voting procedure for the Security Council. With this hurdle cleared delegates quickly adopted the charter, convinced themselves and eagerly began to convince others that 1945 would see the beginning of world peace.

As candidate for Vice President in 1920 Roosevelt advocated United States entry in the League of Nations and became familiar with its purpose and organization. Naturally, the charters of the two international organizations are similar, because they were patterned after the United States Constitution. Avoiding the mistakes of Wilson, Roosevelt obtained the support of Congress in every measure he took in developing the United Nations. But he made even greater concessions to Stalin than Wilson made to Clemenceau and Lloyd George to gain their approval of the League.

The purposes of both organizations are practically identical; the League was "to achieve," the United Nations "to maintain," international security. The charters of both differ from the Constitution of the United States in failing to provide a Chief Magistrate; they substituted a Secretary General with a permanent Secretariat. For two houses of Congress the organization substituted a single chamber called the Assembly in the first, the General Assembly in the second. Membership in the League included all signatory nations and such others as should accede to its charter without reservations; "any member state could withdraw after two years if its obligations had been met," thus the League avoided one potential cause of a civil war. Original members of the United Nations included those who had signed the declaration in Washington in January 1942 pledging themselves to defeat the Axis powers and those who participated in the San Francisco Conference; all peace-loving nations are eligible to join; no provision is made for voluntary withdrawal but members could be expelled for violating the charter. The League made no provisions for amending its charter; the United Nations' charter can be amended by two-thirds vote of the Assembly and the Security Council if all permanent members vote in the affirmative. That is, the charter cannot be amended unless all Big Five states agree. The charter requires that, if a conference to consider amendments has not been held prior to 1955, the question of holding one shall be placed on the agenda of that session of the General Assembly. Both Assembly and Council have to vote to call the conference. As a procedural matter its convening could not be vetoed; but any proposed changes in the charter could be. Preliminary data are being gathered now on the assumption that a special conference will be held in 1956 to consider any amendments proposed.

The charters of both organizations intentionally gave control to the Great Powers; the League through its Council, the United Nations through the Security Council, and for the identical reason, a great power could not be restrained except by a major war which would defeat the object of both organizations.

A Secretary General with a permanent Secretariat was provided for each organization and all expenses were to be prorated among member states. In the League, Wilson invented the mandate system which permitted associate nations that insisted on retaining conquered territory to do so without violating one of his 14 points; Roosevelt, in spite of the flagrant abuses of the mandate system between the two wars, thought up the Trusteeship System of Multiple Ownership of islands and colonial possessions taken from the Axis powers during World War II and embedded it in the charter. He made no objection to Stalin's acquisition of former German and Polish territory, but he made it impossible for the United States to retain islands in the Pacific except as Trustee for the United Nations.

The League only contemplated a World Court; the United Nations provided an International Court of Justice, similar to the U.S. Supreme Court, and regulated the election of judges and directed the General Assembly to encourage the codification of international law. The United States and 35 other nations have agreed in advance to accept its jurisdiction.

A careful comparison of the charters of the League of Nations and the United Nations will show that delegates at Dumbarton Oaks and San Francisco provided a more efficient instrument of international government. The powers and limitations of the United Nations are very precisely defined. Its Security Council has ample authority "to take such action by air, sea, or land forces as may be necessary to maintain or restore international peace and security." The Security Council was provided with a Military Staff Committee, comparable to the Combined Chiefs of Staff that directed Anglo-American forces in World War II, to recommend the necessary forces that member nations should provide, to organize and train these forces and to be prepared to direct their operations against any nation menacing or breaking the peace. This organization can preserve peace, provided that one of the Five Policemen is not the transgressor.

The functions of the principal organs of the United Nations— the General Assembly, Security Council, Economic and Social Council, Trusteeship Council, International Court of Justice, and the Secretariat—are all interrelated, and the Secretary-General is presumed to coordinate its long-range plans to "maintain international peace and security" and "to prevent or suppress war" while these plans are perfected.

The task of the General Assembly, composed of one representative from each member state, is to increase the bonds of friendship among member states. It is required to consider and recommend international policies that will tend to preserve international peace and security. The Assembly will concern itself with basic and permanent factors in international relations to insure that they will promote world order by reducing economic, political, or ideological differences among nations which, unchecked, would produce commercial rivalry, national jealousies and, eventually, war.

The Assembly has been given the hitherto impossible task of creating world conditions in which peace will become the aspiration of every nation. It will labor to increase the standard of living, to seek solutions to economic, social, health, and related problems, and to promote universal respect for human rights and fundamental freedoms. Chapter IX of the charter outlines the means and agencies to be employed, places the primary responsibility of the program upon the General Assembly but establishes under the Assembly an Economic and Social Council of eighteen members as an operating agency to initiate studies and to make recommendations which will tend to remove the economic, social or cultural causes of war.

Conference delegates of the United Nations realized that only force could prevent aggressor or predatory nations from attacking weaker nations; they created the Security Council and made it responsible for maintaining international order. The Council acts for the United Nations, each member of which has agreed to accept and carry out its decisions. To fulfill its duties the Council is organized to function continuously. It has the comparable duties of the President of the United States in defining foreign policy and directing armed forces to support it.

The supreme task of the Security Council is to avert or suppress war, *using force if necessary,* before hostilities can spread. It demands and is given closer scrutiny than other organs of the United Nations. For, in the charter of the latest and most ambitious super State created by all peace-loving nations to avert or suppress war, there is included an organ to recruit, organize, and train land, sea and air forces to preserve the peace by force if necessary.

The Council, if successful, would protect from interruption by war the long-range plans and programs of the Assembly which are expected to reduce the causes of friction that lead to war. Plainly, then, the Security Council must preserve the peace long enough to enable the policies proposed by the Assembly to become effective and thus to convince the world that there are more effective methods of settling international disputes than war. Otherwise, the International Organization will fail.

Under the terms of their entry into the United Nations, all

states obligated themselves to settle their disputes by negotiation, mediation, conciliation, arbitration, judicial settlement, or other peaceful means of their own choice. When disputes begin, the Security Council will first call upon the states to settle their differences by some peaceful means. It is specifically empowered to investigate disputes or any international situation which might lead to friction in order to determine whether the development of the situation will endanger the maintenance of international peace and security and to recommend appropriate procedure or method of adjustment. It can refer legal cases to, and obtain advisory opinions from, the International Court of Justice. Even when using force the Security Council must act in accordance with the principles of the charter, and the organization shall insure that non-member states act in accordance with its principles as necessary to maintain international peace.

The Security Council is not authorized to intervene in matters which are essentially within the domestic jurisdiction of any state in the organization. This wise limitation is designed to prevent the organization from meddling in domestic problems of member states unless they threaten world peace. But this prohibition shall not prejudice the application of measures by the Security Council to preserve peace. Apparently this prohibition would prevent the Council from investigating the oppression of minority groups in states until the internal dispute threatened to break the world peace.

The delegates at San Francisco realized the necessity of prompt action to prevent aggressor nations from starting wars and provided that the Security Council, if a threat to the peace developed, should employ diplomatic, economic or other measures not involving the use of armed forces to halt the aggressor nation. Also, the Council was authorized to call upon member states to apply measures short of war to a recalcitrant state; these measures may include complete or partial interruption of rail, sea, air, postal, telegraphic, radio, and other means of communication and the severance of diplomatic and economic relations. If these measures prove ineffective, the Security Council is empowered to take action by air, naval, and land forces as may be necessary to maintain or restore international peace.

Included in the measures authorized to preserve the peace are demonstrations, blockades, and *other operations by air, sea, or land forces of members of the organization* (italics supplied). This phraseology permits the Security Council to wage war with armies, fleets, and air squadrons in any part of the world.

Furthermore, in order that the Security Council might have forces available for instantaneous action, the charter provides that all members of the United Nations make available to the Security Council on its call and in accordance with special agreement or agreements, armed forces, facilities, and assistance including rights of passage (through their territories) necessary for the purpose of maintaining international peace and security. These agreements shall govern the numbers and types of forces, their degree of readiness and general location. The Security Council shall initiate and conclude these agreements as soon as possible with member states or groups of member states. These agreements shall be subject to the constitutional ratification by signatory states.

Among the armed forces provided, member states shall hold immediately available air contingents for combined international enforcement action. The strength and degree of readiness of these contingents and plans for their combined action, within the limits of the agreements reached with member states, shall be determined by the Security Council with the assistance of the Military Staff Committee. Plans for the use of all the armed forces shall be made by the Security Council with the assistance of the Military Staff Committee. Before the Security Council calls upon a member state not represented on the Council to provide its contingent of armed forces, it shall invite that member state to participate in the decisions of the Council affecting the disposition of that member state's armed forces.

The fixed determination of the San Francisco Conference to use force, if necessary, is demonstrated by the creation of this Military Staff Committee whose functions are to advise and assist the Security Council on all questions relating to:

(a) The Security Council's military requirements for maintenance of international peace and security;

(b) The employment and command of forces placed at its
disposal;

(c) The regulation of armaments and possible disarmament.

The Military Staff Committee will be required to estimate the
strength, composition, and disposition of the forces necessary to
preserve world peace and security and to determine how the forces
placed at the Council's disposal should be employed and commanded. This would embrace the questions of where they should
be stationed and how they should be organized. The decision of
who would command the armed forces was postponed. Obviously
it will be a delicate question and should be left to the Military
Staff Committee to decide for each occasion. During World War
II when Anglo-American forces were operating together, the nation supplying the largest share of the forces furnished the commander. The Military Staff Committee will be responsible for the
strategic direction of any armed forces placed at the disposal of
the Security Council.

The personnel of the Military Staff Committee will consist of
the Chiefs of Staff of the permanent member nations of the Security Council (the United Kingdom, Russia, the Republic of China,
the United States, and France) or their representatives. They are
to invite any members of the organization not permanently represented to serve with the committee when forces of a state not
represented on the permanent committee are participating in the
military operations.

Before resorting to force, the Security Council may call upon all
members of the organization to apply political or economic
pressure to offending states. But, the Council *is* authorized, and
this is a very necessary authorization if force is to be used to avert
war, to recommend appropriate procedures or methods of adjustment at any stage of a dispute which endangers the peace and security. If it deems that a failure to settle a dispute in accordance
with prescribed procedures, or with its own recommendations, con-
stitutes a threat to the maintenance of international peace and secu-

rity, it *should take any measures* (italics supplied) necessary for the maintenance of international peace and security in accordance with the purposes and principles of the organization. This section of the charter places squarely upon the Security Council the obligation to take *any measures* (italics supplied), that is, to use the armed forces of the United Nations, if it appears at any time during negotiations or arbitration that international peace and security are threatened. The Security Council exercises its charter powers on behalf of all members of the United Nations who should assume their share of the responsibility of enforcing measures short of war and agree to make "armed forces and facilities and additional assistance available to the Security Council on call." But, each state will determine by agreement or agreements its own contribution toward world security and fix the quality and quantity of the armed forces, military facilities, and other assistance to be rendered to the Security Council; and the Security Council *can only require* from any state armed forces agreed upon by the state.

Prior to Hitler's invasion of Sudetenland the American Republics had agreed to consult together if peace in the Western Hemisphere was threatened. The crises in Europe in 1939 drew them closer together. In October 1939, a meeting of Pan American Foreign Ministers in Panama established a uniform system of neutrality that favored France and England. In July 1940, Hitler's conquest of European countries possessing territories in the Western Hemisphere inspired them to declare that an act of aggression against one American republic was an act of aggression against all. And when the Japanese attacked United States forces and territory in the Pacific in December 1941, all the Central American states, and Cuba, Haiti and the Dominican Republic declared war on Japan, Germany, and Italy while many South American states broke off diplomatic relations. During 1942 American Republics joined together under the leadership of the United States to resist any attacks in the Western Hemisphere, and before the war ended all except Argentina declared war on the Axis. Argentina signed the Chapultepec Agreement in April

1945, and all American Republics became charter members of the United Nations.

Article 51 of the charter added in San Francisco through the efforts of American Republics reads: "(1) Nothing in this present charter shall impair the inherent rights of individual or collective self-defense if an armed attack occurs against a member of the United Nations, until the Security Council has taken the measures to maintain international peace and security. Measures taken by members in the exercise of this right of self-defense shall be immediately reported to the Security Council and shall not in any way affect the authority and responsibility of the Security Council under the present charter to take at any time such action as it may deem necessary in order to maintain or restore international peace and security. (2) The members of the United Nations entering into such arrangements or constituting such agencies shall make every effort to achieve pacific settlement of local disputes through such regional arrangements or by such regional agencies either on the initiative of the states concerned or by reference from the Security Council."

This article in no way impairs the application of Articles 34 and 35 that affirm the right of the Security Council to investigate any dispute or any situation and the right of any state to bring to the attention of the Security Council any situation that might lead to international friction. But the United States as a permanent member of the Security Council can refuse to vote for any measures that would infringe on the domestic affairs of any nation and can thus prevent European intervention in the Western Hemisphere.

Chapter VIII, Article 52 of the charter, states that "Nothing in the charter precludes the existence of regional arrangements or agencies for dealing with such matters relating to the maintenance of the international peace and security as are appropriate for regional action, provided such arrangements or agencies and their activities are consistent with the policies and principles of the United Nations" which are to maintain peace by averting or suppressing war. Members of the United Nations entering into regional arrangements or constituting such regional agencies shall make every effort to achieve pacific settlement of local disputes through such regional arrangements or by such regional agencies, either on the initiative of the states concerned or by reference from the Security Council. And the Security Council itself is directed by the charter to encourage the development of pacific settlement of local disputes through such regional arrangements or by such regional agencies either on the initiative of the states themselves or by reference from the Security Council. But such action by regional arrangements or by regional agencies cannot be undertaken unless authorized by Security Council.

The plain intent of Chapter VIII is to utilize regional associations, such as the American Republics to preserve peace and security in the Western Hemisphere through the solution of international differences in the Western Hemisphere by the powers of the Western Hemisphere.

At San Francisco it was provided further that, where appropriate, the Security Council could utilize regional arrangements or associations for enforcement action under its authority. In addition the charter specifies that special agreements concerning the number and types of force, their degree of readiness, their general location, and the natures of facilities and assistance to be provided should be negotiated as soon as possible between the Security Council and member states or between the *Security Council and groups of member states* (italics supplied).

The regional plan is amplified by the provision that "the Military Staff Committee, with the authorization of the Security Council, may establish regional sub-committees of the Military Staff Committee." This permits a sub-committee of the Military Staff to act as the General Staff in the Western Hemisphere under the control of a regional sub-committee of the American Republics. The wisdom of this provision is manifest, particularly in the case of American Republics who implemented the Act of Chapultepec in the Pact of Rio that became effective December 3, 1946. In this they agreed that an armed attack on any state shall be construed as an attack on all, and each signatory state agreed to help in resisting the attack.

The United States and Western European Powers utilized Article 52 and followed the pattern of the Rio Pact to create the

North Atlantic Treaty Organization to resist "an armed attack on any of the (signatory) parties in Europe or North America, on the Algerian Department of France, on the occupation forces of any party in Europe, on their islands in the North Atlantic, north of the Tropic of Cancer, or on the vessels or aircraft of any of the signatories in the area." The Senate ratified this Pact July 21, 1949. The other signatories were Belgium, Canada, Denmark, France, Iceland, Italy, Luxembourg, Netherlands, Norway, Portugal and the United Kingdom. Greece and Turkey have since joined.

Similar pacts were made by the United States in the Pacific with the Philippines, Australia, New Zealand, Netherlands, and Japan. Our international responsibilities, therefore, in addition to our obligations to sixty member nations of the United Nations, include Regional Pacts with twenty-one American Republics, the North Atlantic Treaty Organization of fourteen nations, mutual defense treaties with the Philippines, Australia, New Zealand, Netherlands, South Korea, and Japan, and undefined but close relations with Nationalist China in Formosa. The State Department has just concluded preliminary negotiations with Spain for sea and air bases at the western end of the Mediterranean. In the Middle East we have friendly relations with the Arab States and Israel and are establishing a military pact with Pakistan. Another addition was made at Manila in September 1954 known as Seato. This pact binds Australia, France, New Zealand, Pakistan, the Philippines, Thailand, and the United States to act to meet the common danger in case of aggression in the Southwest Pacific.

Returning now to the Rio Pact, if it should become necessary to use force to preserve peace in the Western Hemisphere it is obviously more prudent to have that force supplied by American States. And the conference delegates at Dumbarton Oaks and San Francisco took cognizance of this fact and that similar situations might develop in Europe or Asia. Article 52 provided for an unexpected situation, and in June 1950 it enabled members of the United Nations to unite to defend South Korea against attack by North Korea without resigning from the United Nations. If the present cold war ends in peace and the Security Council, as originally intended, makes full use of regional organizations, its Military Staff Committee can simplify the organization, training, and deployment of the armed forces and reduce its own labors and responsibilities.

The Conference at San Francisco strengthened the provisions formulated at Dumbarton Oaks for the Security Council. It required member states to grant not only assistance and facilities but the rights of passage across their territory to armed forces operating under the Military Staff Committee. This amendment was necessary because, at the Moscow Conference, the Foreign Ministers of the United States, Great Britain, China, and Russia agreed that "after termination of hostilities, they will not employ military forces within the territories of other states, except for the purposes" given in the Moscow Declaration. No state enjoys having foreign troops of any kind cross its territory, but member states must now grant permission. The charter that emerged from San Francisco, although dedicated to the ideal of lasting peace, is generally very practical probably because the delegates met in the midst of war and did not need to be reminded that force is necessary to preserve the peace.

In addition to assuming additional responsibilities, the United States has parted with a considerable portion of its former freedom of action as an independent state. In Chapter XVI, Article 103, the charter provides that in the event of a conflict between the obligations of the members of the United Nations under the present charter and their obligations under any other international agreement, their obligations under the present charter shall prevail. To enable the Secretariat to enforce this provision the preceding Article 102 required that "every treaty and every international agreement entered into by any member of the United Nations after the present charter comes into force shall as soon as possible be registered with the Secretariat and published by it." Article 104 provides that "the Organization (of the United Nations) shall enjoy in the territory of each of its members such legal capacity (authority) as may be necessary for the exercise of its functions and the fulfillment of its purposes." Article 105 further provides that the organization officials and representatives of the member states of the United Nations shall enjoy in the territory of each of its members such privileges and immunities as are necessary for the fulfillment of its purpose." Paragraph 3 of Article 105 permits the General Assembly to "make recommendations . . . to determine the details" of the privileges and immunities it bestows on the organization. In this General Assembly the United States has one vote.

Three new chapters, XI, XII and XIII, were added at San Francisco which must be taken with considerable reserve. These chapters fix the policy of the United Nations toward non-self-governing territories, establish the International Trusteeship System to administer and supervise territories placed under the United Nations, and prescribe the membership of the Trusteeship Council, which will function for the United Nations under the General Assembly, except that the functions of the United Nations relating to strategic areas shall be exercised by the Security Council.

The apparent purpose of these chapters is to provide a method whereby states now possessing mandated territory or non-self-governing territory can voluntarily place such territory under the supervision of the United Nations, which will then exercise its powers in accordance with its policies regarding non-self-governing territories. This would permit any nation which obtained territory previous to the present war, *if it so desired*, to divest itself of its authority and responsibility over such territory. In addition, the United Nations will accept as trust territory "territories which may be detached from enemy states as a result of the Second World War"; and it is the application of the trusteeship system to islands and archipelagoes, such as Iwo, Okinawa, and the Marianas, that is of most concern to the United States, which now possesses most of the islands formerly mandated to Japan and, in addition, other former Japanese islands. Capture of those islands was necessary to enable American forces to defeat Japan. They are now necessary to protect our interests in the western Pacific. Unless the American Government possesses authority to establish and maintain air and naval bases in the islands north of the equator that it captured during the war, it will find it difficult to contribute to the security of the western Pacific as a member of the United Nations or if this organization falls apart to protect its own interests in the Far East.

As early as June 1944, Secretary Forrestal recognized this necessity and inquired of Under-Secretary Stettinius if the President was firmly committed to the innovation of Multiple Ownership. Roosevelt was sponsor of the idea, and the plan was accepted at San Francisco despite army and navy opposition in Washington, for both Stimson and Forrestal regarded these islands as essential "defense posts." Roosevelt had repeatedly disavowed the idea of acquiring any more territory; he was aware of the strategic value of these islands. So he revised Wilson's discredited idea of mandates and devised the more complicated and hypocritical Trusteeship System under which the United States has turned over these islands to the United Nations and received them back with the blessings of the United Nations as a Trustee. Any form of condominium is awkward. It will be impossible to administer naval and air bases as Trustee for some sixty nations with the General Assembly or Security Council authorized to intervene.

Multiple ownership was planned because, for a second time, a President of the United States, without consulting Congress, asserted that, for the present and the future, Americans would never add a foot to their territories. No Caliph of Bagdad ever issued a more arbitrary decree. In our early history many leaders said the Mississippi River would be our western boundary; later others extended it to the Rocky Mountains which they claimed was a natural frontier. Their own initiative and desire for more land inspired Americans to expand their country to the Pacific. Some drove their covered wagons overland; others went by ship to Colon, then on mule back through a jungle trail to Panama, thence by ship to San Francisco; still others sailed around the Horn in their fast clippers. Since 1900 Americans have divested themselves of territory overseas because they had plenty of room within their continental territory. If they ever need or want more land, all proclamations of former Presidents will not stay their advance.

The charter of the United Nations puts no legal obligation on any government to place in the Trusteeship System territories which its armed forces have taken from enemy states during World War II. But President Roosevelt sponsored the system and Dean Acheson, when Under-Secretary of State, agreed with an interpretation of the charter by Alger Hiss, then occupying a responsible position in the Department, that the charter also applied to the Canal Zone and that it was necessary for the United States to report the Zone to the United Nations as "occupied territory." * The American delegation, mostly from the State Department, at San Francisco helped to draft Chapters XI, XII and XIII of the charters. Some of them are still in the Department. They have deposited in the Trusteeship System the Pacific Islands now held by the United States. And already Secretary Dulles has suggested the return of one of the islands, Amami O Shima, to Japan.

Only the United States Senate can restrain the State Department and it should scrutinize closely any further suggestion to give the United Nations control of islands that are essential to the protection of American interests in the western Pacific. Not until Great Britain has agreed to place Hong Kong, Singapore, Malta, and Gibraltar, and Russia to place Port Arthur, Darien, Memel, and Königsberg under the Trusteeship System should the United States place Tarawa, Iwo Jima, Okinawa, or any of the strategic islands or archipelagoes that U.S. Triphibious Forces captured during World War II in the system.

While Roosevelt suggested this application of "multiple sovereignty" of territory taken from the enemy particularly the islands taken by American forces in the Pacific, he was urging Churchill to grant immediate independence to India and to return Hong Kong to China. He did *not* suggest that the immense continental territory acquired by Stalin in Europe and Asia be placed in the System but generously allowed him to acquire former Polish territory for Russia and then recompense Poland with land taken from Germany.

At a Cabinet meeting on January 5, 1945, before the President left for Yalta, Stettinius reported the unilateral action of Russia

* Former Assistant Secretary of State Spruille Braden, *U.S. News and World Report*, April 9, 1954.

in recognizing "the Lublin Committee as the Polish government"; on the next day Roosevelt reported to Congress that the nearer we come to victory "the more . . . we become conscious of differences among the victors." Before Stettinius left for Yalta, Stimson warned him that "Russia would claim control over . . . Poland, Bulgaria and Rumania" incompatible with their independence; and that the captured islands we held in the Pacific should be retained as "defense outposts." Forrestal had repeatedly told Stettinius that those islands should be held as outposts. Yet at Yalta Stettinius made no effort to retain these islands for his country. After his return he reported at a Cabinet meeting on March 13 that the Yalta Conference had been "a most successful meeting," and that there was every evidence "of the Russian desire to cooperate along all lines with the United States." If, in this friendly atmosphere, he made no effort to keep for his own nation these "outposts," he must have either agreed with Roosevelt's new plan or been unwilling to risk a Presidential frown.

Many of the delegates who met at Dumbarton Oaks had witnessed the failure of the League of Nations, of the attempts to limit armaments, of the Locarno Pact, of the Kellogg-Briand Pact, of American attempts to appease Japan and Anglo-French attempts to appease the Nazis. They were undoubtedly aware of the difficulties confronting them and, as Washington is famous for disclosing secrets, they were probably informed of Stalin's criticisms of the proposed organization. Their negotiations were facilitated by the preliminary measures taken by the President and Secretary of State and their deliberations were carried on in a friendly atmosphere, for Congress and the public heartily approved the project.

They went about their task soberly; they provided, first, that nothing in the charter should interfere with the defeat of the enemy states, for the war was still in progress. They next provided means to continue cooperation of the Allies in enforcing the peace terms. Then they invited all peace-loving nations to join in the effort to avert or suppress future wars. The effective work at

Dumbarton Oaks is shown by the few additions to the charter made at San Francisco.

If the Big Five Powers could have agreed upon postwar policies, the charter would have been an efficient instrument of government. The Security Council with its Military Staff Committee, using Regional Committees with sub-staffs, could have quickly recruited, organized, and stationed armed forces in strategic areas that could have preserved peace and security. While the Council preserved the peace, the General Assembly with its subsidiary, the Economic and Social Council, could have initiated measures to create and strengthen friendly relations among nations. The Assembly's program has been undertaken under very adverse conditions, because the driving force that would have made all these things possible was an alliance, based on the fear of the Tripartite States of Germany, Japan, and Italy. Before the Axis Powers were defeated, the moment victory of the United Nations appeared on the horizon, the alliance began to disintegrate.

An International Court of Justice has been provided and is now sitting in The Hague with authority to sit elsewhere if desirable. Its jurisdiction extends to all states requesting it to act and in all matters provided for in the charter or in treaties and conventions in force. It inherited the laws and precedents established by the Permanent Court of International Law and the generally accepted code of international law relating to rights of neutrals and belligerents on the sea. It is authorized to codify presently accepted international laws and by legal precedents gradually it can transform international customs into laws. The General Assembly was directed to encourage the progressive development of international law and its codification. The late Senator Taft considered that "The fundamental difficulty (of the United Nations Charter) was that it was not based primarily on an underlying law." Until the United Nations was formed no international congress had ever possessed power to prescribe such a code. But the charter plainly contemplates the gradual consummation of such a body of laws from previous precedents accepted by the Court, precedents established by the Court, and recommendations by the General Assembly.

The jurisdiction of the Court has already been accepted by the United States which has agreed with most other nations to submit in advance to any of its decisions on purely legal disputes occurring between them. More and more nations will probably submit their cases to the Court. In due course a body of international law will crystallize from world custom and judicial precedents, just as common law did in England. The Security Council with armed forces at its disposal could enforce its decisions as promptly as United States armed forces could those of the Supreme Court. If a legislative body of the United Nations had attempted to create at one session a body of statute laws, it would have been involved in endless debate. Never did the prospect of an international organization to gain and maintain a just and lasting peace seem brighter than in 1945. Russian obstruction had appeared but Roosevelt convinced most Americans and many foreigners that the long sought international organization that would suppress or avert war had been created.

By June 1950 the United Nations had been in existence for five years, the Security Council had no armed forces at its disposition, and it was evident that Russia's policies were threatening world peace. The absence of the Soviet member from the Security Council permitted the improvisation of a unified command to direct the armed forces voluntarily provided by various governments to resist the invasion of South Korea. After the hasty return of the Soviet member to the Security Council, the General Assembly, by stretching its powers and assuming some of the Security Council's, enabled United Nations forces, mainly supplied by the United States and South Korea, to continue the Korean War, to negotiate an unsatisfactory armistice and offer to negotiate a peace. Under Secretary Acheson's deft management the General Assembly provided machinery to circumvent a veto by the Security Council. This at first was hailed as a remedy for the abuse of the veto power by Moscow. It soon appeared that the Assembly was limited to recommending that nations supply quotas of armed forces. Only a few did. As the war progressed, mature reflection convinced Americans that, if the General Assembly could circumvent the veto power of Russia, on a future occasion it might circumvent the veto power of the United States. Enthusiasm for Acheson's plan waned.

Probably the argument that persuaded most Americans to make another attempt to form an international organization when the failure of the League of Nations was still fresh in their memories was the evolution of the United States from a federation of thirteen small independent states. Advocates of the United Nations, basing their hopes on an analogy, argued that, if thirteen states could unite to form one United States, all peace-loving states could merge into a United Nations. They assumed that the Federal Union was consummated in a convention hall at Philadelphia. Enthusiasts anticipated a full-grown United Nations in good working order to emerge from the convention at San Francisco. They forgot that the Constitution of the United States left two questions unanswered. Could a state voluntarily leave the federation and should slavery be perpetuated? They never considered Aaron Burr's attempt to detach some western states from the Union; the Hartford Convention when prominent New Englanders prepared to take their states out of the Union; South Carolina's vain attempt to nullify a Federal law; the unavailing efforts of American statesmen between 1820 and 1860 to find a peaceful compromise between the north and south and avert a civil war. Under the inspiration of George Washington, American statesmen laid the cornerstone of the United States in 1787. It required four years of civil war, the establishment of the longest naval blockade the world had seen, and great land battles—Gettysburg, Vicksburg, and Petersburg—to cement that Union.

If the United Nations is compelled to tread the same stony path, the Korean War is only comparable to Shays' Rebellion, and the next sixty-five years will see world statesmen seeking to find peaceful compromises in various parts of the world while cold wars continue and are interspersed with comparatively small hot wars. Then when a crisis arises that will divide the great powers fairly evenly, say in a ratio of 40 to 60, over an economic, political, or ideological issue, or perhaps a combination of them, for which their citizens or subjects are willing to fight, the history of the United Nations will parallel that of the United States, provided the victor permits or requires the defeated states to re-enter the Union.

If, by some exceedingly favorable circumstance, the United Nations avoids a major civil war, to be successful its charter will have to grow and evolve gradually. No charter could be drawn that would satisfy the requirements of so many different races, with different manners, civilizations, political institutions, ideologies, and religions. It must evolve and the international organization with it.

This evolution of some sixty nations into a United Nations will be more difficult than it was for thirteen small American states whose laws and customs had much more in common. Such evolution would have been facilitated if Churchill's suggestions of first creating three regional associations and then integrating them had been accepted. Inspired by Roosevelt, enthusiasts for the world state deliberately forced events, for many of them realized that their best and perhaps only opportunity to create a universal government was at one stroke when people all over the world were weary of war and ready to accept any plausible proposal for averting or suppressing future conflicts. When the devil is sick, the devil a monk would be.

Stalin repeatedly told Roosevelt that if Great Britain, the United States, and Russia could agree on world policies, they had the power to maintain peace without aid from other nations. Roosevelt apparently never comprehended the converse of Stalin's assertion—namely, that if these three nations did not agree the international organization could not avert or suppress war. With all his zeal for a United Nations, Roosevelt only contemplated that it would suppress boundary disputes between very small nations by measures short of war, and of medium size nations by armed forces of the Big Five. He never explored the problem of using force against one of the five great powers; Stalin's implication and its accompanying paradox are all too evident now. If Great Britain, Russia, and the United States agree, the super State is superfluous; if they disagree, it is helpless.

Chapter 8

Is the World Ready for a United Nations?

Since 1899 little more than fifty years have elapsed. Every known means to preserve the peace has failed to avert or suppress war. Between 1815 and 1914, almost one hundred years, classical diplomacy with three instruments—voluntary arbitration, a rough balance of power, and the concert of five or six Great Powers in Europe—limited major wars to the Crimean, the Franco-Prussian, and the Russo-Japanese and prevented all global wars. The Civil War in America resulted from domestic problems, but the balance of power in Europe deterred possible intervention. Between the end of the Napoleonic Wars and the beginning of World War I only one effort, the Holy Alliance, was made to create a super State; it quickly fell apart and its only permanent result was the announcement by the United States of the Monroe Doctrine which limited European colonization to Africa and Asia.

Limitation of outlets for increasing population placed a greater strain on European peace, but the Foreign Ministers of the Great Powers by 1914 had partitioned Africa, had established an equilibrium in Asia and in Europe, had unified Germany and Italy, and had recovered the Balkan States without the aid of a super State or a global war. Spain, Portugal, Holland, Belgium, England, and France bordering on the Atlantic had obtained a greater share of overseas possessions than late comers like Germany and Italy; but, through the concert of Powers, room abroad was found for them without a war.

In the spring of 1914 the foreign ministers of Great Britain and Germany, Sir Edward Grey and Herr Gottlieb von Jagow had agreed upon a formula that would have removed the last serious source of friction between their countries and would have been satisfactory to Turkey. It authorized the construction of a German controlled railway from Berlin to Bagdad, and reserved for Great Britain its existing monopoly of steamer transport from Bagdad to the Persian Gulf with the additional right to construct a railway from Bagdad to the Gulf at any time in the future. The Turkish Government wanted to develop the interior of the country but lacked necessary funds, and they welcomed the entry of Germany and Britain in the Middle East as a guarantee against a further Russian advance. The untimely assassination of an Austrian Archduke precipitated a war that certainly could have been postponed by the drawing together of Great Britain and Germany, the two most powerful members of the opposing Triple Entente and Triple Alliance.

In the decade preceding the beginning of World War I any civilized European could have taken pride in the peaceful solution of a series of crises by the foreign ministers of the six Great Powers, and regret the pistol shot of an assassin that probably prevented the consummation of the Anglo-German negotiations. These solutions sometimes were obtained by dividing territory of weaker or backward nations that could not resist superior European arms. In such instances the natives usually benefited by exchanging their often ignorant and always despotic rulers for a generally enlightened foreign control. But many arrangements like the Anglo-German-Turkish Agreement, that was never consummated, benefited all concerned and the world at large.

A decade has passed since the founding of the United Nations; it is too soon to pronounce it a failure; evidently it cannot avert or suppress war, so it is not yet a success. In its ninth annual report, the Secretary General admitted "the wide gap between its purpose and achievement." Member nations must depend upon their own armed forces for security. That many nations were unwilling to entrust their future to the untried organization was shown by the haste of the American Republics to provide a regional organization to preserve peace in the Western Hemisphere, and the rapidity with which the North Atlantic Treaty Organization was formed when Red armies threatened western Europe. The formation in September 1954 of the South East Asia Treaty Organization to resist the Communist advance in the south west Pacific shows that the distrust of the United Nations still exists; and the United States, whose President and Congress laid the foundation of the United Nations, has taken a leading part in forming these regional associations.

It was the United States that persuaded the United Nations and a few member states to oppose Communist invasion of South Korea. Their acquiescence was obtained by flying the organization's flag and permitting it and member nations to limit and hamper military operations; wars waged by European allies have often been characterized by the same meddlesome mismanagement. After months of heavy fighting in which South Korean and United States forces suffered greatly, peace in Korea was obtained, but only at the expense of the weaker nation, South Korea, and by leaving thousands of Asiatics in bondage to the Kremlin. To obtain the armistice, United States officers were given pledges they knew would not be fulfilled and the State Department accepted assertions of Russia's neutrality, although well aware of the aid it had given Chinese and Korean Reds. This method of averting or suppressing war under the United Nations was not very different from classical methods long practiced in Europe.

The refusal of France to enter the European Defense Community caused prompt action by Anthony Eden and John Foster Dulles in September 1954 to revive the Brussels Pact of 1948 providing for military, economic, and cultural cooperation of Britain, France, Belgium, the Netherlands, and Luxembourg as the best formula to obtain French approval of re-arming western Germany and restoring her sovereignty. During these negotiations it became evident that the American and British governments were determined to rearm Germany; they will make every effort to gain the approval of the French Government but, with or without such approval, the Anglo-American governments propose to move swiftly toward the rearmament of western Germany, for twelve of her divisions are essential for the protection of western Europe, including France itself.

No attempt has been made to answer the most difficult question of all. Is the world ready for the United Nations? Its objective is a just and permanent peace; to that end everything is to be subordinated, even, temporarily, peace itself, for the Security Council is directed to prepare armed forces and to use them to avert or suppress war.

The charter placed control of the Security Council and thereby the armed forces among the Big Five. This was a practical necessity, but it leaves the future development of the world in the hands of the five most powerful states. We have already seen that when they disagree the United Nations cannot preserve the peace.

Assume that the present Big Five could agree; it would be easy for them to avert or suppress war by the use of, or threat to use, force. They could retain the world as it is or mold it to their own desires. As they are all powerful possessor nations, they would probably wish to preserve their possessions and relative powers. They would surely oppose any reduction in their territory. The growth of all other powers would be almost impossible; and, most important, any effort to reduce their control of the United Nations could and probably would be successfully resisted. The United Nations could easily evolve into the most powerful military despotism the world has known.

Some idea of the probable effect on the world of the United Nations, if it becomes and continues to be successful, can be secured by assuming that it was a going concern in 1750 and that it had preserved the peace and with it the status quo of that time. Then advance the date every fifty years until 1950. And each time compare the world situation. Few if any citizens of the United States would prefer the earlier conditions. Only states who have lost power and prestige or have failed to progress would wish to turn back the clock.

If there is such a person as a citizen of the world, with no feeling of partiality for his own country, would he be willing to fix the boundaries, relative strengths, customs, manners of the nations in a hard mold that could be broken only by dissensions among the Big Five as they are today? Only those who are content with present conditions and are willing to trust to the wisdom and unselfishness of Roosevelt's Five Policemen voluntarily to make future adjustments in the interests of all the nations, can be unhappy over the present rivalries among the Big Five. If there had been substantial accord or even unity of purpose between China, France, Great Britain, Russia, and the United States, today there would certainly be a more peaceful world, but already it would be settling into a permanent condition as changeless as China when it retired behind the Great Wall. All those who think that mankind is capable of building a better world, of creating a more brilliant civilization, should be thankful that dissensions among the Big Five prevented the United Nations from permanently fixing the world in its present condition. What a static political world would look like we do not know. But there is good cause to believe that such a world might well be a stagnant world.

It is true wars may exact a frightful toll from mankind but they may also confer benefits that are usually overlooked. A completely objective history of the economic development of the modern world would have to conclude that a major, in most cases, the main, factor in the rapid industrialization of countries of the western world has been the impulse given by war. The industrialization of the United States began as a direct result of the War of 1812. It is no mere coincidence that the next great spurt in the industrialization of the United States coincided with the Civil War and its aftermath. World War I changed us from a debtor to a creditor nation and gave us unquestioned world industrial primacy. World War II stirred up our economy from the stagnation of the thirties, gave new hope to millions of people and put our industry on a new higher level of activity. As for the stimulus that war gives to progress in industry and agriculture, the advent of atomic power through the war is only the latest and most spectacular example of this process. In the beginning of the Middle Ages the development of metallurgy was inspired by the desire to improve artillery.

Since 1950 the dissensions between the Communist bloc and the free world have made necessary a level of government spending on armaments which has made possible the maintenance of a high level of economic activity throughout the world and has resulted to date in our avoiding the dreaded and long-heralded depression.

On the other side, it has been war and preparation for war that alone has made possible the imposition by the Russian Government of the great sacrifices on its civilian population necessary for its rapid pace of industrialization. A similar process on the same basis is now occurring in China. An interstellar observer might well conclude that war was the instrument chosen by the modern world to secure its rapid development.

Eighty years of peace were enough to sap the spirit of the Romans; happily for Europe, from beyond the Rhine and the Danube, barbarians were at hand to reinvigorate the enervated stock; but if the United Nations preserved world peace for eighty years, only interplanetary invaders could rejuvenate citizens of our world.

Bibliography

The following five books previously written by the author have supplied the bulk of data given in text to support the conclusions offered in this volume:

The Dardanelles Expedition, U.S. Naval Institute, 1925.
High Command in the World War, (I), Scribners, 1934.
The Life and Work of Captain A. T. Mahan, Yale University Press, 1939.
The Armed Forces of the Pacific, Yale University Press, 1940.
The Influence of Sea Power on World War II, Yale University Press, 1946.

Important and direct quotations from other authors are indicated by footnotes in the text.

Collateral material has been obtained from the following books. Where the sources are plainly indicated in the text no footnotes have been used.

Churchill, Sir Winston, *World War II,* 6 vols., Houghton Mifflin Co.
Clausewitz, Gen. Carl von, *On War,* A. S. Barnes & Company.
Department of State, *Nazi-Soviet Relations,* 1939-41, 1945.
Dugdale, Blanche, *Life of Balfour,* 2 vols., G. P. Putnam's Sons.
Eisenhower, General D. D., *Crusade in Europe,* Doubleday & Company.
Goebbels Diaries, Doubleday, Page & Company.
Halsey, W. F., and Joseph Bryan, *Admiral Halsey's Story,* McGraw-Hill Book Company, Inc.
Jessup, P. C., *Elihu Root,* Dodd, Mead & Company.
King, E. J., and W. M. Whitehill, *Fleet Admiral King,* W. W. Norton & Company.
Leahy, William D. (Fleet Admiral), *I Was There,* McGraw-Hill Book Company, Inc.

Mahan, A. T., *The Influence of Sea Power on History*, Little, Brown & Company, 1889.

——, *Naval Strategy*, Little, Brown & Company, 1912.

Mahan, D. H., *Field Fortifications*, Wiley and Putnam, 1836.

——, *Outpost Duty*, Wiley and Putnam, 1841.

Millis, Walter, and E. S. Duffield (Editors), *Forrestal Diaries*, Viking Press.

Morison, S. E., *History of U.S. Naval Operations in World War II*, Little, Brown & Company.

Roosevelt, Eleanor, *This I Remember*, Harper & Brothers.

Roosevelt, Elliott, *As He Saw It*, Duell, Sloan & Pearce, Inc.

Rosenman, S. I., *The Papers and Public Addresses of F. D. Roosevelt*, Random House.

Seymour, C. S. (Editor), *Intimate Papers of Col. E. M. House*, 4 vols., Houghton Mifflin Company.

Sherwood, R. E., *Roosevelt and Hopkins*, Harper & Brothers.

Stimson, H. L., *Far Eastern Crisis*, Harper & Brothers, 1936.

——, and George Bundy, *On Active Service in War and Peace*, Harper & Brothers, 1948.

U.S. Joint Committee on the Investigation of the Attack on Pearl Harbor, 39 vols., Government Printing Office, 1946.

Index